Omri Ginzburg / Out There

Omri Ginzburg

Out There

OUT THERE
Omri Ginzburg

Editor: Ryan Nealy
Translation from Hebrew: Lauren Rozenman
Cover design: Daniel Goldfarb
Hebrew editors: Yoav Keren, Tamar Kaplansky
Writing advisors: Noam Ellis, Ori Rom

First Edition (2.1)
This book is self-published
All rights reserved © 2023 Omri Ginzburg
www.omrigi.com

The characters, places, and events in this book are inspired by my true story. However, due to the sensitive topics it deals with, some of the details have been altered. Most of the characters' names have been changed.

ISBN 978-84-09-50768-9

I am no expert on post-traumatic stress,
I simply wish people to know what I
have been through since the war.

To Mom and Dad, and all
who didn't know how to ask.

AUTHOR'S NOTE

The book you are about to read tells my personal story of discovering and coping with post-traumatic stress disorder (PTSD). The majority of the book takes place during the decade after my release from mandatory service in the Israel Defense Force (IDF). Writing this book served as a therapeutic process and led me to many new discoveries about my PTSD — discoveries that have enabled me to take a few big steps toward the acceptance of, and maybe one day healing from, my PTSD.

I published the book in Hebrew in December 2021 with the main goal of increasing awareness for Combat PTSD among Israelis.

I was born in Israel and lived there almost all of my life. In 2017 I embarked on the journey described in this book. Afterwards, I left Israel and moved to Spain. Here, I've completed work on the Hebrew edition of this book.

After the book was published many people wrote to me about their reading experience and how it affected them. I received messages from people who live among others suffering from PTSD, and people who have PTSD themselves. This is when I understood how little people know about post-trauma and how important it is to make the book available in English. I've decided I want to tell the world the truth and the high personal cost of being an Israeli citizen.

This past year, I've been working on translating and adapting the book for non-Israeli readers — a complicated task that aroused many doubts. Now, after six years living abroad, I've been able to see things in a completely different way.

During the translation and editing process, I've found myself questioning the borders of the state of Israel, the definition of the occupied territories, and if Hezbollah soldiers should be referred to as terrorists or enemy soldiers. Before leaving Israel, I was sure that I had all the answers.

In the end, I've decided to stay as close as possible to the original Hebrew version and tell my story from the point of view of a twenty-something-year-old young man who has just finished his military service.

OUT THERE

I lie in bed and do not move. My heart is pounding and my pupils scan the room searching for a clue that'll give away his location.

Total darkness.

Someone's watching me. I can feel it. He knows I'm here.

It's a competition: he doesn't want me to know he's here, and I'll do whatever it takes to make sure he doesn't know I'm awake.

I can't make any mistake that will give me away.

I lie on my side attempting to regulate my breath.

The tension in the air subsides a little.

But then, out of the corner of my eye, I see the window and my heart races once again.

He's there, a vague silhouette.

Watching me.

I hear a noise from the direction of the living room and I freeze.

The silhouette in the window becomes a clear figure,

then turns vague again. I stare at it trying to see whether he froze as well.

Memories flood my mind and I begin to recreate the dream I woke up from. How exhausting it was. I remember running. A long run. An endless run. The whole time I tried to run faster but couldn't.

I wasn't alone. We were a group of people trying to escape. I was at the front, not as a leader, but like someone who wants to get the hell out first, at the expense of others.

I crossed the fence line and looked back. The moment I turned my head, a shot was fired. The Russian guy running behind me fell at my feet. He lay there without moving, face down, but it seemed he was still breathing. I grabbed his shoulder and turned him to face me, revealing a horrific sight. Most of his mouth was gone and in the center of his face, there was a gaping hole through which I could see the ground beneath him.

I let go of him and continued to run. His body once again hit the ground.

I tried to run as fast as I could, but it was no use. I was running so slow. Almost running in place.

Somehow, I managed to escape.

Others didn't.

I lie in bed, filling in certain parts of the dream and keeping my eyes on the silhouette that is, at times, reminiscent of the tangerine tree outside my window. I can no longer see the figure, but I know for certain: He's **Out There**.

TRAVEL LOG: SETTING OFF

For many weeks I have been preparing my pickup-truck for this journey: a month of traveling throughout Israel, north to south. I have never done something like this before, certainly not by myself.

I dedicate the morning before departure to last minute chores in my garage located in a Kibbutz close by. Work on the truck never ends. That's what it's like with old cars.

Three weeks ago, I traveled to the Golan Heights for the first time with the truck. In a moment of recklessness, I attempted to cross a huge puddle of water. It was by pure luck that I came out with no damage. In gratitude to my heroic truck, I promised to check the condition of the oil in the axles prior to departing on the journey. The axles are the lowest components in the vehicle. If water were to penetrate them, the oil would turn into a gray muddy fluid that could cause problems.

I place a plastic container under the rear axle and open the drainage screw underneath. To my relief, the oil is completely clear. This type of oil has the strongest odor, the kind that remains on your hands for days after. During my military service, those who hung around tanks hated it, but I was rather fond of the smell.

On the way to the workshop, I stopped to buy fresh oil. "Give me the expensive kind," I said to the sales person. Now, I pour it into the cup, measuring 1.7 liters precisely. I can't stand when the car mechanic puts in more than is needed. With a syringe, I draw the oil from the measuring cup and carefully bring it close to the opening. Not a drop spills.

I was afraid to service my previous car myself. Each time I took it for an annual service at the shop, I would cling to the window of the waiting room to see how it was being serviced. I didn't like what I saw.

Instead of measuring the exact amount of oil, the mechanic would bring a barrel up to the axle and begin filling it until the oil would ooze out from the opening. Only then would he run to fetch the cap to quickly screw it back on. Today, I know what to do and how to do it myself. There is no way I would put my car in a shop again.

After changing the oil in the axles, I take a rag, lie down on the car creeper, and roll myself under the vehicle to examine all the components, searching for signs that indicate something is wrong. The pickup truck, is an SJ410K, a rare model of a Suzuki Samurai imported to Israel in 1984.

The truck has a high ground clearance, so there's no need for me to lift it up with a jack to roll under it. I can identify every little change. Each and every screw was screwed in by me. Everything looks fine except for the oil leak from the transmission, which I attempted to fix before. It's a small leak but nevertheless I decide to drain the oil from the gearbox and refill it to make sure the level is sufficient.

With the gearbox filled with fresh oil, I start loading the equipment. I lay down all the spare parts and tools on the floor, including an additional carburetor and replacement belts. Next to them I place the camping gear: a tent, mattress, firewood, kitchenware, two camping burners, a solar panel, and a variety of camping gadgets. Within a few minutes the floor of the workshop is covered with equipment. I know I won't be using everything, but I want to be prepared for every mishap and any kind of weather.

The arrangement of the equipment is critical. I place the spare parts for rare and severe malfunctions in the bottom of the truck's box. On top of it I arrange the camping gear, which will be used every day. On the side panel of the box, I put a bag with towing and rescue equipment, so it will be easily accessible when needed. It's not used often, but I want to be able to reach the items quickly without having to unload everything under the stress of being stranded.

The tiny cabin is the only place that is completely waterproof, which makes it the most valuable piece of real estate on the truck. Even the space underneath the seat is utilized. There I shove the lighting that needs to be available in case I have to set my tent up after dark. I prefer to not get organized in the dark — and not just because it is more complicated.

Loading the equipment takes until the afternoon, much longer than I planned. Before leaving, I fill up the water tank and the spare fuel containers, so I can stay out in nature as long as possible. The truck is heavily loaded. On the way out I pass through the dairy farm and place the truck on their weigh-bridge. It gives a reading of an additional 280 kilograms (617 pounds) on top of the truck's fixed weight. Two-hundred-eighty kilograms of equipment. That is really a lot. At least it will soften the stiff suspension of the old truck.

◆ ◆ ◆

A few minutes later I'm already on the freeway. The little old truck I've restored is the most comfortable place in the world for me. Even though the radio is already 33 years old and struggles to get all the stations, it still does the job, and a sweet sensation of freedom fills the cabin.

At a speed of 70 km/h (43 mph) the noise of the engine competes with the radio, but I can still pick out the sounds of "The Dire Straits," which put me in the right mood to embark on a journey with my truck from the Eighties.

Every once in a while, I turn off the radio to listen to the truck. I know my truck very well, and can identify every single sound: a little squeak from the cable of the clutch paddle, the hum from the screw that got loose again in the right speaker, or the rattle of something that isn't well secured in the glove compartment.

In the past I never had the patience to drive so slowly. Today I enjoy the contrast between the speed of my truck and my thoughts, which never slow down. Even now they are flashing through my mind.

How did I get to 280 kilograms of equipment? In my head I go over the list of equipment in the various compartments of the truck. I review the spare parts, the work tools, and camping gear.

In this truck model, the driver's seat is adjacent to the back of the cabin without the possibility of moving the seat back or putting the backrest down. Behind the seats there's a very narrow gap that I used for storage too.

Behind the passenger seat I installed an air compressor and over it I placed a first aid kit and jump-start cables. Behind the driver's seat — a laptop and, of course, the red bag with my notebooks.

When I think about the notebooks, my heart instantly cringes and my entire body becomes tense. I awkwardly reach behind my backrest and touch the notebooks through the bag, to make sure they are still there.

More and more new cars pass me by. In them are agitated drivers. The workday is over and it seems like everyone is in a hurry to get home. I look at them, all stressed by the endless race against time, while I'm on my way for a lengthy time-out from daily life.

The sun begins to set. Watching the sunset is what I consider true freedom. In the coming month I will probably see all the sunsets. When the time is right, I will pull over and set up a chair to enjoy this beautiful sight that happens every day, and to which I usually pay no attention.

I've told most people that this journey is in honor of completing the restoration of my truck, but the truth is much more complex. The past year was quite eventful: breaking up with Noya, ending the treatment with Gideon after four years, and my request to be discharged from reserve duty service.[i]

All of these added to the endless stream of struggles I experienced in the past decade since 2006 — the

---

[i] After finishing the three years mandatory, Israeli citizens (mainly men) serve in the reserve duty forces and are called up for drills and emergencies.

Second Lebanon War. One of my goals during this journey is to write everything I don't have the courage to say, but wish everyone knew. And this can only be accomplished when I'm by myself. The first chapter will be the text from the notebooks I wrote right after the end of the war. Afterwards, I will write about all that has happened since then.

This trip isn't going to be easy for someone like me, whose biggest fear is darkness. It's not the first time I'm camping in nature, however it is the first time that I'm going to do it alone.

When traveling with friends I'm always preoccupied thinking about the dangers that lurk during our night's sleep. What if someone attempts to steal the cars? Or even harm us? Each time we've slept in the desert I've maintained strict vigilance and woke from every little sound. But, knowing it was everyone's problem calmed me down. This time I am traveling alone. It will be my problem, and mine alone.

◆ ◆ ◆

I drive off route 70 and cross one of the Arab villages on my way to the Hermit's Mill situated on the banks of the Tzipori River. Here is where I'll spend the first night. I drive past fields of grain and can see the village lights become smaller in the rearview mirror.

I reach the mill's parking area. It looks like it's completely abandoned. I have already visited this place when I hiked the Israel National Trail,[i] but many years have passed since then and I feel much less confident than I thought I would. Why didn't I leave my workshop earlier? At least I would've arrived in daylight.

I muster a little courage, grab the large flashlight, and step out of the truck and into the darkness. The village lights are barely visible through the hills to my left. I can't even see a meter in front of myself. Dogs barking in the pitch dark break the silence.

In between barks there's complete silence. I lift the flashlight, scan the area around me, and identify something that looks like a lawn and a few dogs digging into a pile of garbage bags. The truth is, the dogs are less frightening to me. The darkness and the village are my main concerns.

I return to the truck's cabin, debating what to do now. After less than one minute I notice the headlights of a car advancing toward me.

It's probably just some nice hippie guy who guards the mill. Perhaps he will even invite me in, I try to calm myself. But when the vehicle stops fifty meters from me flashing its high and blinding headlights, I am much less optimistic.

A few seconds later the lights turn off, but no one comes out of the car. I don't know whether to step

---

[i] A 1,015 km (631 miles) hiking trail crosses the country from north to south.

out of my truck and walk toward it, or wait for them to come to me.

I decide to wait. He does the same. The minutes pass by and neither of us move. After a while, which seems like an eternity, I notice another vehicle in the distance, getting closer from the direction of the village. This is too much as far as I'm concerned. I start the truck and begin driving toward the exit. On the way, I stop next to the parked vehicle.

The driver seems surprised by the sight of a traveler who came into the compound after dark. "Is it okay to spend the night here?" I ask, even though I've already made up my mind not to. He replies with an Arabic accent, "Come on Saturday, now it's no good."

On the way out my mind is racing. Where do I go? How can I even consider being able to sleep alone in nature? Perhaps I'll find a room in a hostel or even squeeze into the truck's cabin. I enter the village I passed through earlier and I'm no longer sure where I am. The road doesn't seem familiar to me, and the Waze navigator gets totally confused. There is no street lighting here either.

My heart is pounding fast. The dark streets throw me back eleven years. Lebanon. Night. I'm in the command post inside the tank, driving on the side of the valley toward one of the villages.

No, there's no way I've come through here before. This is not the right way. I turn my truck and backtrack. Waze, which in the meantime reset itself, tells me to continue straight at the main square of the village, but turning right seems like a better gamble. Sure enough, after I turn right, I see the exit into the main road.

My body begins to emit heat, as if only now it's allowed itself to slightly release the stress. I open the window, letting the cool air in. What the hell just happened?

The truck accelerates on the main road, and very soon I shift into the fourth and highest gear. The decision is made in an instant: I am continuing north to Achziv. I planned to visit there tomorrow anyway. Maybe I'll find a nice spot to spend the night, and in the morning, I'll wake up to the sound of the waves breaking on the shore.

A car pulls next to me at the traffic light. The lady who is driving seems tired after a long day, but this time I am looking at her with envy. Soon she'll get home and climb into her own bed, while I am about to go sleep in a tent, exposed to all the dangers, alone with my fears. How ironic it is that I have everything to make a campsite more than comfortable, and yet I'd rather spend the night cramped up inside the truck where I feel more protected.

The first thing I see upon arriving at Achziv is the sign which prohibits camping overnight. I swerve with the road next to the water line, looking in vain for a spot to stop at. I then return to the entrance and try coming about it from the other side, feeling like a dog that circles itself unable to decide where to settle.

In the end I arrive at a small eucalyptus grove next to the freeway leading to Rosh Hanikra. The road is noisy and the grove is filled with trash left behind by travelers, but after thoroughly checking the area, I decide to settle. Perhaps here, next to the road, I'll feel a little safer.

I illuminate the area with the spotlight I installed in the back of the truck, start a fire, and pitch the tent. All the while, I hear noises coming from the nearby bushes. It's probably the wind or just a little mouse. And yet, the noises bother me. I don't have the nerve to step away from the truck, turn off the spotlight, or part with my headlamp. Even the sounds of the wood crackling in the fire startle me.

◆ ◆ ◆

I go to get something from the truck, and suddenly someone appears in front of me. I panic and instantly my hearing shuts down, as if someone placed the whole world on mute. After two seconds of horror, I realize there's no one there, only the light from my headlamp shining on the window and reflecting onto the ground. My hearing comes back.

This is what happens when I panic in recent years. I call it "the panic of indifference." Odd. On the one hand, I get emotional about every little thing, to the point that even watching a romantic scene in an idiotic movie is enough to make me choke up and cry. On the other, when I panic it causes a reaction that on the outside looks emotionless.

Instead of jumping, running away, or shouting — I fall silent. Even if I hear a large blast or something heavy suddenly drops next to me, I don't react quickly to the danger. Instead I become pinned to the spot and barely move as if all at once, and contrary to any human instinct, I am overcome with indifference.

However, inside the feeling is different: real panic. It's as if my heart leaves my body for a few seconds and then returns to its place with a powerful bang, after which it starts pounding strong and fast. But there's no external evidence of it.

It used to happen a lot at home. I would sit next to the computer and Noya would suddenly pop up next to me out of nowhere. Instead of jumping in panic, I would just disappear for a few seconds, the world turned off to me. I wouldn't even look at her. And then my heart would return and start pounding.

"Stop sneaking up on me!" I'd lash out in rage. Noya would always say she didn't sneak up, that it's me who was dreaming again, not paying attention. And yet I was angry, without understanding that my reaction was disproportionate and that Noya wasn't to blame.

It takes time for my pulse to settle. This trip isn't going to be easy. I grab a couple of slices of bread with hummus just to put something in my stomach. I fold and load everything that I don't need back onto the truck, and I go inside the tent.

In my sleeping bag I give thanks that a war didn't break out today and close my eyes — but sleep eludes me. Each time I relax a little and begin to fall asleep, strange noises bring me back to a state of alertness.

To calm down I ask myself what exactly I'm afraid of, just as Gideon guided me to do. It's safe to assume that the noises came from a small rodent in the bushes. What are the chances that someone would actually come here and attempt to harm me? Statistics are the most soothing argument. I haven't heard of any traveler having something happen to him while he was sleeping in nature. And in general, what is there to be afraid of in the dark?

Thinking helps me overcome the fear and fall asleep, but my sleep is disturbed and nightmarish. Every few minutes I lift my head and peek outside the tent to make sure that everything's in place and no one is standing there. Several hours go by like this. My body is worn out and I pray for the night to be over. Why won't the sun rise already?

At some point sleep takes over. After a while, I don't know how long, I wake up soaking wet and realize I had a nightmare. This is nothing new for me. I begin recreating the bad dream. In my nightmare I also wake up in the tent.

◆ ◆ ◆

It's morning. I peek outside the tent's opening and find that my battalion in the reserve is getting ready for a drill right next to me. All at once I'm filled with a severe, unpleasant feeling. The guys are beginning a drill, while I'm spending my time having fun on this trip — not to mention, I'm also in the process of being discharged from reserve service.

Contrary to what I expect, the guys are happy to see me. They pass by me waving hello while I attempt to avoid eye contact. I'm so ashamed. I hope the ground will open up and swallow me whole. I need to fold the equipment as quickly as possible, so they won't know I spent the night here. I turn back into the tent and roll up the sleeping bag and mattress, but suddenly the battalion commander comes over to say hello.

I turn to him in embarrassment and try not to look into his eyes. But he's acting as if everything's fine — like no one is angry with me for asking to be discharged. We stand for a few minutes talking as if nothing is wrong.

When he walks away, I turn back into the tent and find that the mattress and sleeping bag are laid back out on the ground. "That's strange," I think and start refolding, first the sleeping bag and then the mattress. But then the deputy battalion commander[i] comes over to say hello. He isn't upset either. I stand and talk to him as if nothing is unusual despite the awkwardness. When he leaves, the mattress and the

---

[i] Also known as Battalion Executive Officer (XO).

sleeping bag are, again, laid out inside the tent. I fold them again.

I have to hide the fact I'm on a trip from everyone, so they won't realize I ditched the drill for my journey. But then Yonatan, the driver, comes over and again I feel uneasy. We talk a little as if everything is fine, and when he leaves, I turn around to the tent — and it's like I haven't done a thing. And it happens over and over again.

I fold the equipment, turn to talk to someone from the battalion, and when I turn back again, everything has been laid out by itself. And each time I feel the pressure build. I start to realize that I don't stand a chance. I can't seem to fold the equipment, and I can't hide the fact that I'm on a trip. Very soon everyone will know. This fills me with terror and I wake up.

◆ ◆ ◆

This isn't the way it was during the first years of my nightmares. Now, I'm able to fall back asleep. After a few hours, I wake up in panic again, but this time from the loud noise of a passing car. First light is coming through the tent's openings, and like every morning, I grab my mobile phone and check the news websites to see if war broke out while I was sleeping.

I get up and fold the equipment without any problems, and ten minutes later I am already in my truck, listening to the hum of the engine come to life.

I don't start driving until the temperature gauge points to at least 40 degrees Celsius. This is a habit I started during my military service. Other commanders would start up the tanks and immediately order the driver to go, even before the engine had a chance to figure out what was going on. White smoke would come out from the tank's huge exhaust pipe while the cold engine stuttered in an attempt to reach the required RPM. I could always hear the agony of the engines from far away. However, my team knew that with each start-up, even for the shortest distance, we needed to wait until the engine woke up before we could start moving.

I am driving on the Achziv shoreline. The sun is shining, there's great music on the radio, and I can feel my first smile coming up. At one of the bays, I stop to make my morning coffee and sit down to drink it facing a flat sea the color of clear turquoise.

What was I so afraid of during the night? I thought I'd already come to terms with ending my reserve duty service — and then such a nightmare occurs and shuffles the deck. What is left to do? Leave Israel?

I continue on to Rosh Hanikra and go down for a walk on the rocky shoreline. I roam around, enchanted by the beds of cyclamen and other flowers I'm not familiar with. I put the experiences of the night behind me and I'm filled with joy for deciding to go on this journey.

A few hours pass and I cross the Upper Galilee in the direction of the Zivon Stream, where I will spend the night. It's been ten years since I've traveled these roads. I used to adore the north — the trees that are green even in the summer, the foggy roads during the winter, the feeling of being abroad — the kind of feeling that can be found only here. But in every trip I've made since the war, I've done my best to go as far south as possible.

The truck swerves through the green landscape and I sing along with the radio. How could I give up on this area for so many years?

Like other beautiful regions in Israel, I only learned to familiarize myself with the north during my military service. I got to know the Upper Galilee and the Lebanon border in depth when we were deployed here, immediately after the war.

Now, every village sign brings up memories. The battalion's headquarters was situated close to Liman. Followed by Biranit, where we kept the tanks. Then Matat, where we went during the drill call-up. Immediately after the turn into Matat, there's a directional sign to Adir Mountain. I recall there's an amazing observation point there. We went up to it at the start of the deployment, after the war was over.

I turn right and start the ascent to the top of the mountain. The narrow road bends through a beautiful grove. The truck works hard to climb and I shift down the gears until I get to first and continue to crawl slowly. To my surprise, it turns out there's no longer a vehicle access to the observation point.

I park the truck and continue on foot. The last time I was here, there was nothing but a few rocks. Now there's a beautiful viewing balcony with iron and glass planks that have inscriptions on them. "This is so nice," I think to myself, and only then do I realize that it's a memorial for the Second Lebanon War. I stand in place. Eventually, I approach the railing with hesitation.

"On the 12th of July 2006, the war broke out," I read and recall that on that date we were still deployed in the Maccabim-Reut sector in the center of Israel. I quickly go through the memorial's timeline, to find the stage in which my battalion joined the fighting. And then I see that on each day of the timeline, they've listed the names of the fallen soldiers. I quickly review the letters displayed on the rusty steel and I locate them: our battalion's four fallen.

The monument reminds me of the notebooks in the truck. This is the perfect time to start writing. I go down to the truck, pull out the laptop and the red bag with the notebooks from the back of the seat, and return to the observation point.

I sit on the ground in the shade of an oak tree, facing the landscape of Southern Lebanon. I place the notebooks on the ground and turn on the laptop. I open a new Word file and save it under the name: "The Past Ten Years." I type the following headline at the top of the empty page:

2006: The War

I look to my left at the worn-out plastic bag. The year is now 2017. A little more than ten years have gone by since I wrote in the notebooks — text I could never bring myself to read. I look again at the names of the fallen on the monument, at the empty page on the computer screen, and at the notebooks.

Under the heading I type, "to complete from notebooks" and I click on the "enter" button until a new page is added to the file. I start writing about everything that happened immediately after the war.

2006-2007: FINALLY SET FREE

Two weeks after the end of the Second Lebanon War. I am twenty-two years old, and in just under three months I will be released from the army.

Avner, the company commander who was wounded in the war, is still in the hospital and I've taken his place as a temporary company commander. It seems that the soldiers, and I among them, don't really digest all that we've been through. But I try to project business as usual. We are running combat procedures before any activity behind enemy lines, we maintain our tanks by the book, and keep a strict morning routine to organize our camp. It's not easy, not for them and not for me.

We are deployed in a grove not far from the border. The residents of Avivim, the nearby village, have stretched a long power line so we can recharge our phones. Although they declared a ceasefire agreement, Israel is still holding onto a few hills on the Lebanese side of the border. At night, the tank squads cross the border fence for stakeouts on these hills. We are all exhausted, but it is very difficult to sleep during the day. The heat is relentless, the shade is insufficient, and there are swarms of flies.

Thanks to a million other administrative tasks that need my attention, I've been able to avoid cross-fence activities. It works well until the battalion commander forces me to join an in-depth patrol.

It's already evening and we are doing our final checks to make sure the tanks are ready for the mission. We get on the tanks and start our movement toward the border fence.

When the war started, the engineering unit made a hole in the fence so our troops could cross into Lebanese territory from a random point to surprise the enemy. Now, we are crossing the fence at that same spot.

When my tank tracks cross the border line, my right leg begins to shake uncontrollably. We drive to the destination hill without our front lights, in complete darkness. All that time my leg continues shaking fiercely as if I have a small engine in my knee that operates independently. When we reach our destination, we use the tank optic sights to scan the area and look for suspicious movements. At dawn we start our movement back toward the border. My leg continues shaking. Only when we cross back into Israeli territory, will the shaking stop.

◆ ◆ ◆

Yonatan, the company commander's driver, knows someone who gave him a key to one of the rooms at the guest house in Kibbutz Manara, a twenty-minute drive from our grove. Every day he takes a few soldiers in rotation for a quick shower and to freshen up a little. When he returns with the last round for that day, I get into the car alone and drive to the room in Manara. But not just for the shower.

The moment I get into the room I take my uniform off and take a quick shower. Five minutes later I am wearing my uniform again. In the time I have left, I sit by the desk in the room and write in my notebook about the war.

I go over each day in my fresh memory and write about the things that happened, exactly the way they happened. I have told no one that I am writing, and the truth is, I have no idea why I'm doing this. Something inside me, an inner urge, tells me that I need to document all that happened in the war. I'd do anything to get one whole hour alone in the room, but in most cases my writing is interrupted by a phone call telling me I'm urgently needed back at our grove.

Six weeks after the end of the war, Avner returns to the company and I go on leave for a long weekend and Yom Kippur[i] holiday. Shortly before the holiday begins, Avner calls me. "Ginzburg, that's it," he says. "Today the last team is returning from duty on the Lebanese side, and after that we are closing the hole in the fence." I feel very relieved.

From the grove we move to the nearby base, from which the tank teams are supposed to leave each night for stakeouts observing the border fence from the Israeli side. On one of the patrols to familiarize ourselves with the area, we go up to the observation point on Adir Mountain, about two and a half kilometers from the border.

The intelligence officer is giving an update on what is happening on the Lebanese side. As we stand there, I suddenly catch a cool breeze of air and I realize that after three years of a mandatory military service and one extra year in the standing army,[ii] my military service is coming to an end. I can literally feel it in my body. For a few moments I can even see the Lebanese landscape not only as a war zone, but also as an amazing mountainous region to travel in.

Despite this feeling, I'm not sure I actually want to be discharged. It's kind of surprising, since I wasn't really motivated during my military service. In the

---

[i] The holiest day in Judaism.

[ii] Officers must sign a minimum of one extra year where they will be part of the professional army.

first two years, from basic training and until the end of officers' course, I hated almost every minute of it.

I agreed to go to officers' course only because I hated the thought that I may end as a common soldier who just follows orders even more. At the end of officers' course I was assigned to command a platoon of recruits at the Armored Corps School. After a difficult and challenging first course and a somewhat boring second, I transferred to serve as a platoon commander in an operational sector inside the Gaza Strip.

There it got to be really hard for me, mainly because I didn't get along with my soldiers. The situation was so dire that one day I went into the battalion commander's office and asked to leave, but Shaul, the battalion commander, laughed in my face. "Did you get confused, Ginzburg? You're the rising star of the battalion," he said. "In eighteen months you'll be leaving for a company commander's course and then the military academy. You only need to decide whether you want a vacation before or after the academy."

Then he explained that there's a group of elite officers in the army, and I am about to become part of it. There was no room for discussion. I turned around and returned to my soldiers.

After eight months I was promoted to the best role in the battalion: Deputy Company Commander of an advanced training company, including all the benefits and accompanying salary terms. But at the end of the first tour we became an operational company, and since then we had been positioned on the West Bank.[i] There, we got an emergency call to join the war in Lebanon.

At no point in my military career did I have aspirations of being promoted in the army. I certainly didn't fantasize about the elite officers' group that Shaul, the battalion commander, insisted I was part of. But, at this moment, with the scent of freedom tickling my nose, the thought that perhaps I shouldn't leave starts to bother me.

In the post war IDF,[ii] they keep talking about preserving the people who took part in combat for the benefit of the next generations, and I completely relate to that. The fact that the commanders during my training lacked real operational experience was very noticeable. There are things that only those who've experienced them can teach.

It is also the first time in my service I feel an obligation to my tank crew that was with me during the war. There are things that only they can understand. We have the strong bond of people who went through a harrowing experience together, and need no words to explain that which cannot be explained.

---

[i] A landlocked area on the west side of the Jordan River that forms the main bulk of the Palestinian territories. Within that area are some Israeli roads and settlements controlled by IDF.

[ii] Israel Defense Forces.

There's also quite a bit of pressure and expectations from everyone, even from higher ranked commanders. On the way back to the base, after one of my recent weekends off, I stopped with Yonatan to eat at the Gome' junction rest stop.

As we sit down, I see the battalion commander with the brigade commander at a nearby table. "Ginzburg!" – The voice of the battalion commander filled the restaurant as he calls me. Yonatan restrained himself from laughing.

I approached their table. "This is Omri Ginzburg, Avner's deputy," the battalion commander introduced me. "He commanded the company after Avner was wounded and led the battalion in the extraction and the evacuation of the wounded. He's the battalion's hero – and now he wants to be released." I felt I would die from embarrassment.

"So, you're the famous Ginzburg," said the brigade commander. "I've heard a lot about you. We need people like you. You can't be discharged right now. The military thirsts for people who went through what you have, who can teach the next commanders and tell them how to deal with war. Ginzburg, I am calling you to the flag! We need you! Your battalion needs you, our brigade needs you, the military needs you."

What a cliché. But after those words I feel like I really have no choice. It's impossible to leave after they called me to the flag. It happens to me quite often during these weeks. I get a strong feeling I mustn't leave, that I am committed to the team, to the IDF, to the next generation.

Still, the indecisiveness doesn't go away. It's like a nagging voice that insists on asking, "What do you really want?" And I don't have any organized or reasoned answer. All I can think of are the moments during my service when I felt I had to get out of here right now. I was feeling like I couldn't stay for even one more day.

It was the same feeling I had that time at the battalion commander's office when I asked to be discharged. When I recall these moments, I am once again overwhelmed by the feeling that I have to get the hell out of here. I imagine myself traveling, having fun, going to the university, taking all my savings from the year in the standing army and establishing a successful business. But how can I disappoint all those people who expect me to stay?

The indecision is relentless until almost the last minute — when I decide to be discharged from the IDF. A day before my discharge, as I pass through the military posts to say goodbye to the soldiers and commanders, I get many surprised reactions. It seems like they all believed I would stay in the end.

Before I leave, I pass through the room to take my equipment and say goodbye to Avner. For a year and a half we've been eating together, sharing a room, commanding the same soldiers, and driving home in the same car. We're both emotional.

"So, are you going to fuck like a donkey?" he finally says, breaking the awkwardness with a dirty phrase as he usually does. We laugh a little. After that I take my bag, step into the car, and along with Yonatan leave the base on the border of Lebanon for the last time. Bye-bye IDF.

◆ ◆ ◆

Two weeks after my discharge, while I'm knee-deep into planning the journey my girlfriend, Shira, and I will do on the Israel National Trail, the phone rings from an unknown number. "Omri? I have a military summons for you following the car accident you had in the Golan Heights," says the voice of a young man from the other side of the line. "I think you are mistaken," I respond immediately. "I was just discharged and I didn't have any accidents in the Golan Heights."

Very soon the conversation devolves into an odd argument. He insists I had an accident and that I need to come in for questioning, and I have no idea what he's talking about. I haven't had any accidents in the army, except for that time I ran the car into a safety rail more than a year ago. "It was in the Jerusalem Mountains and I have already been court-martialed for it," I say. The conversation is beginning to agitate me. When he continues to insist, I hang up on him. I am a citizen now. Screw them all.

Three months into civilian life, I have already taken my SAT test and the days are passing by pleasantly. I bought myself an ATV,[i] which represents the realization of a little dream to upgrade the sense of freedom in my new life. I enjoy fixing everything I know how to, and what I don't know I learn. This civilian life isn't bad.

Still, every once in a while, I am bothered by the thought that perhaps I made a mistake when I discharged myself. Maybe leaving my team and the next generation of soldiers and commanders behind wasn't a good idea. In order to feel a little better about myself, I visit the high school I went to. I want to see if the project for alumni who come and speak of their military service, still exists. It turns out it does. The teacher in charge is happy for me to come and we set a date for me to speak.

I return home and start preparing the materials. I scan the map of southern Lebanon from the old atlas I had in my parents' library. Then I pull out a box of photos — throughout my service I had a simple film camera with me at all times, and I have the stack of photos I developed.

I select some from the pile and scan the photos that will help me tell the story: the preparations of the company in the Golan Heights, unloading the tanks at the Lebanese border, and driving in a convoy on the northern road. There is also a photo I took

[i] An All-Terrain Vehicle or commonly known as a quad bike.

from the slit of the tank inside the famous village of Bint Jbeil[i] during the war.

This is the first time in the seven months that have passed since the war that I'm rummaging through these memories. Up until now, I've completely repressed everything that happened.

A week later I show up for the first talk with the students; two classes sitting together in a big classroom. My presentation is called, "A Company of Tanks in the Second Lebanon War" and my stories are accompanied by my photos. I begin by describing the rush to get organized for the war. I tell them how we prepared the tanks for deployment and how I accessed the secret stash in the spares' warehouse to stock the teams with additional equipment.

The students are quiet and attentive. I tell them how our mission was changed several times and how I felt after the first soldier of the company was wounded. I present a completely different experience than the total fiasco described in the media, and also attempt to refine the harsh stories to focus on tales of heroism. When I start telling the story about Stern's wound and evacuation, my body is flooded with a feeling I'm not familiar with. A kind of unusual excitement, to the point of suffocation.

---

[i] The Battle of Bint Jbeil was one of the main battles of the war and got a huge media coverage. Bint Jbeil also serves as an important base for Hezbollah that controls the southern area of Lebanon.

This feeling stays with me until I change the subject and tell how Shira Nelson and I became the royal couple of the battalion. "It felt as if all the soldiers in the battalion wanted the relationship between us to work," I say. I tell how Avner, the company commander, insisted on replacing me to lead the forces, while explaining to the battalion commander on the radio system, "I promised Nelson that I'd bring him back in one piece." By this stage the students are completely riveted by the story.

At the end of the talk many curious students approach me and I answer their questions. Later, in the teachers' lounge, the homeroom teacher excitedly tells everyone that the lecture was fascinating. "We must make sure we deliver this lecture to the rest of the classes before the students go on their matriculation leave," she says, and I instantly agree. Soon they'll graduate from high school and the majority will join the mandatory military service. Three years for boys and two years for girls.

A week later, when I arrive at the school, the students are pointing at me in the hallways and whispering to each other in excitement. In addition to the program coordinator, a few teachers who've come to listen to me speak are also waiting in the classroom.

I begin to talk about the war and show the photos in the presentation. When I reach the point of Stern's injury that same weird feeling of suffocation overwhelms me, only this time it is more intense. I gag for a moment before I manage to finish the sentence.

Despite this, I return home with a really good feeling. I recall the excited reaction and the riveted faces of the students. I smile to myself when I remember that the part where I tell of my exchange with Avner, one of the students got to the end before me by saying, "because I promised Nelson."

I go through the evening with a sense of satisfaction and I'm looking forward to the next two lectures. But the next day the program coordinator calls me. She starts showering me with compliments about how moving the story is, how fascinating the lecture is, and how grateful they are to me. Then, she suddenly tells me that I don't have to continue with the lectures. "I can feel that it is very difficult for you and that everything is still very fresh," explains the coordinator.

"What? But the students enjoyed it so much," I stutter in surprise and add, "it's very important for me to deliver my perspective on the war to them. So they will have another angle besides the press's version about an army that lost the war and soldiers with no equipment." We make arrangements to speak again later that week. She does not call.

TRAVEL LOG: ZIVON RIVER (PART 1)

I save the file and turn off the computer. It's time to leave Adir Mountain and start looking for a place to sleep. I go back down to the truck, the feeling of suffocation from that lecture I gave in the high school still nesting in my head. How could I have ignored that feeling I had then when I told of Stern's injury?

In the months after my release, I still haven't begun to take in all that has happened. "Release," I say to myself out loud and shake my head. It's more like I've been stuck for the past ten years and I still don't know how to deal with the experience.

As I head down the mountain, I think about the coincidence that brought me here. Of all the observation points in the area, I came to precisely the one place they erected the monument.

A little after Sassa I reach a marking, which directs me to the exit from the Northern Road toward the Zivon River. It's the first time I am about to drive some real off-road route on this trip. I engage the locking hubs[i] and shift into a low gear — another test for the truck I built.

The trail is muddy and the truck slowly climbs the slippery rocks. The back part is sliding right and left looking for something to grasp. I turn the steering wheel to the left and right, and the truck finds a foothold and takes us forward. I stop at a large forest clearing in between hills. From here the trail can be continued only on foot. The sky is clear and the sun caresses my skin until a cooling breeze reminds me, it's only the beginning of March.

March 8, 2017. Thoughts are still wandering ten years back, to the months after my military service. I get settled and continue writing. After all, this is the reason I've embarked on this journey.

---

[i] An off-road car mechanism, which connects the front wheels with the front axle in order to allow all wheels to receive the power from the engine.

2007: THE NOTEBOOKS

I met Shira Nelson during my operational deployment in Northern Samaria, a few months before the war. It was during the time we arrived to start the responsibility handover from the troops who were in charge of that sector before us. At that time, a rumor had spread in the battalion about the many qualities of the officer in charge of the observation unit.[i] Or in the words of Avner, who always excelled in his sexist speech, "There's an amazing blond bitch in the observation war room."

At some point, I walked into the war room accompanied by one of the tank commanders and there I saw a tall officer in a perfectly fit khaki uniform. She had one hand pointing at a map of the

---

[i] A unit that tracks everything that is happening in the sector through cameras and other surveillance means.

sector, and the other holding a military radio. She wore sunglasses on her head that held her perfect blond hair in place.

"Entry is for those authorized only, guys," she immediately made clear. "You can't be in here."

"Hi," I said, "I'm Omri, the deputy company commander,[i] in the sector. This is Daniel, and he's a commander in our company. We came to learn a little about the sector and to understand what you are seeing." In a second, the aggressiveness in her gaze turned to frost. "Can't all your commanders come together?" she replied with the disinterest of someone who doesn't have the patience to explain everything again from the beginning. "I am not going to explain everything to each commander separately. I'll do the overview for the last time, but next time bring everyone together."

Shira went over the maps with us, explained about the sector, and emphasized over and over again the professionalism and seriousness of her soldiers. Daniel and I responded with smiles because of her over-the-top seriousness. When a slight rustle was heard in the war room, Shira lifted a blood-curdling look and blurted, "Is it possible that I am hearing noises around here?"

Deadly silence immediately came over the observers, which made Daniel laugh uncontrollably.

---

[i] Also known as Company Executive Officer (XO) or Second in Command.

Shira kicked him out of the war room, and after a few minutes she ended the conversation and threw me out as well.

A few days later it was my turn to command the company for the weekend while Avner was taking his time off. I loved Friday mornings at the base. Everything's quiet. You start smelling the cooking of the Friday traditional dinner. The soldiers who stay for the weekend clean and organize the barracks. And most importantly — it's the only day they serve hummus and challah for dinner.

But this time there was something more that interested me. When Avner was present, he was the one who went every morning for the situation assessment meeting[i] along with all the commanders in the sector. But that Saturday I went in his place since I was in charge.

The next morning I got to the meeting early and found the battalion commander there. While we waited for everyone else to arrive, I casually asked if the observation officer went home. Shaul, the battalion commander, looked at me with a mischievous smile.

"She's on duty this weekend," he said and quickly made sure that I was aware of the dangers. "Be careful, she will break your heart." Immediately after that, Shira Nelson walked into the board room followed by

---

[i] A meeting to evaluate the current alert level in the sector according to recent intelligence updates.

the rest of the companies' commanders. The meeting was brief and at the end of it, Nelson rushed out to the observation war room.

When I was on duty on Saturdays, I had to remain in operational standby. I spent the entire weekend in uniform and couldn't take off my military boots. I wasn't even allowed to go anywhere without my patrol car and an entourage that includes a driver, a tracker, and a soldier. Regardless, after the meeting I told the others that I had errands to run and went to the observation war room to look for Shira. I requested that she come outside with me for a moment, and asked her out.

A week later I saw her in civilian clothes for the first time. There are very few memories that are etched in my mind like that moment.

She stepped into the military car I took home for the weekend wearing a tank-top, tight jeans with brown leather boots, and the general appearance of a cowgirl — spreading a cloud of perfume around her. We drove to the cliffs over the Ga'ash beach and spent hours on a blanket I threw onto the car's roof, talking and drinking wine from glasses I brought. At the end of the date we kissed.

Shira and I fell head over heels in love. We spent all our shared off duty weekends together and even at the beginning of the relationship we dreamed about going on the Israel National Trail hike together when we got discharged.

Now that I am discharged, I plan the trip carefully and wait for Shira to join me. One weekend, while crashed out on the bed in my room at my parents' house, I tell Shira about the notebooks I wrote at the end of the war.

"Show me," she says. "I want to read it." I go to the drawer at the bottom of my closet and take out the red, worn-out plastic bag from Office Depot with the notebooks in it. I hand it to her and she sits on the bed, leans back against the wall and takes out the first notebook. I sit near her and stare from the side at the first page. I haven't seen these notebooks in months. After we pulled out of Lebanon I shoved them deep into the bottom of the closet and tried as hard as I could to ignore them.

I look at Shira reading attentively, her finger following the words on the page. I try to see what's being reflected in her blue eyes. Is she able to understand my handwriting? What did I write in there anyway? Suddenly the sense of suffocation overwhelms me again, and my stomach is turning — the way I felt during the lecture at the high school. I immediately get up from the bed.

Shira lifts her eyes from the page and looks at me. "I'll be right back," I say and leave the room, closing the door behind me. I go downstairs and step out to water the garden. Then I go to the basement and put all the tools that my father left in a mess back in place. It helps me relax a little.

Less than half an hour later I return to the room and gently open the door, careful not to startle Shira, who is surely focused on reading. I peek in. Maybe she has some feedback for me? To my surprise, I find her asleep with the notebook on her. What? Does she find it boring? I make some noise and Shira opens her eyes and continues reading as if she hadn't been asleep. I get into the bed and lay beside her with my back to her. Shira is silent. She was probably startled by the situation too. How could she fall asleep while reading my notebooks?

A few minutes later my mother calls us from downstairs to tell us that lunch is ready. We get up, I return all the notebooks to the bag, and shove it into the closet. Shira isn't asking to continue reading and I'm not asking her to.

A few months later we embark on the Israel National Trail trip as planned. I envy each solo traveler we meet along the way, but my strong desire to reach the end of the trail holds our relationship together until Eilat, the southernmost tip of Israel. A few weeks after the trip ends, Shira and I break up. It's not painful for me. I've felt it's been over for a while.

◆ ◆ ◆

After the breakup I continue living with my parents. I promised myself a quiet year after being discharged and I have savings from my service, so it wasn't urgent for me to start real life and get a job. But it's not really working.

One morning I sit down to have my coffee in the kitchen, and on the cover of the newspaper I see Avner's photo amongst those receiving medals for their bravery during the Second Lebanon War. The list cites that the "Medal of Courage," ranked the second highest of all medals, will be awarded to Avner. The text also tells the story of the evacuation from Bint Jbeil, in which Avner was wounded in combat on the second day of our operation.

I grab the phone and call Avner, who is still stationed on the Lebanese border. "What's happening, deputy?" Avner answers. I have managed to forget this nickname. "Figure this," I tell him. "You grabbed the first helicopter out of Lebanon, left me alone, and now they are giving you a medal."

Avner laughs. "Trust me. I don't know what they want from me with all these ribbons," he is being modest and adds, "How's Nelson?" I update Avner about the breakup and he, as usual, tosses me a comment about the wild life of a single citizen. He says being a citizen is the highest rank in the IDF. We continue to catch up about the problems in the company, and I'm instantly relieved that I'm no longer a part of it.

Around noon I sit in the back yard with my cousin, Yuval, and my sister, Efrat. They are the same age, five years older than me. They also went to school together and live together in our grandmother's old house, which shares a common yard with ours.

I update them on the news from this morning, and Efrat asks about the story of Avner in Bint Jbeil. I tell them that during the war Avner went into Bint Jbeil with his tank to evacuate wounded soldiers. After the evacuation the tank was hit by several missiles and his entire team was injured.

"Pshh, you're just like Dad. Tell it like a normal person, with details," Efrat says to me. I recall the moment they told me about Avner's injury. From that moment on I was in charge of a company of seventy soldiers.

"To be honest, I wasn't there and don't know much, but I wrote about what I went through in my notebooks," I respond. This is the first time I am telling someone in my family about the notebooks.

"I would really love to read them," Efrat says in a serious voice. "Me too," adds Yuval. I get up from my seat and go up to my room, pull out the red bag with the notebooks, go back down, and hand it to Efrat.

The next day Efrat sends me a text that she's finished reading. I head over immediately and knock on the door. When Efrat opens the door her face is red and her eyes are teary. "I can't believe that you had to go through all this," she says and embraces me, crying. Her strong embrace confuses and embarrasses me. How am I supposed to react?

I mumble something unclear like, "it is what it is," take the notebooks from her and continue to the second entrance which leads to Yuval's unit. He's not home, so I go inside and leave the bag in the living room for him. The next day he also texts me, "I finished reading. You can come take it."

When I arrive, he opens the door and without saying a word hands me the red bag. I take it, not knowing how to react to the silence. After a few seconds I turn around and go home.

TRAVEL LOG: ZIVON RIVER (PART 2)

In the midst of writing I hear voices and lift my head from the computer. Two travelers are walking toward me on the path, approaching the truck. They look at it in amazement. I'm used to this kind of reaction. There are aficionados who are familiar with the history of Suzuki's all-terrain vehicles and are very excited to see it. They know how rare the truck is and how much I worked on it for it to look like this. Others just get excited by the plate that classifies it as a "classic car" and the external appearance which is reminiscent of a matte blue toy truck.

I offer the two hikers a Coke from the fridge. They put down their backpacks and sit next to me. "There aren't many overnight camping grounds around here," says the tall one to his friend, returning to the conversation that they were having before they arrived.

"I'm staying here tonight. It's so beautiful," I say, hoping to somewhat entice them to stay, spend the night around and enjoy a cold drink. But they decide to move along and I resume thinking about the notebooks.

It took several years after the breakup from Shira for me to realize how significant that split second was, when I saw her sleeping with the notebook on her chest — a notebook that contains all my memories from the war.

In one instant, all the emotion I had for her was turned off. Looking back, I can say that I put Shira to an unfair test. She had hardly slept during the last few weeks on duty and she was probably so tired. It wouldn't have mattered what was written there. She simply had no chance of passing this test. And poor Shira, who knew how sensitive the issue was for me, never dared to ask me to try again.

I haven't spoken to Efrat and Yuval about the notebooks since the day I saw Efrat crying, and Yuval's lack of reaction. My apprehension about what was written in the notebooks only intensified — and for seven years I didn't dare tell anyone about their existence. Only after two years of weekly sessions with Gideon, did I give him the notebooks to read.

◆ ◆ ◆

The sun is already setting behind the nearby hills. I shut down my computer and begin my preparations for the night. I lay down a camping tarp and pitch the tent on top of it. Inside I put down the mattress and sleeping bag I bought ten years earlier when Shira and I hiked the Israel National Trail.

I feel better than yesterday. This location feels less intimidating to me. It appears I'm allowed to sleep here, and the nearby trail is much more pleasant than the noisy road I slept next to yesterday. A chain of lights I stretched illuminates my surroundings and I start a fire. Soon I'll have enough coals and I will cook myself some yams for dinner.

A couple of hours later, I'm already lying inside my sleeping bag with a full stomach, ready to sleep. But thoughts begin to bother me. It is so quiet. The only sounds are of crickets and the continuous howls of jackals that seem to be coming from all around the valley. Here and there I can hear the distant barking of dogs. But when all these sounds become quiet, it's totally silent.

A long hour passes and I am still awake. I didn't put out the fire properly, and the wind that changed direction is blowing smoke into the tent. I find it hard to breathe, but I don't have the guts to go out into the darkness and take care of it.

The tag with the instructions about how to pitch the tent is moving in the wind and brushes against its side making a noise as if someone is attempting to undo the zipper. It happens every few minutes, and each time my heart leaps out of my chest and my hearing switches off to the "panic of indifference" mode.

I probably didn't fasten one of the straps on the truck properly, and every once in a while, it bangs against the vehicle's metal and startles me. Perhaps someone is walking around out there.

The hours pass with disturbed and interrupted sleep. Tonight is much colder than yesterday, and despite my thermal clothes I am unable to warm up. They say that in a sleeping bag it's always best to sleep in your underwear. Otherwise the body heat is trapped between the skin and the first layers of clothes, which prevents the air inside the bag from heating up. I'm so tired.

◆ ◆ ◆

I wake up in horror. It is completely dark and quiet outside. A cold wind is penetrating through the opening at the top of the tent. My body is exhausted and my brain is racing at a thousand miles per hour as I lie motionless. I start remembering the dream.

I am backpacking on a trip somewhere in the world. Around me are people who look Indian. They are friendly and eager to help. There's a tall tower overlooking a huge pool with no water in it. I stand at the edge of the pool looking at my bag, which is tossed at the bottom.

In the background there's a heated discussion between the locals and the backpackers. They warn us that we must get away from here. When I look in the direction of the pool again, I see the locals running in all directions. They are being shot at. It looks like there are snipers in the tower, slaughtering them one by one.

My bag is in the center of the pool and there's only one important thing in it: the notebooks I wrote during the war. Suddenly I find myself at the top of the tower. There are a few more Israelis there, and I explain to them, begging, that I need to go down because my notebooks are in the pool and I have no copies of them.

"You don't understand, I haven't managed to read them yet," I say in tears. I start running around in panic in the overcrowded tower, looking for a way down.

The storm subsides and the shooting stops. I slowly go down from the tower through the shade canopy over the pool with a local guy who tries to help me. I can see the bag through a hole in the canopy and point at it. He sees it too and signals to me that he is going for it, but all at once the shooting starts again in full force and he runs back up.

We return to the tower. There are police officers who separate the foreigners from the locals. I immediately understand that the police officers were the ones shooting, and now they divide those who will go free and those who won't. It's clear to me that we're about to die, but the only thing that bothers me are the notebooks that remain down in the pool.

Then, we are in captivity, all the Israelis. Suddenly, school children come to visit. They pass us by as if we're animals in a cage and bid us farewell. The last thing I remember thinking is, "I will never see those notebooks again."

♦ ♦ ♦

I lie motionless in the tent, running the details of the dream through my mind. Why don't I have the courage to read the notebooks? What could be in them that scares me so much? And why don't I remember anything I wrote? Fatigue overwhelms me and I fall asleep again.

The sound of a car approaching wakes me up. The clock displays five in the morning. The noise of the engine reveals it's a Toyota Hilux, a new model. I open the zipper on the side of the tent and cautiously peep through it. The color of the vehicle is dark, but aside from that, it is difficult to say more. The driver is going slowly, in a low gear, and lets the car roll over the rocks.

This is the right way to drive, I think, and pray that he doesn't stop. It's probably the nature reserve ranger, making his morning patrol. He passes by the tent and a while later makes his way back. I am really tired. I haven't slept well in two days and wake up very early. And now I feel the burden of a severe sense of loss left by my nightmare about the notebooks.

The next time I wake up, the sun is already peeking from behind the mountain. I get up to brush my teeth and place a small pot of water on the camping stove. It's amazing how different I feel during the day compared to night time. All the horrible thoughts vanish. Everything looks perfect. The vegetation and the sun fill me with good energy. It's unbelievable how different this place is – how different anywhere is – in broad daylight.

To me, night time means terrible fear, an ongoing nightmare, increased anxiety, and an endless worry that someone will harm me. During the day I am filled with confidence. This place is mine. I've been here since yesterday. The notebook nightmare seems ridiculous right now. A minute before I woke up in terror, I must have snored so hard that the tent shook. I imagine a deer looking in surprise from behind the trees, trying to understand where that awful noise is coming from, and I laugh out loud. The water boils and I prepare my morning coffee.

Afterwards, I go out to roam in the valley and collect twigs for the fire so I can try the outdoor shower I bought. I heat a pot with water on the fire, place the folding pole next to one of the rocks, connect the showerhead to it, place the tube into the pot of hot water, and connect the pump to the car battery. I then take my clothes off, go under the warm flow, and enjoy a shower in my own private valley.

After the shower, I decide to stay here another night and dedicate the day to writing.

2007-2009: ESCAPING REALITY

Every once in a while, the company commander of my new battalion in the reserve calls to update me on an upcoming drill. He says he would like me to participate. Each time he disturbs the tranquility I promised myself. I explain to him over and over again that I was supposed to be positioned in another battalion and that this is a mistake.

For an entire year, Avner and I positioned soldiers to form our future reserve unit. The idea was, once we were discharged from the regular army, we would be assigned to that reserve unit as well. Even Yuval, my cousin, managed to integrate into the same unit. But when I got discharged from the regular army, some highly ranked commander decided he wanted me in his unit, and this is how I found myself in the wrong battalion.

There is also an automatic exemption from reserve duty service in the first year after finishing your mandatory military service. But that didn't matter either. The company commander kept on calling and I started to make excuses.

Last time he asked me to come just for one day so I could get to know the soldiers in the company. I replied that I had a family event and wouldn't be able to come, despite the fact it was an event for a distant relative that only my parents were invited to.

Later, when the first reserve order arrived in the mail, I called him and lied, saying I had a plane ticket for a vacation planned precisely on the dates of the drill. When the date of the drill arrived, I felt bad about myself, so I called and told him that I hadn't gone in the end.

"I don't understand, so can you come now?" the new company commander asked. I could hear the machine guns blazing in the background and it made my stomach turn. "I think we'll meet in the next drill," I responded.

After each conversation with him, a week of thoughts and anger would haunt me. Only now have I begun to understand why everyone leaves for a post service trip to India or South America. They do it to escape the reserve service.

Why is the military so stubborn? So many people get a permanent exemption from reserve service. By the time someone like me comes along – someone who wants to serve – why is it so difficult to just transfer me to another battalion? What's the problem with respecting the law and giving me a year of peace?

I didn't plan on flying anywhere after my release. And photos of friends smoking weed in India didn't appeal to me. But when this is the situation, a vacation abroad couldn't hurt. What's certain is, it will save me the need to make up excuses[i] to get out of reserve duty – excuses that are justified, but still make me feel bad.

A short while later, Daniel informs me that he's going to work selling Dead Sea products out of malls in the United States, and I decide to join. The first week on the job, I get to know Dorin. We fall in love and after several weeks we decide to travel to South America together. It turns out well, since I hated the job and the aggressive marketing anyway.

At a certain point on the trip, I start to feel like I did on the Israel National Trail with Shira. I envy those traveling alone. Dorin and I continue together to Central America, but in Guatemala we decide to break up. I push my return to Israel forward in order to make it in time for the Independence Day celebrations.

I spend the last two weeks alone on a small and beautiful island in the Caribbean, where I create a pleasant routine of a morning run followed by a yoga

---

[i] When someone is abroad he is automatically exempt.

lesson on the beach. Then, roaming around, having tacos for lunch, an afternoon nap, and then back to the beach to watch the sunset. Perfect serenity.

One of the days, I enter an internet-café to video call my parents. My mother tells me about two men in civilian clothes who came to our house looking for me. "They knocked on the door and shouted, 'Military Police. Open the door. We know that he's hiding in the house.' I panicked and didn't let them in," she tells me and adds that the officers left a warrant with a subpoena for an inquiry.

When I return to Israel it turns out that I had been scheduled for several hearings in court on the matter of the car accident (that didn't happen) in the Golan Heights — hearings I was unable to attend of course, because I was abroad.

When the trial date arrives it turns out that all this time they were referring to the accident in the Jerusalem Mountains, when originally they said it happened in the Golan Heights. Now the Military Police want to revoke my civil license for three months. I can't believe this is happening to me again.

"The whole thing is based on the damage report you filled out after the accident," the appointed military defense attorney says. I have no idea what he's talking about. He explains to me that in the inquiry that took place after the accident, they asked me what caused it and I said, "I drove at an inappropriate speed for the curve."

I don't recall ever saying such a thing. The only thing I remember is that I wanted to be done with the post-accident debriefing as quickly as possible so I could go replace Avner who was on call. I didn't place much importance on the inquiry, but as it turns out the military police built an entire case on that one sentence with the charge of reckless driving. I attend court three times, and eventually I'm sentenced to pay a fine. Where do they get the authority to give me a fine? I am no longer a soldier.

To annoy me even more, the new reserve company commander calls me up for a week of training in Tze'elim.[i] Again, I explain to him that I am in the process of transferring to another battalion. "I really don't understand you. Let me be transferred to the other battalion, everyone will be happier." But the company commander is relentless. "Come for the drill. See the company. I promise you won't want to leave."

I no longer have a choice. On the first day of training, I report to Tze'elim. I leave my bag of equipment and my uniform in the car and walk to the gate of the base in civilian clothes.

"You can't go in without an order," the guard at the entrance stops me. Without thinking too much and without saying a word, I sit down on the sidewalk next to the gate. My anger is raging. Why this

---

[i] The main reserve duty training base in the south of Israel.

obtuseness? What's the problem with transferring me to another unit? I want to serve with my soldiers and Yuval. I intend to go head-to-head with the military on this matter.

"Aren't you going to call someone?" the guard wonders. "This is a new unit. I don't know anyone and I don't have a phone on me. I only know that the drill starts here," I reply. "Okay," he gives up. "You can go inside, but next time come with an order."

I enter the base, pleased with my small victory, but concerned about what's to come. I march toward the big hall where the opening talk to the entire battalion is supposed to take place. The annoying company commander is already there.

"Where's your uniform?" he asks without saying hello. "I don't have one," I respond, playing it as dumb as possible, so he'll understand he doesn't actually have a platoon commander.[i] "I have a simple request, it's not complicated. I want to serve, but not here," I add calmly, but the company commander starts explaining again how amazing this unit is and all I need to do is to give it a chance. My pulse accelerates and a strange sense of nausea strikes me, like I could blow up at him; shouting or vomiting.

This lasts for a while until the company commander cracks. "You know what? Never mind. It's pointless. I don't want you here. Good luck," he

---

[i] I was positioned as a platoon commander in the new battalion

says and then turns around and walks away. As he leaves, I look at him, feeling the victory. And this time, it's a big one. His clear attempt to insult me didn't work, and what's important is I got what I wanted. I am being transferred!

A month later the message comes confirming my placement as a platoon commander where I wanted. In the meantime I have already managed to speak with Lavie, the company commander, and Elroei, the battalion commander. "When we're not in training or active we will try to leave the reserve alone as much as possible," Elroei says to me in our meeting. It seems like he understands that there's life as a citizen too. It makes me happy.

Two years have gone by since my release from the regular army and I've begun studying for a bachelor's degree in computer sciences at the Tel Aviv-Jaffa Academic College. During the first semester, the IDF embarks on Operation Cast Lead,[i] in Gaza. My new battalion isn't recruited, but the battalion I was released from is. I got lucky.

I spend the days of the operation glued to the television. The images of the soldiers getting organized prior to entering Gaza remind me of my days prior to the war. When I served in Gaza volunteers came to give out sandwiches and popsicles at the assembly areas. When we were relieved for a

---

[i] A three-week armed conflict between Gaza Strip Palestinian paramilitary groups and the Israel Defense Forces (IDF).

short break during the Second Lebanon War, they waited for us with a barbeque.

I talk to Sila, a good childhood friend and two days later we arrive in Tze'elim to hold a barbeque for the infantry regiment in which a good friend of ours is serving. We organize the grill while the infantry soldiers deploy for a last drill, carrying huge backpacks and heavy combat gear. The scene reminds me of the rows of soldiers in Lebanon. I wonder how many of them fought in Lebanon. Or if they know that their return relies solely on fate.

◆ ◆ ◆

After the Operation in Gaza ends something in me begins to change. One evening, we watch a horror movie at Sila's house. On the three-minute walk back to the car, I become struck with terror. It's a well-lit street in Tel Aviv, yet I feel like someone is watching me and something bad is about to happen. I run to the car, enter it in panic, and lock the doors.

Later, when I park the car at home, I exit quickly and run to my front door without looking to the sides. If there is someone there, I don't want to see him. Later on, I develop the habit of closing my eyes or looking away each time I see a scary scene in a movie.

There are other things I have weird reactions to. One of them is the National Memorial Day.[i]

---

[i] A Memorial Day for the Fallen Soldiers of the Wars of Israel and Victims of Actions of Terrorism.

Following the Israeli tradition, like we do every year, I go with friends to the ceremony at our old elementary school. However, this time it all sounds different to me.

The young students read aloud the names of the alumni who've fallen and tell their stories. After each sentence I feel that something is moving in my stomach. I sit next to Sila, and shrink myself deeply into the chair, trying hard not to cry. One tear escapes anyway. I don't know whether it's preferable to wipe it quickly or to leave it to dry by itself, only so Sila and my friends won't see.

◆ ◆ ◆

During the second semester, after barely managing to get through the first, a surprise comes in the mail — a call-up for six days of military reserve duty scheduled for the end of the semester. I call Lavie, my new company commander. "I don't think I will be able to complete an entire week," I tell him. "My classes are very difficult, and it falls right at the same time as exams." Lavie isn't impressed. "It's always like this. Reserve military service always comes at an inappropriate time," he says. I end the call disappointed.

My father said that as a reserve commander he was always considerate of students, and I was sure I would be treated the same. I'm surprised to find out that even my professors aren't going to give me any preferential treatment, despite the fact that the bylaws are filled with instructions designed to assist those who serve in reserve duty.

One professor even reacts by saying "maybe you just won't go" – something that really angers me. Is this the attitude of an academic institution in Israel? To encourage me to evade my duties instead of facilitating them? As if military duty was my idea.

◆ ◆ ◆

On the first day of reserve duty, I get up early, put on my uniform, and join Yuval for the drive to Tze'elim. The craziness of the drill starts the minute we cross the base's gate — signing for equipment, preparing the tanks, and being pressured by the battalion commander. Everyone is stressed, trying to get organized and start our movements with the tanks toward the firing zone as quickly as possible. After a little more than two years, during which I didn't even come close to tanks, uniform, or military discipline, I managed to forget about it all. Now it comes as a shock to me.

In the mess hall, during lunch, everything looks disgusting. Before I even realize what's happening around me, I find myself standing with a greasy plate in one hand, a disposable knife and a dirty tablespoon in the other. The cook in front of me firmly refuses to give me a large piece of schnitzel or a side dish.

I sit down next to a sticky table with my throat dry from anger, reach for the pitcher of water, and then remember I forgot to take a glass. I get up to fetch one only to discover there are no more. I return to my seat and look at my plate with disgust, feeling as if the frustration is burrowing a hole in my stomach. I wrap the repulsive food between two slices of bread, to obscure the taste, and shove it all in my mouth just to stave off the hunger.

After lunch we return to the tanks to prepare them for departure. When the first tank starts up, the smell of burnt diesel fuel overwhelms everything. It is joined by a cloud of dust created by the powder that falls from the tracks as the tank advances. All at once memories from southern Lebanon start to surface. I haven't smelled a tank up-close like this since the war.

That same day, we go to the firing zone and begin the drill. It's June, in a desert, a million flies, and 43 degree heat (110°F) that exhausts you even if you haven't done anything.

On the third day, upon leaving for the drill with a veteran tank team, the gunner lights up a cigarette inside the tank. Everyone knows it's forbidden to smoke so close to the ammunition.

"Man, did you light a cigarette?" I ask in surprise. "What's up with you? Put it out. Put it out now. This isn't cool." He snaps, "Why should I put it out? I won't. Stop being a checklist supervisor," he raises his voice. A few seconds later we're barking at each other, and then he makes a show of putting out the cigarette and announces, "I'm not staying in this tank."

I call the deputy company commander on the radio and ask him to stop. I get off the tank and approach to update him, expecting him to react in the same way as I did. "Okay, we'll switch your gunner with mine," he decides without paying attention to the gravity of the situation and adds, "We must continue with the drill."

I return to the tank furious. This is driving me crazy. He knows the regulations — there is no smoking in the tank. So what, he can't restrain himself? Why such spite? And why are the other commanders backing him up?

This is not how I pictured reserve duty to be. In the regular army they always spoke of the reservists as being the most professional guys, people who will do everything quickly and efficiently in order to gain a little more time to rest. Instead, this is a group of people nearing forty, who are making an issue out of everything. And their commanders fear them. What a nightmare.

On the way home I tell Yuval about the incident. He says that there are really some difficult guys out there. Deep down I know that with him it would have never happened. The troops love Yuval and that's why they follow him, while I evoke objections.

I barely manage to pass the period of exams after the reserve service. Only with deadline extensions and help from friends do I somehow manage to pull it off.

August 2009. The summer vacation post-freshman year. I accompany a delegation of American youths from the Taglit-Birthright Project — a ten-day free heritage trip to Israel for young adults of Jewish heritage, most of whom are visiting Israel for the first time. I meet them in Jaffa and join them on the second half of their trip — three days down south, followed by two days in Jerusalem.

When we reach Jerusalem, Yariv, the group guide, approaches me and asks whether I would like to participate in a small memorial ceremony. He is planning to have it tomorrow during the visit to Mount Herzl — the main cemetery for leaders of Israel and people who sacrificed their lives for the country. "Maybe you can say a few words about your military experience," he suggests.

The patriot in me immediately signs on for the task. I take a pen and some paper from the reception desk at the hotel and sit down in a secluded corner. A few minutes later I approach Amy, one of the girls in the group, who is also sitting in the lobby. I ask her to proofread what I have written and correct my English grammar mistakes.

Amy peeks at the page in my hand and skims through the first few lines. She then takes it without saying a word and goes to sit in the corner of the lobby. I follow and stand next to her in silence, looking at the tears pouring down her cheeks as she corrects my mistakes.

The next day we start on a visit to Yad Va'shem, Israel's official memorial site to the victims of the Holocaust. Afterwards, we walk to the nearby cemetery, Mount Herzl. We start the visit at the tomb of Yitzhak Rabin, Israel's prime minister who was assassinated in 1995.

From there, we continue to the tomb of Herzl, a political activist and writer who was considered the "Visionary of the State of Israel." Next to Herzl tomb, the ceremony takes place. I am the last speaker. I read what I wrote the night before, and observe that everyone present is deep into the story. At the end of the ceremony they approach me. Some hug me one by one, without saying a word. I feel the tears pressing against my eyes from within, but I hold on tight.

I become more and more restless. Being with the American delegation gives rise to patriotism in me and at the same time, reflections arise about living in Israel. They add to the thoughts that have plagued me the past year and cause me anxiety. I ask Yariv, the guide, to leave the group for a moment to go search for the grave of Oz Tzemach.

Oz was the tank commander in my company when I was the deputy company commander of the advanced training company. When we established the operational unit, he moved to another company in the battalion. On the last night of the war, a missile penetrated his tank and the entire team was killed. A few days after it happened, I saw the remnants of the tank. The team had no chance. Up until today, I haven't visited Oz's grave. In fact, I haven't visited any graves of the fallen that I knew.

I walk around the military plot of the cemetery, find the right row, and walk along it to Oz's tombstone. I stand there, take deep breaths, and stare at the letters engraved in the stone. When I lift my head, I am surprised to see that the Birthright group is standing around me.

"What are you doing here?" I ask Yariv and add, "This is the guy who was my soldier. I told you about him." Yariv's eyes widen in surprise. "I'm here to tell Oz's story to the group," he says. "His older brother is my best friend."

Everything instantly overwhelms me. I feel like in a second I will burst out crying. Yariv tells the group about the coincidence. "This is Israel," he explains. "We all know each other. We are all connected to each other. People here fight together and die together so this country will continue to exist."

Silence falls on the group and Yariv continues to tell Oz's heroic story. He starts by describing the tank, which traveled through a narrow rural road at the edge of a forested valley. In a second I am thrown back to that valley, the one I was in myself.

I can literally see the path we created for our tanks. It reached the main road of the village. I can see the sharp turn to the left and the road with the lowered backyards on the right. I remember the tank that slid into one of those yards after crushing the picturesque fence. It was right before the intersection where I saw a sign with the word STOP in its center. The Israeli stop sign is just an image of a hand. This one reminded me of the Playmobil kit I had as a child.

As Yariv talks, more and more details continue to flood me. The sights of the beginning of the war comprised of short and delusional moments when I felt like I was on a pastoral trip in the south of Italy. I am surprised to discover that I remember the colors of the fences, the pot plants in the windows, and even the feeling I had when noticing that "Stop" sign.

I lift my eyes to Oz's headstone, look at the letters of the name, and the date he died. "He's gone," I think to myself, feeling as if I am only now beginning to comprehend it. Only now, three years after the war.

This thought opens the floodgates. I start crying like I have never cried in my entire life. Bitterly sobbing, my entire body trembles, releasing something that has been festering inside for three whole years. I hide my face in embarrassment, not knowing what to do. The crying is uncontrollable. Sights of the Lebanese village continue to overwhelm me, and with them, the moments of horror I experienced.

Yariv continues to talk about Oz. I reach out to the headstone and touch the letters engraved in the stone, without actually understanding what I am doing or why. My sobbing only increases. And then, out of nowhere, Shiran, the paramedic of the group, approaches and hugs me. In that moment, the hug means the world to me. I feel like she's the only one in the group that can understand me. She's my age, an Israeli who was raised here and served in a combat unit. Only she knows what I am truly going through at this moment.

My fingers continue to feel the letters, lingering on sharp edges. I sob continuously. Where is this coming from? Oz wasn't even a good friend of mine, but the crying doesn't stop even when Yariv finishes talking. The group continues to stand quietly by the grave. There's complete silence, in which only my crying is heard, growing increasingly stronger, until I can't take it anymore and I storm off to the lavatory.

I wash my face and take deep breaths for several minutes. It takes me a while to get composed. I'm embarrassed by the group's reactions and looks. When I return, they are still very quiet, as if they are shocked. Some of them approach and hug me. No one is talking.

◆ ◆ ◆

From Mount Herzl we go straight to Ben Gurion Airport, to catch the flight that will take the Americans in the group back home. There's an unusual silence on the bus. The past hours created a great bond between us and saying goodbye at the airport is very emotional.

The thoughts and memories from the war accompany me my entire way home. Suddenly I am thinking of Klein who was a tank commander in the company back then. How come I never stayed in touch with him? I am such an asshole. That same evening I text him.

"What's happening, bro?" — as if we talk every day.

"Wow, man, you have no idea how happy you made me right now," Klein replies.

I tell him that I just spent a week with a group of Taglit. "You know how it's supposed to be. Great fun with plenty of American girls. But somehow I managed to turn the experience into a difficult one. We concluded the trip on Mount Herzl, at Oz's grave. I remembered our 'great escape' after the run over incident," I write to Klein regarding the retreat battle led by our company.

"You really moved me right now," Klein replies. "Since the war, I sometimes recall some of the events. I remember in particular when they asked you to evacuate a fallen soldier and you immediately called me on the radio, asking me to come with you. I felt like you trusted me no less than I trusted you, and I will never forget it.

"More than that, at the end of the war, when we got back to Israel, you jumped on me with such a tight embrace. I will never forget that hug. What a commander you were. You organized the entire company in a German-like order, and held everyone by their balls. We have to get together for a beer. I remember everything. I trust you and appreciate you very much. I love you."

"Let's speak when you get back. I would be happy to meet up!" I write. And then, after a slight hesitation, I add, "I think I am a little confused with myself lately about the whole war." This is the first time I'm telling someone else about what I'm going through — perhaps even myself. Klein's reaction surprises me. "I'm the same way," he writes. "Why do you think I escaped Israel like that? Studying in London wasn't my first choice, I just needed time off from Israel. When I come for a visit we must meet."

♦ ♦ ♦

That same summer I move to live alone for the first time in my life. Efrat, my sister, has left the residential unit in the backyard and I take her place. I don't want to be dependent on anyone.

With what's left from my reserve savings I buy my first car, a second-hand Suzuki Jimny. It's a small off-roader with a weak engine, but it definitely does the job. I feel like I'm sixteen-years-old again, when I bought my first dirt bike and went riding every day after school. The hum of the little engine that exerts itself while I squeeze out every ounce of horsepower it has to offer. The strong wind that hits my face, and a rush of adrenaline into my veins. The ultimate freedom and independence.

The experience of my first car is similar. I start going out with it on long desert trips with my friends. I'm always in charge of preparing the route and navigation. This is a big task: to plan the route in advance and then deal with navigation throughout the trip. But at least there's a better chance of seeing animals before they run away.

On the first night trip to the Golan Heights, we enter an abandoned Syrian village. All at once leading the convoy becomes a huge disadvantage. Throughout the drive I feel as if a million eyes are looking at me through the broken windows of the empty buildings. Behind every little turn I imagine someone standing in the middle of the road, waiting to surprise us. I have never felt like this before. I don't tell anyone about it.

◆ ◆ ◆

At the start of the second year of my degree, rumors start about an operational reserve duty activity that will last for a month precisely during the exam period of the second semester.

I call Lavie, but he makes it clear to me that the other two platoon commanders approached him with the same problem, and he has no solution. Every time I imagine the upcoming reserve service, I get stomach aches and nausea. It can come from nowhere, and all at once. If for one moment I am not busy and my thoughts begin to wander, I instantly get the image of dressing myself in uniform, signing for a weapon, and going on a nighttime operational activity.

Over time the stomach aches become a daily issue. Despite living close to my parents, it seems that living alone doesn't help my sense of security. Instead of advancing in my classes, I picture myself dressing in uniform and I instantly become nauseated. Instead of studying, I just sit at home and stare at the screen.

After two more weeks I start waking up at night. My mouth is dry and my body, frozen, like I'm paralyzed in bed. I know that someone is out there, waiting for me to make the first move. Sometimes then tension keeps me awake. Only when the promise of light penetrates through the shutters, can I calm down enough to fall asleep again.

Most mornings I don't recall anything from the night before. The memory pops up by surprise at some point during the day, and then I try to understand what happened. How could it be that I was so scared in my bed, in my own home?

During the day everything looks so safe, and I don't attribute much importance to it. I am focused on my goal to complete the semester successfully, and when I have a clear goal I know well to ignore any factor which bothers me, or push it aside.

At the beginning, he appeared only on the days I thought about the reserve service. At some point, he started visiting just like that, for no reason. And then every night.

The more the sleepless nights accumulate, the more exhausted I become, and waking up in the morning becomes impossible. I sit in classes for hours on end staring into space, picturing myself in uniform, commanding soldiers, attempting to understand who the hell is he? Why is he stalking me at night?

TRAVEL LOG: ZIVON RIVER (PART 3)

The sun begins to set and I start to get organized for the night. Each time, starting a fire is a test. Will I make it on the first try? The fire catches right away igniting the dry leaves and twigs. But when I put the thicker branches on, they refuse to light up and the fire dies. When I attempt to separate a few coals to heat a pot of water for pasta, all I get is a great deal of smoke. The dying fire doesn't come to life even after blowing on it.

By now I consider skipping dinner and going to sleep, but eventually I decide to cook the pasta and sauce over two camping burners. While the meal is cooking, I once again light up pieces of paper and leaves, add twigs and branches, and this time the fire catches properly. I sit in front of it with the cooked pasta and manage to enjoy the moment, despite the darkness surrounding me.

After I put away the equipment and brush my teeth, I make sure that the fire is completely extinguished. This time I also remember to cut the pesky label off the side of the tent and to tighten the straps of the bag on the truck. Tonight, there won't be any unwanted noises.

After last night's cold, I decide to give the "sleeping in underwear" method a chance. I take off my pants and slip into the sleeping bag. Before I fall asleep, I am flooded by thoughts of the time following the war.

In the first three years after Lebanon there were several signs. I ignored them all and continued to run away and suppress them. And each time, I chose something else as a problem to blame.

The former company commander was unable to understand that I was assigned to the wrong battalion. The new company commander didn't allow me to finish the semester. I even managed to blame the professors who wanted me to invest more time in my degree. They were all gunning for me.

All the signs pointed to the same problem, but I didn't have the nerve to admit I didn't want to go to reserve service. The military police that contacted me at the beginning of my breakdown turned into the enemy as well. How is it possible that a civilian, formerly a brave officer who fought in Lebanon, should pay for the vehicle damage out of his own pocket? I didn't understand then what significance this accident would have later on, when I would seek the help of the military.

My attempts to suppress continued, but the post-traumatic stress that I hadn't yet acknowledged, didn't give up so easily. Once I started waking up, feeling that there was someone out there watching me, it all escalated so fast.

Someone was trying to harm me, and I had nowhere to run and had no one to blame. "He's out there," where did that term come from? I try to remember, but all I can think of are the countless nights I lay motionless for hours, convinced that if I move even an inch, he would hurt me.

Indeed, nothing makes sense in this situation. Night after night it turned out that there was no one there. Nothing bad was happening. And still, I was convinced that a great disaster was imminent.

Despite the heavy thoughts, I somehow manage to fall asleep.

◆ ◆ ◆

I wake up suddenly from a noise that sounds like a large group of people approaching me. I lie motionless in the tent and hear them whispering. I count at least twenty people walking on the path. They then step off and walk around the tent.

God! This is not another nightmare, it's reality! It's all real. There are people surrounding my tent. Not one or two, but many people in the dark. I am completely surrounded. What's going to happen? What are they planning? What am I supposed to do now?

My eyes watch frantically but my body is paralyzed. I can't see anything through the tent sheet. I take a deep breath and, with a swift motion, get out of the sleeping bag, open the tent's zipper and peek into the darkness. The sight before me floods my entire body with a feeling I couldn't have imagined even in my worst nightmare.

In front of the tent's opening are four-armed people. One of them kneels in a shooting position right in front of me. His rifle and his face, covered in camouflage paint and aimed at the valley. His magazine is loaded into the rifle. Another person, also kneeling, is a little farther away, and the remaining two are lying prone a little ways behind him, their weapons aimed in the same direction.

I'm confused and panicked, in my underwear, and in the company of armed soldiers. Without fully understanding what I'm doing, I ask in a hesitant stutter, "What's happening, guys?"

"Everything's fine. We're watching over you," one of them answers. I pretend this answer satisfies me. I close the opening of the tent and lie on top of the sleeping bag. I hear them walking around me, literally around my head. My heart is pounding a million beats per second.

One of the soldiers whispers his location over the radio system, but I don't hear the one answering him on the other side. Perhaps he's wearing a headset. I can almost see it in my mind's eye.

When they continue their movement, I once again freeze in terror. My eyes look around frantically. I have no idea if they all continued on or if several of them are waiting in ambush next to the tent. I have a feeling that there's another one out there and he's lying right beside me. Earlier I felt someone position himself to my left, and I still haven't heard him move away.

The thoughts are relentless, as if attempting to break down the situation into the smallest components. Which unit could it be? Wait, what unit even trains in such a small group, and in an area that isn't defined as a firing zone?

The realization slowly seeps in. This is not a drill. When the soldier said earlier "everything's fine, we're watching over you," I thought he was kidding. Indeed, this is what we used to say to civilians. But we're really close to the border with Lebanon. This is probably a real operational activity.

I lie in the dark thinking about the Hezbollah men who easily crossed the border fence in 2006 to carry out the kidnapping[i] which led to the war. Who knows how many of them cross the fence every night searching for targets.

Very quickly the thought turns into self-flagellation for my poor handling of the situation. How did I not ask him whether it was a drill or operational activity? Whether it was routine or an emergency? How did I not ask if I have something to worry about? And what would I have done if they had answered me in Arabic? What's certain is, even if they're still around, there's no way I'm going out now to ask them what I didn't ask earlier.

It looks like I will not be falling asleep tonight and I haven't got the nerve to pack the equipment and escape. I lie with my eyes open and listen to the silence. Every once in a while, some noise breaks through and I try to determine whether or not they're still close. A few hours later, I'm still in the same position. Could it be that they are too? What, not even a slight movement?

I feel exactly the way I did on those hard days, when I would wake up from a nightmare and feel that he is out there, looking at me. Only this time it's real. I'm not in my bed at home, but lying alone in the dark, five kilometers (three miles) from the Lebanese

---

[i] Hezbollah, a terror organization from Lebanon, that kidnapped the reserve soldiers, Eldad Regev and Udi Goldwasser, may they rest in peace.

border, and God knows what is happening around me. Let the sun rise already so I can get the hell out of here.

I don't know how or when, but I fall asleep. It's still dark when I wake up from the noise of an approaching vehicle. The clock shows 05:19. The engine sounds like a D-Max pickup truck I used to drive in the military. The sound of the antenna tapping on the metal leaves no room for doubt. Only the military off-road vehicle drives with a deployed antenna pounding on the body.

I open a peeking slit but am blinded by the headlights and can see nothing. After the truck passes the tent, I notice it is indeed a military D-Max and in its back seat there are several bobbing heads of sleeping soldiers. It's probably related to the soldiers who were here earlier.

I'm cold and so tired. My throat is very dry, from the cold, or perhaps from the nightmares I forgot. This too happens to me a lot.

When the sun starts to come up, the tent warms a little and the air inside seems to become brighter. I snooze the alarm clock, close my eyes and manage to sleep a little.

♦ ♦ ♦

When I wake up everything seems a lot less frightening. And still, after the visit from the soldiers, I need a break from camping. Today I'm going up to the Golan Heights. I intend to drive the route of the Dishon River and from there continue to Kibbutz Ein Zivan, where I will enjoy a shower and a good night's sleep at Tabenkin's, another good friend.

The thought of seeing Tabenkin makes me hurry the organization and after a short while, the truck and I are on the road again, traveling among huge carpets of daisies speckled with anemones and cyclamen.

It is precisely inside all this beauty around me that I remember the days I scorched this road with tank tracks. It is here that we erected the battalion's assembly areas during the war. It is here that I organized the company in the convoy that I entered Lebanon with — and in some ways, never left.

Tabenkin is working when I arrive at his house. He takes a break to have a coffee with me. "Who takes a month off to travel in this small country?" Tabenkin asks from the kitchen with his back turned to me.

I update him on my recently ended relationship with Noya and about my wish to celebrate the conclusion of my truck project. But he can tell I'm hiding something and continues to dig, "I've known you for quite a while. You really don't know how to rest or roam around aimlessly." I smile without saying a word.

Tabenkin lets me get away with it this time and the topic of conversation changes to memories from an off-road trip we took together in the mud of the Heights. How will I ever be able to publish what I'm writing during this journey if I can't even tell a good friend about my PTSD? How can I publish something like my notebooks when I can't even bring myself to read them?

Tabenkin goes back into his study and I step out to the balcony with my laptop.

2010-2011: COMBAT PTSD CLINIC

I continue to wake up at night in complete paralysis and fear, feeling like someone is out there. There's no other choice, I need to speak with someone. The first person I share this with is Sila, my best friend. We grew up together and he could always point out things about me that I wasn't able to see.

Despite our closeness, I can't find the words to describe what I'm going through. I don't want him to think I'm just trying to get out of reserve service. In a telephone conversation I tell him that in the last few weeks I have been unable to sleep. I also share that as more time goes by, I am increasingly distracted by the upcoming reserve service and it's impacting my studies.

Before the call I pictured Sila's surprised reaction, but he is not surprised by anything I say. "It's anxiety man," he names it, and insists I need to speak with a professional — a psychologist such as his mother.

What does that even mean — anxiety? In any case, I don't think I have that. In general, his words aren't resonating. Sila goes on talking to me about anxiety in our following conversations too. Each time I listen a little more closely, but I do nothing with it. I feel like what he's describing is really not me. I'm fine. A psychologist is for people who are really screwed up, and it certainly doesn't coincide with my plans economically speaking.

I'm working very little during my studies in all kinds of casual jobs so I can maintain my car. I plan each expense carefully, so where will I find the money for psychologists? If I ask my parents they will surely help, but there's no way I'd ask them. How will I tell my father I need a psychologist due to something relating to the military? What will I say to him – that I don't want to do reserve service and I have excuses? These thoughts help me ignore the situation and somehow, I manage to go on as usual.

One morning I wake up, exhausted and extremely tired, like every morning, and I drive to the college for another day of mid-semester schooling. Thoughts about the reserve service fill me right from the beginning of the drive, even before I exit my hometown of Kfar Saba. "What will people around me say if I don't show up for the upcoming operational tour?" I think — and the next thing I know, I find myself in the parking lot of the college.

I sit in the car confused, looking side to side, not understanding how the hell I got here. In the morning it takes nearly an hour to get from home to the college, but I don't have a shred of memory from the drive — which route I took, what was playing on the radio, whether there were traffic jams. How long have I been sitting in the parking lot? I have no idea.

The thoughts that filled my head as I left the house placed me in a hypnotic-like state, and from that moment on I drove on autopilot, like I was sleep-driving. How could I drive like this? How did I not have an accident? How is it even possible to not remember what happened a moment ago?

The feeling of no control bothers me immensely and is manifested into agitation and impatience toward my fellow schoolmates. I don't notice until I accidently overhear a conversation about me. "Leave him. He's grumpy again." Again? When else have I been grumpy at school?

Another week passes and despite my attempts to convince myself it's nothing serious, the situation isn't improving. It's getting worse. I haven't slept properly for more than a month and I can barely function. I don't do the homework in any of the courses, I just copy it from other students before the beginning of each class.

I try to talk to Lavie again to explain that I am very stressed from my studies and can't handle an entire month of operational tour. But Lavie doesn't understand me and insists that there's no other solution. I must report for reserve service.

♦ ♦ ♦

Toward the end of the first semester I crack. I realize that if I don't speak to someone, I might not pass the exam period successfully. And again, I walk circles in my room, while searching for the right words to ask Sila for help. Finally, I call him.

"It's time to talk to your mother. It is possible that something isn't quite right with me," I admit for the first time out loud. I ask him to give Dita a little background information to make it easy on me when I call her. That same night she invites me for coffee at their home.

When I get there, Dita takes me to his older sister's room, which has been converted into a clinic. I tell her everything that I've been through the past few months. Dita knows what I'm talking about. She tells me that she is very familiar with the issue and that it's a shame it's not treated properly in the military. Her gaze is full of compassion. It seems like she is torn between wanting to hear more as a professional, and the urge to get up and give me a motherly hug.

Instead, she tells me that she'll confer with a good friend of hers about making sure I start treatment as soon as possible. By the next morning I receive the phone number of the IDF's Unit for The Treatment of Combat PTSD. I didn't even know there was such a thing.

I'm not able to sleep that entire night. What am I supposed to tell the people in that unit? What am I even suffering from? Anxiety? In the movies they call it shell shock or PTSD, but they're talking about people who are completely dysfunctional. And what if they want to discharge me completely from the reserve service? How will I tell Yuval and my dad? I don't really want to get out of the reserve service. I just want them to let me finish the semester in peace.

The next day, I call the number that Dita gave me. "Combat PTSD Clinic," the voice of a young soldier says over the phone. "Hi," I stutter, "I got your phone number, ehh... I have some issues with the reserve service and it seems to me that I need to talk to someone. I am going through some issues that are a little weird lately," I add with a great deal of effort.

"Okay," she says in a tone I can't quite figure out. Then she asks bluntly, "Were you under fire? Were you shot at?"

"What? What does that mean?" I ask baffled, trying to stall for time to understand what I'm supposed to say. My head is buzzing with a million thoughts.

"During your military service, were you shot at?" The soldier on the other side of the line sounds short and impatient. "Because we only treat those who were under fire," she says.

"Ah, I think so, I was in the war," I stutter.

"Not 'I think so.' Were you shot at or not? Were you under fire in some kind of situation? Because otherwise we simply don't treat it," she repeats. I can just imagine her rolling her eyes.

I run events from my military service through my mind. During the war no one actually shot at me — that is, not at me personally. But during my military service an improvised bomb exploded right next to me. Oh, and there was the time a missile flew right over my head. On the other hand, it's not certain they were aiming at me. Maybe the charge that blew up on my tank in Gaza counts? But the truth is that no one was sure it was a charge, and technically it isn't considered "shooting at me."

Perhaps the missile that flew over my tent in the Gaza strip counts? Wow, I have no idea, I think to myself. I never felt like someone was shooting at me. But it looks like only one answer will move me to the next step.

"Yes, I was shot at," I reply after a long silence. I feel like I'm lying. She isn't particularly interested.

"Okay, so I am scheduling an evaluation appointment for you," she responds, this time cheerfully. "Can you come on Thursday at eleven?"

"Yes." I listen to her arrival directions without really understanding what's happening, and hang up.

I have no idea what to do now. Is this how it's going to be? "Were you shot at?" Up until yesterday I hadn't told anyone anything and suddenly they ask me over the phone what happened to me during my service? And now, this soldier will write it down in some case file and everyone will be able to read this information about me?

I feel like my head is about to explode. I don't really know if I was under fire or not. No one ever pointed a gun at my head or stood in front of me with a weapon, so I think I wasn't shot at — certainly not like my father was when he fought Egypt in '67 and in Syria in '73.[i]

In a week I'll go to that evaluation session. What will I answer if they ask whether I was shot at? All I want is for them to approve my treatment and cancel my upcoming reserve service. Wait, did I just lie to her in order to get out of military reserve service?

I tell no one I made an appointment with the Combat PTSD Clinic, and my thoughts are relentless in the week leading up to it. Will they be writing down everything I say? Will there be a file with my name on it? Will they write down that I don't want to do reserve service? Indeed, this unit is part of the IDF, there is no real confidentiality, and every low-level soldier who answers the phone has access to the files.

---

[i] In The Six Days War and The Yom Kippur War.

A moment ago, the military wanted to revoke my driving license because of some sentence I said five years ago. Now I am supposed to tell them what I am going through at night and what happened in the war? For what purpose? So five years from now they can judge me for what happened there?

♦ ♦ ♦

Thursday arrives. I park outside the gate of the Tel Hashomer base close to Tel Aviv. I walk in and follow the instructions of the guard at the gate. I enter the one-story building, cross through a narrow corridor filled with windows, and arrive at an old classroom plaza — a strange combination of a primary school and a derelict healthcare clinic in a forgotten suburb. I knock on the door of the admissions office and tell the receptionist I've arrived. She looks up at me. "Wait here. In a minute you will go in for an evaluation with Guy Shulman."

I sit down on a chair in the corridor flipping through newspapers tossed on the table without actually reading them. Each time one of the doors opens, I lift my head to see who comes out. I'm terribly anxious about the possibility I will run into someone I know here. I imagine all kinds of possible scenarios for such an encounter and attempt to prepare my reaction — some story, in case one of them comes to pass. Eventually, a large bald man in civilian clothes comes out from one of the rooms and asks me to come in. Guy Shulman.

For more than two hours we sit in a nearly empty room with only a writing desk and two old chairs. At first, he asks about my childhood and my life up to my enlistment in the IDF. I describe the normal childhood of a slightly mischievous boy, the kind who looks for thrills here and there, getting into shenanigans. Nothing unusual. A normal life in a family where everything was "just fine."

Shulman is not satisfied. He dwells on every detail and continues to ask about family members. What do my parents do for a living? What kind of relationship do they have with my siblings? He then focuses on my father's military service and asks whether he was diagnosed with PTSD after the Yom Kippur War.[i] I am surprised by the question and reply that he wasn't.

When we move on to my military experience, I describe a very motivated soldier without any unusual difficulties. I try to share as little as possible regarding the war in Lebanon, but he's relentless. He asks invasive questions about the turn of events during combat and attempts to find out what specific event impacted me there. I don't recall a specific event, but his questions lead me to recall when I was exposed to large amounts of blood and live fire while I had command responsibility. Stern's incident.

I respond carefully, making sure to provide as little as possible. My head echoes with the experience

---

[i] In '73, during the Yom Kippur holiday, a war began, when the Arab coalition jointly launched a surprise attack against Israel.

of the accident in the military vehicle. What if I say too much and they end up blaming me? I try to move on to another subject, and after a while, which seems like an eternity, I notice that it's working and feel very relieved.

Shulman moves on to the period after my release. I tell him about the mistake in assigning me to the wrong reserve service battalion. I also tell him how the orders occupy my mind and distract me from my studies. I tell him how I wake up at night with a strange feeling and I'm unable to go back to sleep. At the end of the meeting Shulman says they will review the details and update me about the next stage.

I leave there with a bad feeling, as if he forcefully extracted details I didn't want to share with anyone, ever — surely not with someone who is somehow related to the military.

A few days later, Shulman calls. "We currently do not have an open spot for individual treatment," he says and offers me group therapy with other patients in the unit. "Think about it and let me know," he concludes. I hang up the phone.

Even during the evaluation with Shulman, I sensed that something was happening against my will. I don't want to tell anyone else about the war and the decisions I made during the course of it. Talk about it in front of a group of strangers? No way. It sounds like a bad idea.

A few more days pass before I call Guy Shulman to reject his offer. He asks me to think about it a little more.

◆ ◆ ◆

With the evaluation still weighing heavily on me, I am thrown into the exam period of the first semester. The black cloud of my upcoming reserve service is still hovering over me. The emails from Lavie continue to arrive, and each one brings a long, sleepless night followed by a day of fatigue.

At some point I break. I ask Lavie for a meeting, and several days later I arrive at his home for coffee. Before I even open my mouth he starts talking about the assignment and training. He goes on and on about tasks, goals, and what he expects of me in my role as platoon commander. Only when he finishes, is he kind enough to ask me how I feel.

I remind him that the deployment falls during the exam period and there's no way I will be able to make up for the gaps in my studies. I barely survived the last exam period, and that was without being absent. I tell him I'm unable to sleep at night or concentrate during the day — that it is difficult for me to think of myself as under deployment or in charge of troops once again. I even confess that since the war, something has changed in me. "I really feel that I'm unable to come for the assignment at this time," I conclude.

Lavie attempts to calm me down. He says it's difficult for him as well, and that he too carries things from the Second Lebanon War. "But there's nothing we can do. The battalion must meet its assignments."

I continue to insist and tell him that I can't come. But Lavie continues, as if I haven't said anything. "Try," he says. "After the deployment period starts, we'll see what can be done with your studies."

I leave the meeting frustrated. Lavie didn't listen to a word I said. He only blurted out the usual catchphrases that commanders recite when a soldier has a motivation problem or fears. I know, because I myself recited those same slogans to soldiers.

The night after our meeting is the hardest I've experienced yet. I toss and turn in bed, preoccupied, and don't close my eyes even for a second. Each time I picture myself wearing the uniform I'm overcome with severe nausea. I wish I could simply disappear somehow from the world. "But then I'd miss the exam period," I think. No, this isn't a good solution. One thought after another, and hovering over everything is the question, "What the hell am I to say to Lavie?"

When the morning comes, I take the laptop into bed and write a long email to him that describes, in detail, all that I've been going through lately:

> I don't even know where to begin, but after long conversations and a great deal of reflecting, I have decided that I cannot go on like this anymore. I need therapy. Why is it

that every time I'm about to enter the reserve service I'm unable to sleep at night, to study, or concentrate when driving? It weighs on me all the time and lately I'm realizing that maybe my stress doesn't just come from my studies.

The difficult part, which is why I have delayed getting therapy for several years now, is dealing with you, with Yuval, with my father, and friends in the company. I have long talks with my soldiers in which I convince them that we need to continue coming to reserve service, despite the fact that it sucks. How can I tell them that I'm not coming? How, knowing that they will have a harder time because of my absence? Yuval will go, and I will stay here?

It simply doesn't make sense. I can't keep suffering for months with every reserve service order. There are plenty of nights that I can't fall asleep because I can't stop thinking about the military and worrying about the war that could break out tomorrow.

When we get together, I'm unable to tell you what I really want to say. So I've laid it all out here. Now you know that we have a problem.

Lavie, I am sorry for dropping this on you and hope that you'll understand.

I finish the email and send it to Lavie without reading what I've written. The next day at noon, when the phone rings and Lavie's name comes up on the screen,

I get filled with hope that he understands. However, despite having read the email, Lavie implores me to come anyway. "I have no other solution," he says. "All the officers have problems, and I really need you." I barely manage to utter a word. The call ends and I sink back into my fears.

◆ ◆ ◆

A call-up drill is planned for the following week. All the soldiers in the battalion will receive an automated surprise phone call and they'll need to report to the base up north right away. When we arrive at the base, we'll have to prepare the tanks for mobilization as soon as possible — a deal of twelve hours, and then we will go back home.

Waiting for that phone call raises my anxiety levels to new heights. It comes when I'm on my way to college. I'm driving on the highway and the phone rings. When I answer, an automated message says in a robotic voice: "Hello, this is a recorded message. This is the reserve unit of — Omri Ginzburg. You need to report to — Yiftach base, immediately."

I disconnect the call and continue driving as if it didn't happen. I park in my usual parking space at the college, and turn off the engine, but I don't step out of the car. When I imagine myself putting on the uniform, packing a bag, and driving north, I am overwhelmed with severe nausea again. I can't seem to banish this image from my head or the feeling from my stomach.

In class I am unable to understand a word. The phone in my pocket vibrates hysterically. These are the group messages of soldiers reporting that they're on their way, and of commanders who are rushing me to arrive quickly. Every now and again I take the phone out of my pocket and peek at the messages. The stress is building up, buzzing in my body until I can't take it anymore and I run out of class to the bathroom.

I pace in the small bathroom back and forth, feeling like my body weighs a ton and a half and my feet are glued to the floor. I wash my face in the sink, trying to relax, but all at once my stomach turns. I run to the nearest stall and throw up my breakfast.

Immediately after, I call Guy Shulman's private phone number. Maybe the Combat PTSD Clinic can help.

I tell him what happened. "I'll take care of it," he promises. I leave the bathroom and the building to get some fresh air.

A few minutes, later my mobile rings again. "You don't have to go. I will notify the battalion that you are exempt from reserve service for the following year," Guy gives me the news. He says that he'll speak with the commander of the unit and find a solution for my individual treatment. I am flooded with such relief that I can barely hear the rest of his words. Exempt for a year? In a second my body returns to its normal weight. My stomach settles. I can breathe again.

Less than a minute passes before the first pestering thought sneaks back in. Wait, how will I explain to everyone that I'm not coming to the drill or for the deployment? What will I tell the other platoon commanders? I'm about to really screw them over. And what about Yuval? And what about my parents? Very soon thoughts return and run in every possible direction. I can't take it anymore. I am so tired. I grab my bag from the classroom and leave the building. That's it. I'm going home.

I decide to tell the rest of the platoon commanders myself that I won't be coming. A few days after the telephonic drill I call them to set up a meeting, but two of them refuse to meet with me. Moran, who was my commander in officers' course, tells me that I have pulled a really dirty trick, and Idan, a kind of quiet geek, who I actually got along with, says I screwed them over and he doesn't understand what I was thinking. Only Ofir, who I have known as the cool platoon commander — a worn-out guy who only wants to complete the tasks and go rest — agrees to meet.

I go with him for coffee. He also tells me that I've screwed them over, but assures me they will manage and that everything will be fine. I share all that I have been through recently and he admits that he, too, has nightmares from time to time. "In my opinion, everyone who was there carries a heavy load," he says. His empathy surprises me.

After the meeting with Ofir, I call Ori. He was a tank commander under me and we always had a special relationship, which came from both of us being fed up. Even in the mandatory service we spent many hours complaining about how shitty being in the military was. Since we started the reserve duty, I've been the one who always encourages him to come so we can both sit and complain together. Because of that, I hesitate now before calling him. It's obvious that talking to me will cause him to leave as well. And truly, Ori identifies with what I am telling him.

It turns out that, just like me, he gets nauseous whenever the callup letters arrive. He tells me that sometimes he starts crying for no reason and that he completely fell apart when his parents' cat died. He asks me a load of questions about the process that led to my exemption. He eventually determines that he really needs to go to the Combat PTSD Clinic too. Oddly, despite everything I already know about myself, when he describes his symptoms, I get the feeling he is just looking for excuses — that he has no issues and just wants to get an exemption.

There are many more people I need to talk to about this — especially Dad, Yuval, and my uncle Yossi, but I don't know where to start.

A few days after the phone call drill, I run into Yuval in our common backyard. He says nothing about it, only asks if I'll make it to the coming deployment. When I tell him that I probably won't, he simply says, "Okay." We don't speak of it more than that. What a relief that I don't have to explain. I say nothing to my parents, however. I have no idea how to start the conversation.

◆ ◆ ◆

A few days later Guy Shulman calls to inform me there's a possibility of beginning treatment with the commander of the unit.

"Does he wear a uniform?" I ask.

"Yes, he's a military man," Shulman answers.

"I don't think it's a good idea," I say with a trembling voice. Shulman says that at the moment there's no other option and asks that I give it a chance. I reluctantly agree, feeling I have no choice.

The exemption lifts a heavy load from my heart. For the next three weeks I'm finally able to focus on my studies, even though I still wake up at night every once in a while, panicked and feeling someone is there with me.

These nights, when someone is watching, waiting for me to make a mistake, are like small wars. I mustn't fall asleep, but he mustn't know that I'm awake either. No matter what position I wake up in, facing the wall or the ceiling, I remain frozen, terrified. I don't dare move a finger.

◆ ◆ ◆

When the reserve service date arrives, I remain at home. I tell my parents I was under some pressure lately and that's why I've been released from the assignment. They don't quite understand and ask what I'm feeling. I explain, impatiently, that I'm stressed in my studies and unable to sleep or concentrate. "They released me this time, and that's it," I summarize.

A few days later I return to the Combat PTSD Clinic for my first meeting of individual therapy. While waiting in the hallway, I examine the people walking around. Some are soldiers and some are in civilian clothes. Why are they here? Did they fight in Lebanon? Maybe in the operation in Gaza? Or are they just trying to find an excuse to get out of reserve service?

On the billboard in front of me is written, "Aspire to heal, mostly will ease, and do the best." I read the sentence several times and don't understand what they are trying to say. The receptionist calls my name.

"Come," she signals me to enter the room behind her desk. I go into a cramped, barely lit room, which has a desk covered with papers. In the room there's one window covered by a semi-transparent red sticker so no one can see in from the outside. The wall is covered with inscribed photos and thank you plaques. On the side there are two worn out armchairs that look out of place and in between them a small, low table.

"Come, take a seat," the unit commander calls me in. He's a tall man wearing a standing army uniform adorned with the rank of major, combat pin, parachute wings and a brown Golani[i] beret. He sits in front of me and introduces himself as Kobi, the commander of the Combat PTSD Clinic. He grabs a large notebook and begins with an explanation about the unit and the service it provides.

"We have group therapy, which is the most recommended in the unit, but you elected not to participate in it." Kobi notes in a tone that sounds a little critical, as if implying that I have to appreciate that the unit commander himself is sitting in front of me. "Let's start with you telling me about yourself, from childhood to present. From there we will try to figure out what the problem is and how to solve it," he says.

I find myself once again telling the story of my life to a stranger. I tell him about my childhood and then move on to describe, in bullet points, my military service from enlisting to my last role, in the war. Kobi writes everything in his notebook. I keep thinking about the young receptionist outside the room who can read it, and the military police investigator who will be able to peek at my file. I make sure to omit details which can somehow hurt me later on.

The unit commander also focuses on Stern's injury incident from friendly fire.[ii] I leave out the fact that I

---

[i] One of the IDF infantry brigades.

[ii] When our forces fire at our forces by mistake.

was the one who approved the shooting without making sure that Stern's tank crew members were inside the tank. The unit commander doesn't say much. At the end of the meeting, he asks me to set another appointment for two weeks from now.

◆ ◆ ◆

On my way home I run into Yossi and Orit, Yuval's parents, who live close to us. As I fear, they are surprised to see me. "What are you doing here? Aren't you in reserve service?" Orit asks. "I received an exemption this time," I answer, but Yossi isn't convinced.

"An exemption? How does an officer get an exemption so easily? What, did you leave Yuvali alone?" he says without realizing the sensitive topic he's stressing. At that moment all I want is for the ground to open up and swallow me.

"The truth is, I'm dealing with all kinds of stuff from the war," I finally say and look down at the floor. "I felt like I couldn't go this time." For a few seconds, that seem very long to me, no one speaks.

"It's okay to rest for a while," Orit breaks the awkward silence. "I am sure they can manage without you this time." The feeling that I'm cheating fills me up again, as if I am a spoiled kid who thinks he deserves to stay at home while the others are stuck doing checkpoints somewhere in the West Bank.

I continue to go to meetings at the Combat PTSD Clinic. At the beginning of the third session, the unit commander informs me that we've completed the introductory stage and that it's time to define the actual problem.

"I can't function. Something in the reserve service stresses me out."

"This is not the problem, it's only a symptom," the commander determines.

"Perhaps the problem is that I can't sleep at night?" I suggest hesitantly.

"You're asking me? You are the one who needs to define the problem," he answers firmly. I don't know what to say and find myself spending the rest of the session in this weird situation. He asks me over and over again to define the problem, but I have no idea what he wants from me.

The next sessions aren't much better. At the beginning of each he asks whether I have thought about it. Do we know yet what the problem is? I fail to answer again and again. Sometimes I am forced to admit with shame that I don't know, and other times I try to answer, but the commander determines, "This isn't the problem."

Longer portions of each session go by in complete silence. I stop trying and we just sit in front of each other for 45 minutes without saying a word. With this annoying silence I get increasingly angry at the unit commander, toward the uniform he wears, and everything he represents. I don't want to talk with him anymore.

One night, at a birthday party for one of my friends from school, I meet a girl named Tal. I take her phone number and call her the next day. The conversation is so good that I drive to her in Jerusalem that same evening and we spend the night together. The connection between us is amazing and already on that first night I tell her about the Combat PTSD Clinic.

Tal, a master's degree student in psychology, shows interest in what happens in the sessions. I tell her about the long silences that I can't understand. Tal says that there is such a therapeutic approach, but it is considered old fashioned. Very soon we become a couple.

By the sixth session the patience of the commander of the unit has run out. "I want us to talk a little about the relationship between you and your soldiers," he starts the conversation. "How would you describe yourself as a commander?"

I am so thirsty for a conversation after the prolonged silence between us that I reply honestly, "I was a little harsh as a commander, especially in the operational company."

"What do you mean by harsh?"

"I was very strict, mainly about readiness and alertness. I was also quite agitated when something would go wrong, and to tell you the truth, even when it didn't," I admit.

"In general, I was an agitated commander who took everything personally." The unit commander nods as he hears this. I continue, "When I was a platoon commander in the operational company, one of the soldiers spoke on his phone during a stakeout in the tank. Completely against regulations. It was forbidden to even bring a phone."

"How did you find out?"

"I heard him talking when we were on stakeout. I asked him if he had a phone on him and he said he did, but that he didn't use it. I asked him for it and saw an outgoing call he made two minutes ago." The unit commander continues to nod.

"And what was your reaction?"

"I took it personally that he lied to my face. Later on, the company commander and I gave him detention, and because of it he didn't get time off for 28 days."

"And how did the team react to it?" the commander is interested to know. I tell him about the shunning. "They were not pleased with the punishment, so they decided to not speak to me. I remember I saw them on the train on the way to the base and I said 'hello' and 'have a good week,' but they didn't respond. On that day we went on an operational activity, and they only responded to commands and reports. I didn't take it so hard. I continued to conduct myself normally. I was, perhaps, supposed to feel bad about it, but the truth is that I felt a great relief."

"Really?" The commander asks surprised, "Why?"

"Because they finally stopped behaving like kindergarten kids that needed to be watched at all times. As part of the shunning, they tried to be the best they could, so that I'd have nothing to complain about. After a few days they got over it." I think for a moment and add, "Actually, the soldiers were never good friends of mine. I was always closer to my commanders, a rank or two above me."

The commander nods again. "Were there other incidents of soldiers who were angry at you?" he asks. "I had an incident with soldiers from Givati[i] support company who was serving with us on the tour," I respond. I tell him how the soldiers who were with us at the military outpost would go to sleep and leave the tower guard empty.

"We were in the middle of the Gaza strip, protecting Israeli civilians and ourselves. I tried to speak with the soldiers but it didn't work, so I went directly to their company commander. The soldiers didn't like that at all. Everyone at our mini-base was angry with me and didn't speak to me. When I had some time off duty and went home a few days later, I found out that a bill of 100 shekels was missing from my wallet and someone had smeared gum on my dress uniform that was hanging on the wall. Do you get it? This is what an officer in the IDF gets. Even my own soldiers were better than the soldiers from Givati."

---

[i] One of the IDF infantry brigades

The unit commander looks at me for several seconds in silence. "Soldiers who ostracized you, snitching on soldiers from another battalion, agitated all the time, don't like your own soldiers. I can really understand them," he says. "I wouldn't want to be one of your soldiers either."

How do I even respond to something like this? Does he really think that or is it some kind of provocation? From his look and tone of speech it seems like he's really angry at the way I handled the situation. Maybe he feels protective of the soldiers and the insult slipped out by mistake? The words are stuck in my throat. Neither one of us says another word until the end of the session.

On the way home his words continue to pound inside my head. Perhaps I was a shitty commander. The other commanders in the platoon really loved me and those who outranked me, appreciated me. I think my soldiers counted on me when it came to operations too. Something in the unit commander's response doesn't add up.

After a few nights of waking up in terror, I tell Tal what happened in the last session. "What?" Her eyes widen. "I'm shocked! This guy is an idiot!" From her reaction I understand it was truly unusual and decide to share it with Dita as well. Her reaction is unequivocal too. "You have to get out of there," she says in shock.

The next day I call the Combat PTSD Clinic and inform the receptionist that I will not be attending any more sessions. A little later the unit commander calls and asks that I at least come for a summary talk. I agree, and arrive at the meeting calm and at peace with my decision.

When he asks why I wish to stop the therapy, Dita's and Tal's words echo in my head. I reply calmly, "Your reaction to my relationship with the soldiers was emotional and unprofessional in my opinion." Before he has a chance to respond I tell him that generally speaking, walking onto a military base and sitting in front of a person wearing a uniform makes it more difficult for me, and maybe it's best I get therapy outside the army.

The unit commander tries to convince me to stay, and again says that they have the most experience treating these conditions. He doesn't bother to apologize or even explain the things he said in the previous session. In any case, I am determined to get away from there. Within ten minutes I'm outside feeling an immense sense of relief.

Dita is glad to hear the news and recommends a private psychologist she knows well. The thought of spending money on this bums me out. Maybe I need to find a way to make the army pay, I think. If the army broke me, why shouldn't it pay for the repair?

◆ ◆ ◆

One night I open the browser in private mode and Google for a lawyer who deals with claims against the

Ministry of Defense. I click on one of the first results, and in a move that surprises even me, I leave my details on the website. I change the name and city of residence, only the phone number is correct. I quickly close the window, delete the browsing history, and go to sleep as if it never happened.

The next day, I am awakened by a call from an unfamiliar number. I collect myself and manage to utter a "hello," which sounds almost normal. The man on the other side of the line introduces himself as a lawyer from the website and suggests we meet for coffee. We schedule a time for later in the day.

After our conversation, I stay in bed and begin to think about what exactly I'm going to tell him and how. The thoughts stay with me until the afternoon. It is pouring rain on my way to the coffee shop. While driving I try to formulate the little speech I will give to introduce him to the story. What will I tell him? The last time it was part of therapy, but this time we are talking about a strange person from the internet. How will I even recognize him?

The coffee shop is packed with people. I stand at the entrance and scan the space. Next to one of the tables there is a big man sitting in a tailored suit. His hair is medium length, grayish, and smeared with some greasy product. I can see the expensive eyeglasses from here. It's obvious to me that this is the man. He looks quite shady. Our gazes lock and he waves hello to me. When I approach his table, he gets up, shakes my hand, and gives me a hug that lasts a little too long. We order coffee and the lawyer introduces himself and tells me he's handled many cases against the Ministry of Defense.

"Would you like to tell me more or less what this is about?" he carefully puts out feelers.

"I have been feeling a great deal of stress lately," I say, hesitantly. I still haven't decided how much I'm going to reveal. "Lack of concentration and sleeping problems..."

"Ah-ha, sleeping problems, anxiety," the shady lawyer completes my words, as if to signal to me that my story is familiar to him.

"I turned to the Combat PTSD Clinic and they approved therapy, but the therapist wasn't very professional, and I couldn't deal with the fact that he was wearing a uniform," I say. The lawyer continues to nod. I lower my head in embarrassment. "I want to go to therapy, but I can't afford it and I don't want to tell my parents."

"Don't worry, I will help you get everything you deserve," the lawyer announces with confidence. He starts listing my rights, detailing the options at my disposal. "This is not a simple process, but I will accompany you step by step throughout the entire thing," he promises.

I hesitantly inquire as to how much it will cost, hoping he will take my situation into consideration. "Opening a file and collecting materials will cost 750 shekels (approximately 210 USD). After that we will need to prepare an application which will cost another 1,500 shekels, and at the end there's a minor percentage from the compensation you will receive. But leave that for now," he says and gives me a compassionate look. He holds onto my hand as if we're old friends.

"Let's start by getting to know you better, and most importantly, help you. It is so hard for me to hear what you're describing. I only want you to feel better."

The lawyer pays the bill, and we leave the coffee shop. The rain has stopped and we both stand in the cool air. "You deserve proper treatment. You deserve compensation. I will walk with you through the process and we'll receive all that we need from them," he says emotionally and again gives me a strong, way-too-long, hug. I turn and walk away with a sense of disgust. All I want is to shake off his hug and his fake attempt to protect me. We just met, what's that all about?

I get into the car, close the door and remain seated in the dark driver's seat. What was it, all of it? I feel used, but I don't quite know why. I feel an urgent need to wash my hands, as if his touch soiled me. In my head I play over the things he said. It feels like he wants to make me look worse than I am in order to extract more money with the lawsuit. He doesn't want me to get therapy, I think; he needs me to get money. I have never before experienced such a feeling.

The meeting causes me to take a step backwards from the whole lawsuit and therapy matter. I don't have the energy to start telling everything to yet another person.

◆ ◆ ◆

I manage to complete my degree and start working as a software developer at a sought-after company with a great salary and good benefits — something I have dreamed of throughout my studies. I tell myself that perhaps I should simply try to concentrate on the new job.

A few months later, when I've already grown accustomed to the office routine, a call comes in from Elroei, the battalion commander. He points out that we haven't spoken in a while and he'd be happy to get an update on my wellbeing. It's been nearly a year since we spoke, and I know that my exemption is about to expire.

The next day we meet at the coffee shop next to my place of work. I order a cup of coffee and Elroei orders a Coke. He drinks straight from the glass bottle with his thick lips creating such a vacuum that they almost rip from his face when he puts down the bottle.

"Before we start, I feel the need to apologize," says Elroei, and explains that he wasn't aware of my condition last time and that Lavie was wrong to pressure me instead of understanding the situation. I feel relieved. This is the first time someone from the battalion understands. Or so it seems.

"But I have a proposition for you," the battalion commander continues with a mischievous smile. "You really don't have to accept it, but if you want to come back to the reserve service a little, I'd be happy for you to be our training officer. It's time to refresh the positions in the battalion anyway."

Elroei waits for a few seconds to examine my expression and takes another big gulp from his drink. I think about how to respond. When I hesitate, he emphasizes, "This could be a good role for you. No soldiers, no operation company, and no tanks."

Pros and cons are already racing through my mind. This really is an easy job. I would just come for some of the days and walk around during the training without a great deal of responsibility. On top of that, I would be close to Yuval, I wouldn't be sleeping in the field, and I wouldn't have soldiers. On the other hand, the previous training officer always got into the tank with the battalion commander during training. And in war time too.

"Elroei, I know how it works," I finally say. "When the drill begins, or in an emergency, you will immediately ask me to join you in the tank. And I have no idea how I'll react to it. And mainly, I don't want to have the feeling that it's even a possibility."

Elroei smiles. "It's not going to happen," he says. "I give you my word that you won't be stepping onto any tanks, not during drills and not in an emergency. Wait, don't give me an answer. Think about it and we'll talk in a week or two. Okay, I've got to get going," he announces and stands up, leaving a five shekel coin on the table. "Think about it."

Eventually, I take the job. The first few months are pretty good. During this time, I've been to reserve service for several one-day drills. I enjoy always knowing what's about to happen, as part of the battalion's leadership. Even when they start talking about the upcoming training, two whole weeks in Ze'elim, I'm not especially bothered.

Now that I'm a training officer, I won't be going on tanks, and I don't have annoying soldiers who will act up. What's wrong with two weeks that remove you far from your daily routine, stress at work, chores at home? No cellular reception and being unavailable? I begin to understand why people like going on reserve service.

♦ ♦ ♦

About two months before the training, I decide to break up with Tal. The relationship that started really well has been slowly coming apart, especially from my side. I feel I've lost interest and miss the feeling of being alone without frameworks and without anyone expecting something from me.

Tal takes the breakup hard. "I can't believe this is happening to us. Our relationship is great, you're just scared," she tries to convince me.

For an entire month after the breakup Tal continues to chase me with letters and offers to meet.

I refuse them all until she lets it go. But then, about a week before the reserve service, I start to crack. I miss her. I call.

Tal, who's just moved to a new apartment, invites me over. We sit and drink coffee among the boxes, getting updates about each other's lives. I'm so happy to see her and talk to her about the upcoming reserve service. Before I leave, Tal confesses that she just started seeing someone new. She escorts me to the parking lot and we kiss outside the building.

"You can't just come over in the middle of my life and turn everything upside down for me," she says, attempting to snuggle into my arm the way we used to curl up when we slept together. We stand there for several more minutes, then I drive home.

The next day, a Thursday morning, I put on my uniform and drive with Yuval to Ze'elim to prepare the training that is about to start the following week. I coordinate a few classes that will be delivered to the staff and try to complete small insignificant tasks. I chase the officer in charge of the bunker to get the ammunition ready and find the battalion's allocation of markers. And of course, I take care of Elroei's obsession for a working projector.

And all this time, my mind is somewhere else. I can't stop thinking about Tal and the mistake I've made by breaking up with her. I have to talk to her. I have to explain to her that I was wrong, that everything is clear to me now, and I want us to try again.

My phone doesn't stop ringing. Every second, someone calls and adds another redundant task to my endless list of assignments. How can I be stuck here in Ze'elim when the one thing I want most is to talk to Tal? On the weekend I'll be returning home, but Tal is going away with her family for three days, so we won't be able to get together. She told me this when we met at her apartment.

At lunch time I walk to the mess hall. I take the plastic tray and a beige colored "meat[i]" cup, which is greasy as if someone dunked it in the fryer. Again, there are no forks, so I take a tablespoon instead.

I load some potatoes in a glowing sauce from the serving plate and approach the cook. He places a thin piece of schnitzel, dripping with fat, on my plate with an expression of "it is what it is." I walk among the filthy tables searching for a familiar face, and finally sit down next to a few officers from the battalion. Everyone is complaining about the food. No pitcher has water in it. What a repulsive mess hall they have in Ze'elim. And why is there never a fork to be found?

At dusk, when everyone is busy, I shut myself in one of the classrooms, take a piece of paper, and begin to write to Tal. I write to her that I'm in reserve service and I feel like shit because I can't be with her. I tell her I want us to try again and that I'm most

---

[i] Mixtures of milk and meat are forbidden according to Jewish Kosher laws, which the military follows. Beige colored dishes are reserved for meat, blue is for dairy.

likely a coward like she said, but now I understand it and want us to get back together.

I go over what I've written while my mobile phone continues to vibrate in my pocket. Eventually I answer. "Where are you?" Elroei asks. "I need you to prepare the classroom with a projector for a talk with the brigade commander." I add a few more words to the end of the letter, fold it, and shove it in my pocket. I then straighten up the chairs, collect a few empty soda cans left on the floor from the previous lesson, erase the board and make sure the projector is working.

The talk with the brigade commander, who I know from his previous roles, starts with a round of introductions. "I'm Omri Ginzburg and I am the training officer," I say when my turn comes. "I know who you are," the brigade commander responds. "The question is, how does the person who was Avner's deputy during the Second Lebanon War, who has gained so much operational experience, get to be a training officer? There's a problem here that needs to be checked," he throws a half-smiling, half-serious look at Elroei. "This is for another time," Elroei replies.

At the end of the introduction round the brigade commander moves to talk about the threats from the northern border. "One lesson learned from the Second Lebanon War, and Ginzburg can surely back me up here, is you always have to be thinking that tomorrow war will break out," he says and stares at me. "When you go to bed at night, you need to know that tomorrow there's war. When you wake up in the morning, you need to know that perhaps over the course of the day, or tomorrow, war will break out. You need to be sure at every moment that you've done everything you can possibly do to be prepared for the war that will begin tomorrow."

I'm becoming increasingly enraged. What kind of a country is this, that you need to go to sleep thinking tomorrow there will be war? Every night, before I go to sleep, I give thanks that war didn't break out today. Every morning, the moment I open my eyes, I check the news and am grateful that war didn't break out during the night. Terrible things have already happened while I was sleeping. What does he want? That every day, all day, every night, I will live my life as if tomorrow there's war? What kind of life is that? Does that seem normal or healthy to anyone?

◆ ◆ ◆

After the talk, we disburse to go home for the weekend. I leave the classroom full of rage and walk with Yuval to the car. Why do I need to be in the army? Why do I have to wear this uniform? How am I going to survive a week of this shit, eating this disgusting and greasy food?

Like every training, Yuval drives there and I drive back. We don't talk the entire way. As is common for a member of the Ginzburg family, Yuval is not a great talker, surely not on issues relating to emotion. He didn't ask about my exemption from reserve service, and even when I got back he didn't ask about my assignment to a training position. When you think about it, even when he returned my notebooks he didn't say a word. What's wrong with him?

Eventually Yuval falls asleep and I'm able to delve into thoughts about the letter to Tal, which is burning a hole in my uniform pocket. I imagine over and over the moment she returns from the family vacation, finds my letter in her mailbox, and straight away calls me to tell me she loves me.

The moment we get home, I rush to take a shower and head out with the car again. I stop in front of the entrance to Tal's building, run to toss the letter in her mailbox, and drive away with a huge sense of relief.

On the weekend, I feel like a soldier on leave and go out for a drink with friends. As Saturday night approaches, so do the Saturday blues.[i] With a complete lack of motivation and a great deal of anger at life, I pack my bag for the training. On Sunday morning at 6:30 Yuval and I get into the car and drive back to Ze'elim.

Toward noon the tanks' platform[ii] and assembly areas are swarming with soldiers running around like

---

[i] The work week in Israel starts on Sunday.
[ii] Parking lot and service area.

ants. I see many familiar faces here. It's always fun and exciting to meet the guys.

But then I hear one of the tanks start up. The driver steps on the gas pedal, and revs up the engine so high that a cloud of dust and diesel fumes fills the area, throwing me all at once back to Southern Lebanon. Weakness overwhelms me, and my stomach turns. I need to get out of here. What's with Tal, she was supposed to be home by now. Is it possible she hasn't seen the letter? Why isn't she calling?

I pull away from the tanks' platform and go up to one of the classrooms in the training building, hoping to find a quiet spot. Fortunately, I'm in charge of the classrooms and that's why I always have the key. I lock the door behind me, sit on a chair at the front of the dark and messy classroom and stare at my mobile phone. There's no sign of Tal, and I text, "Hi, did you happen to come across the gift I left for you?"

I continue going in and out of the messaging screen waiting for a response, which doesn't arrive. I imagine the sound of the incoming text message, but nothing is happening. The nausea that came over me earlier has passed, but I'm being filled with a very bad feeling.

For me, it boils down to the fact that I can't be with Tal right now. I don't want to be here, I don't want to wear this uniform, I don't want to deal with tanks and ammunition as if it's the most important thing in the world. I don't want to continue living even one more day as if there's war tomorrow. All I want is to be with Tal. I could be with her right now instead of all this. Thoughts continue to inflate in my head, and I get even angrier until the sound of an incoming message brings me back to reality.

"Don't write to me anymore and don't come over. I don't want you in my life," Tal texted me.

A 64-ton weight lands on my chest. All my internal organs flip. All at once I feel it rising. I grab the small trash can next to the board and throw up. Luckily, it had a bag inside. Seconds later, the soldiers who've arrived for their talk knock on the door. God, take me away from here. I hear them gathering outside asking where the training officer is and where's the key to the classroom. Bug off, I say without a sound.

A few moments pass and I realize I have no choice. I carefully tie the bag with the vomit in it, place it in my backpack and leave the room. What should I do now? The sound of the tanks' engines is at full volume by now and the heavy smell of diesel again makes me nauseous, sending me to the bushes behind the building with vomiting spasms.

I have nothing left to throw up. I slump down to kneel, grab my head between my hands, and I feel like the loneliest person in the world. To make it worse, my phone doesn't stop buzzing with message alerts. Elroei has already called twice, and I didn't answer. I have no clue what to do. Who will I talk to about this? With Yuval? With my friends who know nothing? The only person who knows everything in detail is Tal. I have no one else to talk to.

I call her and she answers right away. "Didn't you understand what I wrote to you?" she asks purposefully. I feel the chill blowing through the line.

"Tal, I am in reserve service right now," I respond with a trembling voice. "I'm having a really bad time here."

"I told you. I don't want you in my life! Just when I had something good, you came along and ruined it. Don't call me, don't write to me, and get out of my life for good," she stabs at me and disconnects the call.

I couldn't have anticipated this turn of events even in my worst nightmares. My phone continues to ring. Elroei sends more and more messages about the projector that's needed for the battalion commander's talk. I feel like screaming. Who cares about the fucking training and the fucking projector right now? I want to go home.

I try to collect myself and walk toward the tanks' platform. On the way I throw the vomit bag in the large bin. At the exact moment I cross the road, a garbage truck passes by leaving a trail of horrid stench behind it. I wonder if the driver is asking himself how it could be that the army's garbage stinks more than any other trash. Again, my stomach turns and I hurry toward the nearby toilet, but the door is locked. What is it with locking all the toilets? What do they want? For people to not take a shit?

I run to another building. Fortunately, it's open. At the last second, I reach the only toilet stall open in Ze'elim and throw up inside the bowl, which is already clogged with shit and toilet paper. God, how I hate the military.

I wash my face, calm down a little, and go buy a can of soda from the vending machine. I tell no one what I'm going through. I tell Elroei that I forgot my mobile phone in one of the offices. I continue with the training, but all I really care about is calling Gideon, the psychologist Dita recommended.

TRAVEL LOG: GOLAN HEIGHTS

Tabenkin leaves the study and goes to the porch. "Shakshuka[i] for dinner?" he asks. "Of course," I answer. When he goes to the kitchen I close my computer and delve into thought.

I recall the day after the hypnotic drive to the college. I then realize for the first time how impatient I can be toward others. However, the fact that I understand this doesn't mean I'm able to avoid this behavior. It happens today too, and the main problem is that I can see it only in retrospect, two days after the incident and with a few more people to apologize to.

Following the nights that I felt there was someone out there, I would walk around like a tight spring. If someone were to say something out of place, I'd use

---

[i] A typical dish of eggs poached in a sauce of tomatoes.

it as a reason to lash out. And this is even before I began to remember the nightmares. From there on, it only got worse.

I've blamed so many external factors in order to hide my post-traumatic stress. I couldn't handle the fact that something in the world made me want to avoid the military. So, I found other reasons and people to blame. Why should I go to reserve service if I wasn't assigned to the right battalion? And after they moved me to the right one, it was the reserve service that prevented me from accomplishing my studies.

I was convinced that if I went to operational deployment, I would fail the degree. But when I had no choice and I found myself in the reserve service, I had to find someone or something else to blame. So I picked the easiest target. I will get Tal back and then the army will be the only factor that separates us.

Tal was smarter and knew to stay away. She knew that only total separation would save her from me. Thinking about it now, my inability to reach her to talk, even for a minute, is what sparked my obsession.

The letter to Tal was just the opening shot. When the reserve service was over, it was no longer possible to blame the army, so all my energy was directed at the new task — getting Tal back. I vaguely remember there were more attempts to contact her. It only ended when Tal turned to my sister, Efrat, and asked her to make sure I was alright. I was so embarrassed by the situation that I stopped trying.

To this day, the last phone conversation I had with Tal is the low point in my life. It was probably the turning point as well. Gideon would be the first to kick off a process of understanding and accepting myself.

◆ ◆ ◆

After the Shakshuka, Tabenkin and I head to the local pub. We sit at the bar and order two beers. It's the weekend, but the dark pub is completely empty, and all we have to do is watch the bartender work until he brings us our beers and places two shots next to them.

"Cheers," says Tabenkin. "Cheers," I answer and we click our glasses. Each of us takes a big gulp and before I manage to put down the glass Tabenkin asks, "So, what are you writing about?" I smile and he continues with confidence, "Well, I've seen your laptop screen." I think for a moment and then answer, "The truth is, I have started writing a book."

This is the first time I am telling someone about it. From that moment, and even before we manage to get wasted, I reveal everything to Tabenkin, who didn't even know about my PTSD.

For two hours, and with a great deal more alcohol, I tell him about the period after the military service. I share the fear I have when someone comes at night. I tell him about my attempts to avoid the reserve service and the path of tribulations I went through with all the review boards.

When I finish, Tabenkin stares at me and finally says, "Let me understand. How much of a masochist can you be? With all your fears and nightmares, you chose to go on a journey and camp outside to write a book? Stay in the kibbutz, we will organize a room for you. It looks to me like you've suffered enough," he laughs.

"You have no idea how much," I say and tell him about the first nights on the journey and the soldiers who surprised me at Zivon River. "But it is something I've always wanted to do. I have never gone on a journey on my own and every time I've traveled with girlfriends, I've dreamed of being alone."

Tabenkin thinks for a few seconds. "And the entire ten years you have dealt with everything on your own, banging your head against the wall — isn't that a journey alone?" He asks naturally and resumes drinking his beer. I continue to stare at him for a few more seconds, thinking about his words. I recall different points in time when I didn't tell anything to anyone — about the nightmares, the lack of concentration, or the review boards. How the hell did I cope with everything on my own?

◆ ◆ ◆

The following morning, I pack up my gear and leave for an off-road drive along the barrow line overlooking the Syrian side of the Golan Heights. I drive the paths that go between mine fields, pass under the wind turbines, and arrive at an observation point where there's an old Centurion ("Shot") tank. The tank was placed there in memory of the '73 Yom Kippur war that took place in the Golan Heights. It's the same tank my father used in that war when he got wounded.

I park in the shadow of the tank, and start to heat water for coffee. I sit down, open the laptop and start to write about Gideon.

2011-2012: GIDEON

I am sitting with Lavie in his car, parked outside my house. It's already the middle of the night. I can't understand how it's so late. The battalion is anticipating an upcoming drill. It will be the first drill for Lavie as the battalion commander, having just recently replaced Elroei in the role.

Lavie presents me with the assignments for the upcoming drill. "The tanks arrive at the Elyakim base on Thursday morning and need to be unloaded from the Tank Transporter.[i] We need two tank drivers, a tank commander, and an officer," Lavie details. There are always unpleasant assignments before the drill starts. Since I was reassigned as the battalion's training officer, I'm the one who usually ties up all these loose

---

[i] A truck carrying tanks on top of a trailer.

ends. As far as I'm concerned, this is the cost I have to pay for the favor Elroei did when he transferred me to the training officer role — a role that is considered a privilege for more experienced officers.

"The truck with the equipment also needs to be unloaded and we have to arrange a team to guard the tanks over the weekend," Lavie continues. "Next month we have the operational deployment in the south of the Golan Heights. I thought that perhaps you would join my team for the first week. What do you say?"

I'm shocked. "I haven't notified them at work, and besides we already talked about me not coming when the battalion does operational activities. This was my arrangement with Elroei when I took the role and he promised that it would be the same with you."

Lavie's request makes me feel like I can't take it anymore — that something inside is about to blow up. Enough, I want to be discharged from the reserve service.

Lavie goes on talking about the preparations as if I've agreed and the subject is closed. All I can think about is how I'm going to screw them over at work if I disappear for a week without prior notice. This feeling reminds me of the stress during my exams period.

I can't hold back anymore. "I'm not coming, enough. We've talked about it dozens of times, I am not part of the battalion anymore. Stop calling me," I say firmly. I leave the car, slamming the door. When I lift my head and look to the other side of the car, I see Elroei suddenly. He stands close to the car nodding his head again and again, as if signaling that I did the right thing. How did Elroei get here?

I ignore this improbability and turn around without saying anything to him. I start walking back toward the house when all of a sudden Lavie steps out from between the parked cars on the street to argue. How did Lavie get transported outside of the car? What's going on here?

I start running toward my house. I look back and I see Elroei, still standing next to the car nodding like a bobble-head dog on a car dashboard. This gives me permission to run faster. Lavie appears, again out of nowhere, in the middle of the street and tries to block me. I try to accelerate, but I am running in place. I attempt with all my might to deliver movement to my legs, to push hard, increase my strides, but I continue to run slowly. The harder I try, the slower I run, and the more Lavie appears.

It's pitch dark outside and only a few lampposts illuminate small sections of the street. Each time I leave an illuminated section, I return to the same spot and start all over again. Once I realize I'm in a loop, the cycle finally breaks and I succeed in reaching the fence of the house. I have no more energy. Lavie is right behind me and I don't have enough time to open the gate. If I slow down, he'll catch me. I have no other choice but to jump over the gate. With the rest of my strength I try to leap. I send out my right leg to the far right and push hard with my left leg, which stays behind. Everything is in slow motion.

While I'm in the air I feel a strong blow in my right foot. I look down and see that I've stumbled onto the fence with my foot. The slow-motion releases and I fall with a quick roll over the fence, into the dark yard. Time stands still. It is completely dark. Someone is looking at me.

I can see the front door of my house from this distance. It is lit with a single yellow bulb, which focuses the light on the entrance step in front of the door. I crawl toward the door, attempting to make as little noise as possible. Perhaps this way, whoever is looking at me will not pay attention.

When I get close, I notice a female figure sitting on the step at the entrance. Her back is turned to me. I continue to crawl toward the door and recognize Tal's hair. What is Tal doing here? If she's here so late, she probably wants to tell me something. Maybe she finally realized that we should be back together again?

I approach Tal, entering the illuminated area of the entrance, but she doesn't turn around. I stand next to her, put a hand on her shoulder and try to turn her to face me. Nothing. I try as hard as I can and fail. Her body is stuck in the same position and she doesn't react. I feel like I'm in a loop again and it's lasting too long.

Just then, it releases, and Tal slowly turns around. Her shaded face is gradually revealed by the entrance light. First the forehead, then the eyes, the nose and the...

◆ ◆ ◆

I wake up in bed panicked. The room is completely dark. I am frozen and can't get unstuck. My mouth is dry again. He is out there, looking at me, waiting for me to fall asleep again. I mustn't show that I know he's there.

I begin remembering the details of my dream: the conversation with Lavie in the car and Bobble Head Elroei. Feelings of frustration, anger, and failure fill me. Why couldn't I run faster? And why did Elroei stay quiet? Why not help me convince Lavie?

The fear remains. Who's the one standing there looking at me? What does he want from me? One thing about the dream leaves no doubt: I know why Tal didn't have a mouth. It's like in cartoons, when they shoot someone in the head and you can see straight through the hole to the background. Just like that, only a lot less funny.

This is the first time I've woken up in the middle of the night and succeed in recalling a dream. This is more nightmare than it is dream. I can't seem to break free of the position I woke up in.

Old, late-night apartment noises make my heart jump every few minutes. The wooden shutters in the bedroom, the refrigerator's compressor, and all kinds of weird creaks. My throat is parched, but there's no way I can turn to the water bottle next to the bed. I have no idea what time it is, but I have no intention of turning around to reach the phone either – or exposing myself with the light of the screen.

After a few long, tense hours, I hear the birds starting to chirp. Any moment the sun will come up and I'll be able to start relaxing.

It's longer than I expect before the first ray of light penetrates the bedroom, shining on the wall next to the bed. The warmth passing between the shutters delivers a calm to me, and I fall fast asleep.

♦ ♦ ♦

At 7:30 in the morning the alarm clock goes off. I drag on a few more snoozes, then try to get myself out of bed. I've forgotten everything from the night before and wake up normally, only tired and more exhausted than usual.

I dress quickly, brush my teeth, and prepare to go to work. Keys, wallet, sunglasses, and I'm ready to leave. I walk down the path that leads from the front door to the gate of the yard – and then I recall the nightmare.

I stop in my tracks. It all happened here, on the street and at the entrance to my house. In one second my home turned from a safe and protected place to a scary crime scene. I look at the path and the entrance to the house and get a glimpse of the nightmare patiently waiting in the depths of my memory. After a few seconds I continue walking and arrive at my car. I sit in the driver's seat and wait for the fragments of terror to assemble into the whole story from last night's nightmare.

◆ ◆ ◆

While I sit with a cup of coffee and the office's morning quietness, I think to myself, "Could it be that every time I've woken up in the middle of the night, I was having a nightmare?" Enough, I need to give in and get help.

During lunch break I call the psychologist that Dita recommended. "Hello, you've reached Gideon Bar. I am unable to come to the phone right now. Please leave a message and phone number and I'll get back to you as soon as possible," the voicemail answers. "Hi Gideon. My name is Omri. I got your phone number from Dita. I would appreciate it if you'd call me back," I respond in a slightly trembling voice and hang up.

Toward the evening Gideon calls me and suggests we meet. We schedule an appointment for later in the week. That night I go through the pile of documents I've collected: the evaluation from the Combat PTSD Clinic, the therapy summary, and the business card of the shady lawyer.

It's been more than a year since I was at that clinic. It seems so long ago. I try to think of what else I can bring for the meeting with Gideon, and remember the red plastic bag hiding deep in my closet. I open the closet door. Maybe I should let Gideon read the notebooks I wrote at the end of the war? If he reads them, I won't have to tell him about the war myself. I'd better not, I say to myself and shut the closet.

◆ ◆ ◆

That week we meet. Gideon shares a clinic with two other psychologists in a house on my street. It's a minute's walk from my house, which is located in the yard of our family complex. I still haven't told my family about the therapy, and I hope no one sees me. If someone from my family happens to pass by they'll immediately stop and ask me where I'm going. Then I'll need to come up with some excuse. And if I know our neighborhood, it is likely the neighbors will also wonder why the Ginzburg son is walking into the psychologists' clinic.

I go in and sit on the leather couch in the old living room. This house belonged to the Lerman's before it became a clinic. For 27 years I've been living in this neighborhood and pass by this entrance, but this is the first time I'm seeing the Lerman's house from the inside.

It seems like most of the furniture remained there after the family left the neighborhood, and inside the clinic is an atmosphere of a home that no one lives in anymore. Next to the living room there's a big dining table loaded with many objects. The window reveals a wild garden that hasn't received any attention for years.

After a few minutes, Gideon escorts a young man from his office to the front door. I scope out Gideon and the patient through the corner of my eye. I wonder if he too had issues from the army. He looks younger than me. Perhaps for him it's really fresh, from Operation Cast Lead in Gaza.

Gideon comes to the living room and gives me a strong handshake. "What can I get you to drink? Hot? Cold?" he asks. "A glass of water," I answer shyly. Gideon pours me a glass of cold water, and for himself, a glass of Coke that seems to have gone flat.

We enter Gideon's office and I sit on the chair. He organizes a few things on his desk, and after that he throws his heavy body on the therapist's chair. "During our first introductory meetings I will write a few notes for myself. After that, the conversation will flow more freely," says Gideon. I nod in agreement, hoping he won't stay silent now like the commander of the Combat PTSD Clinic.

"Dita referred me to the Combat PTSD Clinic as the quickest option to get treatment. It didn't work out so much, and now I want to start individual sessions. I'm also going to ask the Division of Disabled Veterans to finance the therapy," I say to Gideon.

"Okay," he says. "Take into account that the process of the Disabled Veterans can take a long time and it's not certain that it will succeed. Also, how should I put it delicately? The journey to be approved as a disabled veteran in Israel is not the most pleasant."

"Yes, I have already encountered several difficulties with the Combat PTSD Clinic," I say and recall the first phone conversation with that soldier.

"I suggest that we start the therapy. At the same time, I will help you with your application to the Disabled Veterans Department. If we succeed, they will cover all our costs. If we are not successful, you will pay the discounted rate, which the Disabled Veterans Department pays me." The deal that Gideon offers relieves my concerns and I agree immediately.

◆ ◆ ◆

We begin with an introductory session. "I'm 27 years old. I was born in Kfar Saba and grew up literally here, down the street. I have two older siblings: Ofer, the oldest who is 11 years older than me, and Efrat, who is five years older than me. My grandparents arrived in the neighborhood by the 1930's and they had chicken coops next to the house. A little after my sister was born, my father and his brother, Yossi built adjacent houses on my grandparents' farm with a common yard instead of the chicken coops. This is how we grew up, my family next to our cousins.

"All of my best friends lived in the neighborhood. We spent most of our time in the orchard that surrounded the neighborhood. Almost every day, at four o'clock in the afternoon, we would set off with our bikes to roam the orchard. And when it was the right season, we ate oranges straight from the trees. Later on, the orchard transformed to fields where they grew strawberries and watermelons.

"I think it was during summer break between the third and fourth grade, when I was about nine, that I went to work with my father for the first time. From that year on, I saw any school vacation as an opportunity to work with him. All my friends would go to summer camps and I went with my dad to work. Almost all my family members worked with my dad before and after their military service."

Gideon cuts me off and asks with a smile, "What does your father do that everyone wants to work for him?"

"My father has a workshop for metal coating, not something fascinating, but he's always paid handsomely."

"What's so fun about working when everyone's hanging out at the beach?" Gideon is interested to know, and I explain. "The truth is I liked the money. I would save a lot without having a defined goal. I remember, I would go down to the living room in the evenings holding the petty cash box with the money I'd saved from working. I'd spread the bills and count the money in front of everyone. 'Look at how much money this boy has!' they would say. 'You'll be a millionaire,' someone else would add."

"And what did you end up doing with all the millions?" Gideon asks and we both laugh. "I bought new bicycles, a home theater sound system, and at the age of sixteen — a motorbike. When I had some larger sums, my dad kept my money. On the wall in the kitchen he had a shelf where he would keep the letters and certificates he needed to file. There was also a plaid notepad where my parents' savings plans were detailed.

"Among all the numbers and words there was a little spot for me. There, at the top left corner, was a small frame and in it, my current balance. At the end of each vacation period, Dad would erase the previous balance and update the new one according to the money I had earned. 'I'll be your bank,' he used to say. 'Whenever you need money, I'll give it to you.' Each time he would organize the paperwork, I'd ask to see the plaid page. I'd stare at it for long minutes and calculate how much more I could earn, just so I would have more."

"How was life with the common yard?" Gideon asks. "There aren't many families who know to get along in such close proximity." It seems like he's looking to find where I'm hiding problems. "The truth is, everyone got along pretty well. The common yard was always bustling with life — playing football, barbequing, and building a treehouse. Our back porch was next to Yossi's porch.

"My uncle, Yossi, worked for many years at the bank, and was always dressed nicely. During the week he would come back from work in his elegant clothes and immediately go out to the porch to smoke. My dad and Yossi had two lawn chairs, one next to each other in the space between the porches. On Friday evenings, they loved resting on those chairs, each on their own side. On the weekends, Yossi used to sit on the lawn chair with shorts, shirtless, and with the stump of his amputated leg peeking out."

"How did your uncle lose his leg?" Gideon asks, surprised by the casually tossed detail.

"My uncle was injured in the Yom Kippur War by a shrapnel and lost his leg. My father was also injured in that same war when his tank caught fire," I tell Gideon. He continues to nod with a serious look on his face.

"Do you know how your uncle was injured?"

"The truth is, I don't know any details. They always told me it was from shrapnel, but nothing more than that. He was like that when I was born and it never seemed unusual to me. The first time I realized it wasn't a normal sight was when my friends came over and asked him, 'Where's your leg?' Yossi would always laugh and reply with the same pre-prepared answer. 'The leg? It went for a walk.'"

"And what about your father? Did he ever talk about his war injury?" Gideon asks.

"I spoke with my dad many times. During my childhood he would often share stories from the reserve service. The more I matured and the more I asked, the more he would tell. We used to go with him to Latrun, to meet his friends from the war and visit the tank's museum. He always took me to see the tank he had during the war. He would patiently explain the roles of the tank's crew and say with great pride that all crew members are needed in order to operate it."

"So all your siblings are also devoted to the armored corps?" Gideon continues to question.

"My brother served as a 'pencil-pusher' in the logistics corps and my sister as a welfare Non-Commissioned Officer. Yuval, Yossi's son, enlisted in the armored corps five years before me, and stayed on for a long permanent army service. I remember my dad was very proud. The whole family would go visit Yuval at the base on Saturdays. Yuval was always selected as the top soldier of his platoon. He also stayed on to serve as a commander in the command course like my father..."

"And you, did you want to be selected as a top soldier like your father and Yuval?" Gideon interrupts me.

"I wanted to become a combat pilot, and after I didn't pass the medical screening I tried a special unit of the Navy and the paratroopers. When I ran out of options I went along with tradition," I laugh and continue my story. "When I enlisted in the armored corps, Yuval was already in the company commanders' course..."

Gideon interrupts me again and asks, "Did they make trips to visit you all over the country too?"

I smile. "Mom and Dad came to visit me at every possible opportunity too. During my basic training they came all the way to the settlements in the West Bank. Later, during Commander's Course they drove all the way to Shizafon base at the end of the desert. When I was in an operational unit, they skipped between the Gaza border and the Lebanese border. Nothing stopped them. They would get up early in the morning on a Saturday, fry the schnitzels and go wherever I was."

"Why didn't Ofer join the armored corps? He didn't have the right medical profile rating?"[i] Gideon attempts to understand why my brother didn't continue the family tradition.

"He had a profile rating of 97. My mother always said that Ofer was the homey type, but it's probably because he simply didn't want to join."

"Simply didn't want to? What did your father think about his firstborn child becoming a pencil-pusher in the Logistics Corps instead of being a brave combat soldier in a tank?" Gideon asks a question that never occurred to me.

"My parents were supportive. I don't remember any time that there was criticism over Ofer's choices."

---

[i] A score from 21 to 97 indicating the medical state of a soldier. A score of 82 and above, qualifies one to join combat units.

I continue to paint a picture of our normal family, when deep inside I realize I don't have the real answer.

Later, I tell Gideon about the therapy at the Combat PTSD Clinic and the unit commander's words that made me end it.

"And what do you think? What kind of commander were you?" Gideon asks.

"I don't know why I was so agitated and hard on the soldiers. I wanted everyone to get home safely, without any unusual events. I truly believed in the rules and the fact that they could keep us safe. Besides, I didn't take the commander at the Combat PTSD Clinic seriously."

Even now, talking to Gideon, I try to defend the decisions I made as a commander, perhaps in the attempt to show him — and myself — that I'm at peace with my way.

"And yet, it's still insulting when someone tells you he wouldn't have wanted to be a soldier under your command, especially if he's a 'big general' in the army. Weren't you offended?"

"I know I did the right thing for the soldiers," I answer without hesitation.

Gideon insists, "How is Mr. Confidence so sure of himself?"

"Regarding the specific case of the soldiers from Givati I received a clear answer. After the incident of the snitch and the bubblegum revenge, they were transferred to the infamous Philadelphi Route[i] on the border between Egypt and Gaza.

"On one of the busy Sundays at the central bus station, I saw one of them. He sat with the soldiers from my team at that time. I had no energy to talk to him and preferred to stand a little behind.

"Later that day, my crew member told me that one of the Givati soldiers who loved sleeping instead of going up to the guard post, was injured from a missile that hit his post on the Philadelphi Route. And guess what? He was sleeping during the event and didn't notice a terrorist approaching the post.

"It strengthened my belief that my 'snitching' and insistence with the soldiers were justified. And if this wasn't enough, when we arrived at the base, I found a 100 shekel note on the floor, the exact amount stolen from my wallet." I smile, pleased by the coincidence.

◆ ◆ ◆

Gideon and I continue to talk about the military service. I tell him about the different roles I had and the difficulties that started after my release — mainly upon receiving my reserve duty orders.

"Do you want to be discharged from the reserve duty?" Gideon asks. I don't reply immediately. Each time someone asks me this question I feel like they're

---

i Infamous for many deadly attacks on the IDF that controlled the area until the Israeli disengagement from Gaza in 2005.

trying to test whether or not I'm trying to dodge[i] and don't actually have a real problem.

"At the moment, I am a training officer in the battalion. It's much better than the role I had before. Sometimes, I still find it hard to go to reserve duty, but I don't want to stop serving, in spite of the difficulty." And so, in two sentences, I sum up a big problem that Gideon and I will be talking about a great deal more.

The session lasts for more than an hour and we schedule another appointment for the following week. Gideon recommends that I write a personal letter and attach it to the request form I'm going to submit to the Disabled Veterans department. The deal that Gideon offers me and his willingness to help, leaves me optimistic for our next meetings.

It seems that since my last encounter with the commander of the Combat PTSD Clinic, something has changed. I don't know if it's related to the time that's passed and the insights that were slowly sinking in, or if the increasingly frequent night terrors have made me understand that there's no other way. I need to start talking and sharing.

◆ ◆ ◆

For the second meeting with Gideon, I bring the forms together with the letter I wrote. I wait for him

[i] Dodging draft. People who choose not to take part in the obligatory 3-year military service in Israel or in reserve duty.

in the Lerman's living room until he finishes with his current session.

Gideon leaves his office and escorts a young teenager to the door. I wonder what his problem is, he still hasn't had the chance to serve in the army. Gideon approaches me and offers something to drink. We go into the office and he closes the door behind himself, places the glass on the small table, and throws his body on the chair. I give him the letter so he can go over it before I send it with the application forms.

Dear Sirs,

My name is Omri Ginzburg, I served in the military as a tanks' deputy company commander. I took part in the Second Lebanon War, during which I replaced the company commander after his injury. During the war I made a great deal of operational decisions, one of which caused the injury of a commander in the company. The memories of that event, together with the feeling of guilt, disturb me to a great extent. The smells from that night never leave me.

Since my release in December 2006, I carry a heavy load from the experiences of war. However, the more I try to suppress the thoughts and avoid triggers that remind me of those experiences, my condition only gets worse. After many failed attempts to cope with the symptoms myself, I decided to seek help. I turned to the Combat PTSD Clinic. They recognized my problems and I was offered therapy with the unit commander. Unfortunately, the therapy wasn't successful. Going to a military base and talking with a therapist in uniform, during hours that did not conform to the schedule of a civilian, prompted me to discontinue the treatment. I thought I would be able to continue on – to deal with the heavy load myself. I even attempted to return to reserve service in a non-combat role.

This last reserve service in October was especially difficult for me. I thought I would be able to cope with the continued service in a non-combat role, but I was wrong. The smell of dust from the tanks took me back to the depths of Lebanon. Images from debriefings brought back the nightmares. And the disturbing thoughts and night terrors returned.

About two weeks ago I contacted a private therapist to continue treatment and try to solve my problems. All these issues cause me to lose sleep and bother me on a daily basis. After a session with the new therapist, and with his recommendation, I turn to you for recognition and assistance in financing the therapy.

Gideon finishes reading the letter, and points out that, through writing, I can clearly describe things that perhaps I still don't have the courage to say. "What's the name of the commander who was injured?" he asks. "Stern," I reply.

Gideon nods his head with a serious expression. "And Stern, how is he these days?" he asks, and I tell him that after the injury, Stern came to visit the company a few times. Since my release from the IDF we haven't seen each other.

Gideon asks about the injury, and for the first time in my life I share the details of Stern's incident with a stranger. I tell how we finished clearing the route to Bint Jbeil,[i] and positioned ourselves on the outskirts of the village with our two tanks close to one another. A moment later, a bullet shot by an IDF sniper hit Stern's face.

"And why do you feel responsible for the incident?" Gideon asks. "Because I was the commanding officer in the area. When other forces joined us, they reported that they were going to shoot. I did nothing in order to prevent this injury." I pin my gaze on Gideon trying to extract any piece of information from his expression and body language.

He seems surprised by the blame I've taken upon myself. "But what could you have done?" Gideon asks calmly. "I didn't make sure that everyone entered the

[i] A village in south of Lebanon where one of the main battles of the 2006 Lebanon War took place.

tanks, and I didn't try to identify the force coming to us before I approved the shooting."

Gideon looks at me and pauses for a few seconds. It appears that he too is attempting to ascertain from my body language what he can and can't ask. "And why, in your opinion, didn't you tell Stern to go into the tank?" he finally asks.

I take a deep breath and exhale with a heavy sigh, then respond in uncharacteristic honesty, "I was actually asleep. One of my crew members woke me up because the force that was joining us called me on the radio. They reported that they were executing a shooting. I didn't even have a clue what they wanted from me so I approved them to proceed." I stare distractedly at the floor between me and Gideon. The session ends and we schedule another appointment for the following week.

◆ ◆ ◆

The next day I drive to submit the forms at the Disabled Veteran Department. I approach the gate with my car and the guard signals me to open the window. "Can I see your disabled veteran card?" he asks.

"I don't have one. I'm here to submit forms." He examines my ID card, then opens the gate and directs me to admissions. I drive up to the small roundabout and turn right according to his instructions. The parking lot is empty, but I have a hard time finding a spot since all of the spaces are marked handicapped. Am I supposed to park in a handicapped spot too?

I step out of the car and walk toward the admissions office. Outside the admissions hall there are several older people sitting, some with an indication of a physical disability, and some without. I wonder if they have issues from the wars of their generation.

The security at the entrance is reminiscent of an international airport. I approach the security worker standing behind the counter. She wears a beige security shirt and from her right ear dangles a white cord that goes under her clothes and connects to the communication device attached to her belt, next to the firearm.

"I came to submit forms," I say and place the stack of stapled papers on the counter. She takes out the earpiece and stamps the forms:

10-1-2012 | Claim Received

And that's it. Five and a half years have gone by since the war.

♦ ♦ ♦

The wait for the Disabled Veteran Department's response lasts forever. In the meantime, I make sure to attend the sessions with Gideon, who continues to ask about my family and childhood in the shared yard. I tell him about the basement at my parents' house, which was filled with old tools that my father collected over the years, or were handed down from my grandfather. It was my favorite place as a child.

Every once in a while, I would go down with my dad to fix some broken toy. We would dismantle, reassemble, glue, and paint. My dad had a solution for every problem and he always thought of an original idea to fix what was broken. Our basement was like a grownup playroom that only my dad and I loved. No one else was interested in it. Mom came down very seldom and she'd berate us, "When will we get rid of all this junk?" She was unable to see the magic and the possibilities the different tools gave us.

My dad doesn't know how to put things back in place and everything was always messy. Once every few weeks, I would go down there and organize it — hang all the wrenches on the wall according to size, arrange the hammers, sort out the screws according to screw type, empty the trash, and sweep the concrete floor.

Each time I would attempt to improve the location of the tools. Things that weren't used I would place into deep, less accessible storage and the tools in use I would hang in an orderly fashion on the walls. I once built shelves for the tools, right under the emergency exit from the shelter[i] to the basement.

When Dad got home from work, he immediately removed all the shelves I put up. "You can't block the emergency exit from the shelter," he explained. "This

---

[i] Every house/apartment in Israel must have a protected room built of reinforced concrete.

exit must always remain open. What would we do during an emergency if we have to open the emergency exit and haven't moved the shelves? We don't want to find ourselves stuck inside."

Another time, I left my bicycle blocking the main entrance to the shelter. Dad immediately told me that the passage to the shelter must remain open at all times and that there has to be room inside for all of us. Ever since, I always make sure the passage to the shelter is open and the emergency exit isn't blocked.

I would also help my dad change the water in the emergency tank down there. After we watered the tangerine tree with the old water, we would refill it again and make sure to place a new sticker with the date we changed it.

He was also meticulous about checking the old telephone that was placed on a shelf in the shelter. He wasn't satisfied with only picking up the receiver and hearing a dial tone, but he'd also make a call to the other line installed in the house.

The other line had one phone, in the study on the second floor. Dad would call from the shelter and we would hear Mom leaving her cooking and running up the stairs to answer the unusual phone call on the other line. Every time Mom answered, he would make up something new to say. "Mom, we smell wonderful aromas, but can't figure out what's cooking," or "we just wanted to make sure that there's enough schnitzels for everyone." She would laugh and hang up.

We also used to check the shelter door. Dad would go into the shelter and I remained outside while he made sure that the door closed well and it could be opened from the inside as well. He wasn't flippant about this either. I would look at the steel door slam shut and see the handle on the outside turn until it was completely locked. Then he would open the door and show me there's a hammer in the shelter in case the door jams. And if this wasn't enough, he would get in the shelter with me, show me how he closes the door from the inside, and let me try to release the handle with the heavy hammer. The mechanism was so well oiled that even as a little child I succeeded in opening the door.

And, of course, all the checks must be made in the correct order: first checking the phone line and only then locking the door, so that if we get stuck, we can call Mom and ask for help.

I never attributed any importance to it. But now, telling this to Gideon, it seems a little unusual to worry at such a young age about the next war. It also connects with my military service. The army is built on its preparedness for an emergency. This is one of the first principles taught to combat soldiers. They rouse you from bed to defend the base. They conduct nightly readiness inspections to check that the magazines and canteens are full. Each time you go off the tank you need to make sure all the switches are adjusted according to the post-operation checklist.[i] Otherwise, we wouldn't be ready, just like if a war breaks out and my bicycle is blocking the entrance to the shelter.

Since the beginning of my military service the operational readiness and these values have resonated with me. From the very first week of basic training the commanders gave me the nickname "the officer." I never broke guard duty and was always surprised when people would fall asleep, listen to music, or eat on their watch.

When I received an assignment, I would find a way to deal with it. I spent many long hours on guard duty thinking about responses to scenarios that could take place at that moment. Where could a terrorist come from? What would I do if I get shot at right now? What would I say on the radio? Where would I take cover? Where could I go so the terrorists won't see me? If we were in the middle of the desert or securing an event in the center of Tel-Aviv, I would think for hours about all the possible scenarios. After years of alertness in my childhood, the military instructions seemed completely natural to me.

◆ ◆ ◆

Gideon asks again what my dad used to share about the wars he served in. I respond that he loved telling

---

[i] Set of actions that make sure that the tank is set and ready for departure to battle.

stories about the military at every opportunity. Most of the stories I knew by heart. When I was in officers' course I was asked to prepare a paper on any topic I wanted. I chose to interview my dad about the Yom Kippur War and his injury. I thought I already knew everything, but was surprised to discover many more details about his military service. It was the first time he told me the whole story. It's also the last time we've spoken about the war.

Dad, just like me, was rejected in the final step before the trial period of combat pilots' course and enlisted in the armored corps. Like me, he also went into the tank commanders' and officers' courses immediately following basic training.

While writing the paper I found out he was a deputy company commander during the Yom Kippur War. I didn't know then that I, too, was destined to be a deputy company commander in the Second Lebanon War.

Unlike me, he got wounded in the battles of the Golan Heights. On just the second day of the war, his tank got hit by a shell and he got shrapnel in his lip, but continued to fight. On the fifth day of the war, during the battle of Khan Arnabeh,[i] beyond the Syrian border, my father's tank got hit by another shell on its rear end, probably by friendly fire.

---

[i] The battle to conquer The Bashan Salient in southwestern Syria during the 1973 Yom Kippur War.

As a result of the impact, electrical shorts started inside the tank, which led to the explosion of the ammunition. The engine stalled along with the turret's ability to traverse. The tank caught on fire, and Dad, along with two crewmen who were with him in the turret, managed to escape.

The fourth crewman, the driver, remained trapped. The cannon got stuck right over the exit from the driver's compartment. When Dad found out the driver was stuck, he ran back into the burning tank and manually cranked the turret until the driver successfully got out. While Dad was inside the tank his face got burned.

Gideon keeps interrupting me with questions that make me look at things from a different perspective. "And what did your dad feel after he sat in the burning tank and manually turned the turret?" Gideon asks. I realize we never really spoke about that. "The conversation ended with the same technical descriptions, 'we did what needed to be done,' this is what my dad used to say," I reply to Gideon, a little embarrassed that I'm unable to answer such an important question.

"Why don't you ask him?" Gideon suggests something simple, but it sounds impossible to me. How do I start such a conversation? Will he even want to talk about it? Perhaps he prefers to not remember? Why should I be the one to evoke things he has repressed for so many years?

Gideon asks to hear more details about Yossi's injury, and I realize I've never heard my uncle talk about it. When I tell Gideon about our family history, I begin to understand how much impact dad and Yossi's injuries had on my childhood.

◆ ◆ ◆

Gideon and I continue to meet once a week. During one of our sessions, we talk, again, about my older brother's military service. As usual I point out that he was a pencil-pusher because he was afraid to be a combat soldier.

"Why do you disrespect it so much? Maybe Ofer is the brave one and you're the coward?" Gideon tosses into the air. It takes me several minutes to digest. "You both grew up in the same house, in a constant state of alert from the fear of war. In the shadow of your father's and uncle's injuries. And probably in the shadow of some repressed post-traumatic stress as well," Gideon continues. "It was expected of both of you to continue this glorious tradition of a fighting and coping family. You grew up to die for the army and it never occurred to you that there's another option. Your brother, Ofer, had the courage to say 'no' to combat service." I am silent. In one moment Gideon manages to change my entire perception of Ofer's choices.

"Did you ever ask Ofer why he chose to serve in the logistics corps?" Gideon asks, but I don't answer.

"Did you and Ofer get to talk about your service? Did he ask you about your experiences after the war?" Gideon continues to rattle my thoughts.

Gideon's on a roll, and begins summarizing the conclusions from our last sessions. "You disrespected the draft dodgers. You were raised on the idea that wanting to be a combat soldier is good and not serving in the military bad. You believed that there's no justified reason to not want to serve as a combat soldier. Something changed in the war, and now you're the one who fails to cope with combat reserve service. The inner conflict is what makes it so difficult for you to cope with this new situation. Is it possible that you can't accept the fact you want to be something you were raised your entire life to hate?"

So accurate. In one moment everything becomes clear.

◆ ◆ ◆

A week later, on the way to another meeting with Gideon, I pass by my parents' house to say hi. Mom, as usual, sends me to my old room to check the mail that has accumulated there. Among the letters from the credit card company and pension reports, there's a letter from the Disabled Veteran Department. Finally, my summons to the review board has arrived. They will determine whether I'll be reimbursed for the sessions with Gideon or not.

Oh, no. Now I'll have to explain what this letter is all about. The address is the same for all of us. The postman puts all the letters addressed to the Ginzburg family in my parents' mailbox. My parents were probably surprised that an envelope with the insignia of the Disabled Veteran Department is addressed to me, and not to Yossi.

I go back down to the living room with the bundle of letters in my hand. My parents sit on the couch, following me with their eyes. "How are you?" Mom asks.

"Everything's good."

"Is everything alright?" she asks, probably in an attempt to receive a different answer.

"Yes, I started seeing a therapist."

Just like that, I drop the bomb in the middle of the room.

"What's wrong sweetheart?" Mom asks in concern. Psychological therapy is not a topic we discuss at home — ever. Like many other things we never talked about. And in general, the overall consensus is that psychologists are for people with serious problems. So, when I suddenly come to my parents and tell them that I've started seeing a therapist, either the situation is drastically severe or I don't really need to see one.

"I have some issues with the military that I don't exactly know how to handle," I respond with a slightly shaky voice. I wasn't ready for the question and don't know what words I should use. On the one hand, I want them to know that something is happening. On the other, I don't want them to think it's something serious and to worry. That's why I didn't want them to see the letter — certainly not before I did.

"Who are you seeing? How did you get to him?" Mom moves to the technical matters, which probably make her feel more comfortable. "A guy named Gideon," I respond. "He works in a clinic here at the end of the road, in the Lerman's old house. Sila's mother made the connection for me." The fact that it's related to Sila's mom and that the meetings are here in the neighborhood, should reassure her. "You go every week?" she asks in an attempt to estimate the seriousness of the condition. "Once a week."

"I remember, we also had people that couldn't forget the sights," Dad joins in the conversation. "Even during the war, there were those you could tell had been affected. Some came out of it and some didn't," he shares in a failed attempt to alleviate the situation. "So, what's wrong with you? You don't want to go to reserve service anymore?" he asks, perhaps because he doesn't have the nerve to ask what's really interesting him.

"I do want to go, but it's difficult for me," I respond. There's a heavy silence in the room.

"And what's wrong with you? What do you feel?"

"I think I have some nightmares occasionally," I reply vaguely. I still don't know what I want to reveal to them. I glance at my watch. "The truth is, I'm going to Gideon right now. Don't worry, everything's fine."

Dad thinks for a moment and then asks, "Do you need something? How much does the therapy cost? I want to give you money." How does one respond to that? I have no idea what I need.

"I'm not paying him now. Gideon said we'll submit a claim to the Disabled Veterans Department and they'll reimburse him. He has many patients that pay through them." I manage to get it out somehow. Mom looks surprised. "What, and just like that he's not asking for money?" she asks. "Yes. If they don't pay him, I will repay him for everything," I respond and begin to head out. "Well, I'm off. We'll talk later."

♦ ♦ ♦

I leave them alone in the living room. During the short walk to Gideon's clinic, I notice that my shirt is soaked with sweat. I wonder what they think. Dad is probably telling her about his friends who carry problems from the war — the standard stories about commanders who suffered shell shock and made excuses why they couldn't join the combat with their tanks. This is how shell shock looked in his view — cowards who didn't do what needed to be done.

There is, for example, his story about one commander who reported on the radio that his tank was broken and he couldn't move forward. When Dad went up to the tank himself and asked the driver what the problem was, the driver told him that everything was working well. There's also the commander who told him he had problems with the radio and again, when Dad came up to the tank, he found out that everything was in working order.

On the way to Gideon, I read the letter from the Disabled Veteran Department. It gives a date I need to report to the review board to establish my disability percentage. What does disability percentage have to do with it? I just want them to pay Gideon for the therapy so I won't have to pay for it myself.

TRAVEL LOG: ATLIT

I was very preoccupied with money at the time. As if financing the treatment was the most important thing. Back then I didn't yet understand how much I needed the official recognition in order to allow myself to be someone I had always hated.

I close the laptop, organize the coffee set, and continue to think about the nightmare with Lavie and Elroei at the entrance to my house; a nightmare that starts with my fears of reserve service, builds up to my great hope that Tal will come back to me, and ends with Tal being injured just like Stern was. What power the PTSD has, to pin Stern's injury on Tal. His injury, which I blame myself for, and which stands in the center of my PTSD. It reflects total lack of control, the feeling of failure, and mainly a great deal of luck for getting out of there alive. To this day I walk around with that feeling. Why did they shoot him and not me?

Along with my thoughts of Gideon, Tal, and Stern, I pack the gear onto the truck. I give one last look at the Centurion tank that father was so proud of, and step into the truck to drive toward the south of the Golan heights.

When I put the truck into fourth gear, the pesky thoughts begin. I still need to look for a place to camp. I am preoccupied with the familiar dilemma of setting it up. Is it better to take advantage of the last hours of daylight and settle in comfortably or is it best to wait for nightfall?

In setting up early, you can see your surroundings well and where it's best to put up the tent, but you also expose yourself. If, by chance, someone comes by, he will see me from a distance, understand that I'm getting organized for an overnight stay, and could come back under the cover of darkness.

Settling down after nightfall reduces the chances that such a thing will happen, but it is harder logistically and maybe even more frightening. I've had enough of this proximity to Lebanon and Syria, it's time to skip over to the beach.

With the setting sun in the background, the truck and I flow through the bends of the beautiful road overlooking the Yarmuk river. Low gear, high RPM, light strokes on the breaks, and thoughts that wander far away, to my dad.

I'm so sad that I've never really spoken with him about the war. The conversations always remained on the level of stories about tanks without equipment and going into battle without sights adjustment — conversations that never evolve beyond that.

How come we've never spoken about the experiences that truly make an impact? About the sights of the wounded? About the smell of blood and the pain he experienced during the long hours of waiting for an evacuation with burns on his face? What goes through your mind when your entire face is scorched and you don't even have a mirror to comprehend what you look like?

What do you think about when you're sitting in a tank that is going up in flames, turning the traverse manually for thirty seconds or more while the skin on your face burns up? What kind of a relationship develops with the man you've risked your life to save? I've never asked these questions in the past, and since the war there's no chance I will.

Even with my mom I haven't managed to speak about these things. Since they saw the letter from the Disabled Veteran Department, they ask every once in a while, "How do you feel?" And I respond, "Everything's fine." They ask, "Does the therapy with Gideon help you?" And I answer, "Yes, of course."

It's not a lie, the therapy does help, but the answer still comes out impatiently because what I really want to say is that I feel like shit. Truly crap. And I don't know how to deal with it, and it's never a good moment to bring up the issue. Each question like this floods me with overwhelming emotions that I can never express in words. Certainly not to Mom. It seems to be my main motive for writing about what I have been through since then.

My parents met two years after the Six Day War of '67. Did Dad tell her something about that war? In the Yom Kippur War, he went into battle in the Golan Heights, and Yossi in the Sinai sector. Dad came home burnt and Yossi came home without a leg. Did they ever talk about that? Did any of them talk about what really happened there?

What did Mom feel 33 years later, when she sent her son – also a deputy company commander in the tanks – to a war in Lebanon? What did she go through every night, looking at the names of those fallen on the news? And how about when the criticism over managing the war began, and she knew her son was still there at that moment?

How do you handle such fear? And what would she have thought if she knew that while she was lying in bed worrying, I was racing in a tank at full speed, closing my eyes and praying to not go over a charge that would blow my entire crew to pieces? Which is worse? Knowing or not knowing? And who's more afraid? Dad, who was in battle and knows exactly what it's like there, or Mom, who can't really imagine the horror?

At the end of the descent from the Golan Heights I imagine Dad's tank battalion driving in front of me toward the highlands. What a mess must have been on Yom Kippur — shelling, dozens of vehicles stranded, military vehicles, reserve service troops driving their civilians' cars — a combination of chaos and uncertainty. How come we never truly talked about it? How did he fail to warn me about what was going to happen?

◆ ◆ ◆

After two and a half hours of slow driving, I arrive at the Atlit beach. The sun has already set and a full moon is illuminating the shore. I find a nice corner between two low tamarisk trees.

In the distance the sound of a Purim[i] party is heard. After the incident with the soldiers in Zivon River, it is soothing to know that there are people around. I'll be able to sleep better here, and maybe I will even pop over there during the evening.

I set up my tent with double the number of pegs because of the winds anticipated during the night. The camp fire lights on my first attempt and I soon sit in front of the flames with a bottle of beer in my hand, watching the tomato sauce for the pasta bubbling in the pan. The trance music from the party fits together with the song of the waves. Such a delightful moment.

---

[i] A Jewish holiday in which people wear masks and costumes and are encouraged to drink wine.

The third beer and full stomach translate into tiredness, and the idea of going to the party fades away. It isn't supposed to rain until tomorrow, but I prepare the camp for it before I get into my sleeping bag. I put the chair into the back of the truck, load the remaining wood for tomorrow, and cover it all with a tarp. I can hear the sounds of the party in the distance. I feel safe and quickly fall asleep. Toward midnight, a strong wind wakes me. Once every few minutes a wave of sand hits the side of the tent, but it holds up nicely.

At two in the morning, I wake up again when a pile of sand penetrates the top ventilation opening and lands on me. I cover the phone with a sweatshirt and pull the sleeping bag over my head in an attempt to hide. I go through the next three hours in short snoozes and countless awakenings. Every few minutes a strong gust of wind deposits sand in my ears or the wall of the tent bangs against my face. The sun starts to come up, but another hour goes by before I break and decide to forego the sleep and start the day.

I step out of the tent and see that the wind has covered my tracks and the tire marks of the truck. The sand is perfectly arranged around me in small waves. The music still plays in the distance. The wind becomes stronger and the tent loses its shape. I have to fold everything before it is blown out to sea. I struggle with the tent and just shove everything in an untidy bundle into the bag. I use the remaining firewood to build a wall around the stove to make coffee. What a terrible night.

The clouds arrive earlier than expected. I pack up the truck and change my shirt. A reminiscent feeling engulfs me when I push my head through the collar and the scent of mom's laundry softener fills my nostrils.

The truck starts up easily and I start racing along the dunes parallel to the shore line, picking up speed in a second. The truck cruises like a race boat over the small dunes. A few fishermen wave hello to me in the distance. They seem to be excited by the unique look of the truck.

I stop at the top of a dune, the sea spread out before me, and go out on a short walk. I take a dip in the freezing water while keeping an eye on the truck to make sure no one approaches. The wind gets stronger and with it the waves of sand. I return to the truck and sit in the passenger seat, watching the waves of the sea and sand pass before me. I feel safe and protected, enjoying the winter atmosphere. A good time to continue writing.

2013: FIRST REVIEW BOARD

Twelve long months after I submitted my application to be approved as a disabled veteran, I report to the review board. The address on the summoning letter leads me to an office building with peeling paint on Shaul Ha'melech Street in Tel Aviv.

I press the filthy button of the lift and wait. When it arrives, three people step out of it. The first man looks like a sloppy lawyer, wearing a suit a few sizes too big. Next to him, a woman who's invested a little too much in her external appearance. And a little behind, her son, a young man who looks neglected, wearing a training suit.

I step off the elevator on the third floor, walk down the hall following the signs for "Review Boards," and arrive at the waiting room. A guy in his mid-twenties takes my ID card and asks me to wait. I sit down on one of the plastic chairs.

Around me there are other people waiting their turn, most of them in groups of three. Only I am by myself. Every trio is comprised of a lawyer, a representative parent, and a current or potentially future disabled person.

I look at myself and I feel like I don't belong. I am alone, wearing black jeans, a hooded sweatshirt, and black boots. The guy in charge of the queue chats with the lawyers about his private life and his successful business. The lawyers whisper with their clients and give them last minute tips — what to say and what not to.

The rooms of the review board are in another part of the floor and can't be seen from here. Every once in a while, a trio comes out from the far side of the corridor and I am able to overhear a sentence or two as they pass in front of me.

"You shouldn't have said that. You can't say you're feeling much better," one of the lawyers scolds his client. The mothers and fathers look worried, but allow the lawyers to manage the situation.

Each time the guy running the queue checks his lists, I hope that he'll call my name so I can be done with it.

"Omri Ginzburg, who's that?" he finally announces.
"I am."

"Room 303. Take a left at the end of the corridor, third room on the left after the door."

I get up from my chair and walk along the empty corridor. It has pale cream-yellow walls and white doors. The door jambs are gray and seem like they were painted hundreds of times. Room 303 is open and I peek in. "Should I come in?" I ask.

"Yes. Sit down. We'll be right with you," answers one of the review board members. I walk in. In the center of the room there's a lone student chair. I sit down. In front of me, behind a long and narrow table, sit the three members of the board: a woman who's looking at me with a motherly gaze, a man with gray hair who looks like he's already seen everything in his life, and another guy, a little younger, who's examining every move I make.

Next to them there's a young woman sitting in front of a computer. The man with the gray hair passes a few stapled pages to the rest of the board members. "Let's start with you telling us a little about yourself," he says kindly.

◆ ◆ ◆

The meeting ends after ten minutes. The girl next to the computer hands me the protocol and a feedback form. "We would be happy for you to fill out your opinion of the review board members," she says.

I take the pages, leave the room, and start walking toward the elevator without writing anything about anyone. I take a deep breath and try to understand the weird feeling that overtakes me — a kind of mental fatigue and a raggedy physical feeling. I am sweating profusely, my shirt is soaking wet. I feel weak and achy, my mind is troubled, and thoughts are flying in every possible direction.

The elevator is already waiting for me. I press the button and the doors open immediately. I leave the building and walk toward the car. The street is noisy and stifling, with the stench of exhaust and the honking of nervous drivers. I have no air.

I widen my steps to reach the car as quickly as possible, just to escape the commotion. I step in and immediately close the door. And suddenly it is quiet. The car's familiar smell soothes me a little. I take a few deep breaths and try not to think about anything. When I calm down, I start going over the review board's protocol, attempting to recall what I even told them.

I am twenty-nine, living in Kfar Sava on my own. I've worked for a software company for two and a half years now, and get along well at work. After I was released from the reserve service, orders began to arrive.

At the beginning, I kept looking for excuses to evade and even tried to transfer to a different unit. About three years ago I realized that something was wrong. Every call up letter brought on a strange nausea. I would hold the letter in my hand and feel my stomach turning. Later on, it started bothering me on a daily basis. Reserve service takes me directly back to the events of the war. The worst situation was about three years ago, when I was facing an operational deployment.

I couldn't sleep at night. I was really troubled and barely functioning. Today there are many other things that take me back to the war. It could be a headline about the tension with Iran, scary movies, or certain smells. I have nightmares about endless pursuits in which I try to kill someone or they try to kill me. I always wake up in fear and worry that there's someone looking at me.

The more stressed I am, the more severe the symptoms become. During the exam period for my degree, I couldn't bear the stress so I sought treatment.

My most difficult moments come when I'm alone, especially when it's dark. Each morning I'm thankful that war didn't break out during the night, and each night I am grateful that war didn't break out during the day.

My relationship with my parents isn't simple. The truth is, with my dad it's even difficult.

He was in the armored corps as well. The hardest thing I've had to cope with is the shame from my dad. I live in conflict. I feel guilty and I'm ashamed to say it to my dad.
I turned to a lawyer in the past, but I felt he was trying to extort the system, so I decided to come here and tell my story myself.

It wasn't until now that I realize I've revealed several of my most hidden secrets, the ones I've never told anyone. Not even to Gideon. I feel like I was coerced to speak, but part of this coercion was self-inflicted. I forced myself to be as miserable as possible. I have never portrayed myself as such, but this sick situation made me feel like I had to. If I'm not miserable enough, they won't help me. It is me who needs them. I have never been so dependent on someone else's decision.

I put down the review board's protocol on the passenger's seat, start the car, and go home, agitated about the traffic jams. I arrive home and go straight to bed without taking my clothes off. All I want is to disconnect from the world.

◆ ◆ ◆

The wait for the review board's decision lasts forever and along with the anticipation, the frequency of my nightmares rises. On days I'm exposed to a headline related to security tension or a news report about a wounded soldier, I know I'm going to have a difficult night. I'll wake up drenched in sweat and scared, knowing that someone is watching me, wanting to harm me. When I lie frozen in bed I try to recreate the nightmare, not always successfully.

The dreams begin to repeat themselves. A large part of them center on my feelings of failure and fear — an attempt to reach a goal unsuccessfully. More specifically: countless failed attempts to kill the one in front of me, an enemy or a good friend. In most cases I try to squeeze the trigger and nothing happens. My weapon simply won't shoot. And even if it does, I can't make a hit. And if I do hit something, the bullets don't have an effect. Those in front of me continue to fight.

In a lot of dreams, I need to lead a group of people. My task is clear, but I always fail and someone who isn't supposed to get hurt does. Each time I wake up in panic, accompanied by a sense of failure. The nightmares are so real and sometimes they even last in the long hours I lie motionless after waking. Not sleeping, not awake. Waiting until the sun starts to come up.

Even the days after the nightmares are hard. Sometimes it takes me two or three days to recover and break free from the feelings of guilt and failure. Some people get to the office after they drop off their children at kindergarten. I arrive after I've spent the whole night trying to kill someone. And I've failed over and over again. And everything is so realistic that

I feel like someone who's living a double life:
Nighttime Omri and Daytime Omri.

It becomes a ritual. I sit silently in front of the
computer at work. The moment everyone goes to
lunch and the room is empty, I call the Disabled
Veteran Department. I try to find out if a response
has arrived from the review board. I know the answer
will come by mail, but I can't bear the thought of my
mom seeing the letter before me.

I give the soldier my file number. She replies,
"Omri? Hold on. I'm checking," and she puts me on
hold. I pin the receiver to my ear waiting for the
news. On the other side of the line I can hear the
annoying and whispered voice of the host of
Galgalatz[i] radio station.

The wait lasts for several long minutes, during
which I pray that there will be an answer. Eventually,
after she checks what's happening with my file, or
maybe she only pretended to check, the soldier comes
back and says, "No, there's no reply yet." I've heard
that sentence dozens of times, and dozens of times
I've asked, "Is there a way to find out what the status
is? Because it's been a few months already..."

"No, there's no way to find out," she always replies.

At first, I'd call once every two weeks, but very
quickly it's become part of the routine at the office
and I've started calling almost every day.

---

[i] One of the most listened-to Israeli radio stations, operated by the
IDF.

Today, the wait lasts for an especially long time. Leonid, who sits in the office with me, has already returned from his lunch break with a cup of coffee.

He sits in front of the computer. "Who are you talking with Omrigi?" he asks quietly, and I smile as if I'm hiding a secret.

"Omri?" The representative at the call center returns to me, "The case is waiting for approval with the Compensation Officer." This is an answer I haven't heard before.

"Thank you, but what does that mean? There's an answer?" I ask in a way that Leonid won't understand who I am talking with.

"I don't know. You need to wait for an answer. Other than that, nothing is written here," she says impatiently and ends the call.

"Who isn't giving you an answer, Omrigi?" Leonid asks again.

"Some test I took, nothing to worry about," I blow him off.

I try to understand the meaning of the representative's words. A Compensation Officer is the one who pays, isn't it? Does that mean I'll get something? Will they pay for the therapy? How long is it going to take? I can't wait any longer.

◆ ◆ ◆

That same evening, I have a meeting with Gideon and tell him about the phone conversation. It seems like he thinks it's good news, but doesn't want to say it outright.

At one point he even slips. "Your story is touching and you're a charming guy. Why wouldn't they approve disability rights?"

Each time the words "disability rights" come out of his mouth I immediately remember my uncle Yossi. Yossi has disability rights because he doesn't have a leg. My dad also had temporary disability rights because he was totally burnt in the tank and underwent skin grafting. But me?

Because of a few nightmares I will receive disability rights? Can't they just give me a voucher for a few therapy sessions and be done with it?

During that same session I talk to Gideon about the days after the war. We were dumped for a few weeks in a grove next to the village of Avivim until the IDF made the final withdrawal from all the territories in the south of Lebanon. Gideon asks about the mood of the soldiers in the company after the cease-fire. I tell him that no one really digested what we'd been through.

"And did you continue to do operational activities inside Lebanon even after the war?" Gideon asks. "The soldiers did. I barely did," I answer and recall how I managed to evade the repeated entries into Lebanon. "And didn't you command the company at that point? You told me that the company commander was wounded and evacuated to the hospital."

Images I've managed to forget run through my mind, but it's hard to find the words. Finally, I say, "I commanded the company, but I bent over backwards to not get on a tank and cross the border."

Gideon, who was an officer in the combat engineering corps, is surprised by the answer and continues to badger. "And did it work out for you?" he asks.

I tell him about the only time I entered Lebanon after the war, how my leg wouldn't stop shaking until we crossed the border back into Israeli territory. "Did this happen to you before, your leg shaking like that?"

"Once, after an IED (improvised explosive device) blew up under the tank when we were on stakeout in Gaza." I had already completely forgotten about these incidents, and while talking to Gideon, I recall even the smallest details. He continues to ask about the weeks after the war, and eventually I tell him about the notebooks.

I describe to him how I would sneak into the room at the guest house in Manara, sit down at the dining table, and write about everything that happened during the war. I knew it would be a heavy subject, but Gideon tries to not make a big deal out of it. He beats around the bush, asking unrelated questions, until finally he addresses the issue.

"What prompted you to write? Have you written before?" Gideon asks gently. We both know this is just an opening question that will be followed by many more.

"At the end of the war I felt an inexplicable need to write it all down. I was afraid I'd forget things that happened or that I'd remember them differently, so I simply sat down and wrote."

"Have you had the opportunity to read what you wrote since then?" Gideon asks.

"The truth is I haven't," I respond, and tell him how I carry the notebooks with me everywhere I go. "When I lived with my parents, when I traveled in South America, and even today. They are still inside the red plastic bag from Office Depot that I got the day I bought them empty."

"Have you ever shared the notebooks with anyone?" Gideon asks, perhaps out of anticipation that I'll suggest he read them. "Very few people," I answer. I tell him about Shira Nelson, who fell asleep with the notebook in her hands, about Yuval's indifference, and about the embrace and tears of my sister, Efrat.

"Why do you think that Yuval said nothing?"

"Because that's Yuval. He doesn't talk much. He's the genius cousin and the perfect officer. He probably had criticism about my actions. Maybe he thought I wasn't professional enough."

Gideon seems surprised. "That's what he thought when he read your notes about the war? That you weren't professional enough?" he asks.

"I don't know. If he didn't say anything, it's because he didn't feel comfortable saying what he thought about what we did over there."

"Are you sure he read everything? Perhaps he didn't even finish reading?"

I try to picture a situation in which Yuval puts the notebooks down halfway through. "Why would he stop in the middle?" I wonder.

"Could it be that Yuval found it hard to read about the combat? Just like you find it hard? Like you're afraid your dad will find it difficult to talk about the war?" Gideon asks. I keep silent.

He looks at the clock and so do I. We have exceeded the session time by a lot. "We'll have to finish," Gideon says with his soothing voice.

◆ ◆ ◆

The session ends and I leave the clinic. When I get home I go to the closet and open it. In front of me there's a row of buttoned shirts, sorted from dark to light. All the buttons are facing to the left and all the hangers are open toward the back of the closet, ready to be pulled out quickly. The arrangement of the hangers makes me laugh. It reminds me of our family shelter's organization.

Under the buttoned shirts there's an orderly pile of bedding. I reach behind the pile, feel my way around, and pull out the red plastic bag with the notebooks and the operational plan book[i] from the war. I return to the living room and place the bag on the table. First thing, coffee, I say to myself and go to the kitchen. I return to the living room with the coffee and sit on the sofa in front of the plastic bag and the plan book.

The plan book is made from two hard sections, 20 by 30 centimeters stapled to a flexible strip that allows it to open up like a book. It's wrapped with a transparent nylon sheet. Between the nylon and the cover, there's still a layer of dust. The cover has a piece of paper attached to it with the writing "Operative – Deputy Company Commander." I open the double Velcro strap that secures the binder, and a cloud of Lebanese dust rises in the air. This is the first time I've opened it since the war.

On the left side of the binder there's a code map covered in nylon, and on top of it, three slides of the last operation we carried out in Lebanon. A terrain brief, on which the movement axis of our company is drawn in blue marker. The enemy brief, with no markings on it. And the friendly forces brief, also empty.

The slides are held together with some black insulation tape that was applied in haste. The movement axis is partly erased and filled in with

---

[i] A small binder containing all the information required prior to going into battle.

corrections. On the right side of the plan book there's a table with a list of the company's tanks. It includes a column with the tanks' numbers and a column with the mechanical faults. Some of the tank numbers are erased, probably due to last minute changes.

I examine the list and recall all the faults we couldn't fix during the battle. Some tanks went out of commission after they were hit by a missile and their crew was wounded. Nearly all the tanks had their radio antenna broken. Some lacked equipment and had problems in the gunner's systems.

Next to the tanks' list there's another table with various data about each tank in the company: fuel, ammunition, food, water, and a column of kilometers. I completely forgot that every day I would collect an assessment report from the crews.

The kilometers' column is almost completely empty whereas the fuel column of each tank is filled with erased numbers: 1200, 800, 500, 300, 100 and completely empty, underlined twice for emphasis. During operational routines it was prohibited to start up the tank if there was less than 700 liters of diesel, but during the war we drove on fumes.

I remember Roman's faltering tank on the last day of the war. We crossed the fence back into Israeli territory and just at the entrance of the parking area the engine died from lack of fuel. Then I remember Klein's steering fault and the extraction of Stern's tank.

I close the briefing binder and place it on the table. I peek into the red plastic bag, pull out one of the notebooks, and quickly flip through all the pages without reading a word.

Why do I need to read it right now? Nothing good will come of it. I put the notebook back in place, go to the bedroom and shove it all back into the dark corner behind the pile of bedding. It is clear to me that I'm about to pay for this unnecessary curiosity with another night of terror.

◆ ◆ ◆

Like every Saturday, I arrive at my parents' house a little before one in the afternoon, loaded with bags of dirty laundry and empty plastic containers from last week's leftovers. I toss my laundry into the hamper and organize the plastic containers in the pantry. Then I go to the second floor to collect the clean laundry.

The laundry is arranged in an orderly fashion on the old couch in the hall. The buttoned shirts are ironed and on hangers, all facing the same direction. Between the folded clothes and the back of the couch, the letters that have arrived this week are waiting for me. Among the letters from the bank, advertisements, and bills, I see it. A letter from the Disabled Veterans Department.

My heart is beating fast. Can it be that after a wait of five months, there's finally an answer? I open the letter and sit down on the couch.

Your claim for recognition of disabled rights from 10.01.2012 – Decision.

I hereby inform you that after examining your claim and the results from the medical examination, I've come to the conclusion that your PTSD (Post Traumatic Stress Disorder) mental disorder occurred during, and as a result of, your military service.

The Medical Review Board, in their meeting on 16.1.2013, has set the rate of your disability at 20%, according to the following specifications:

Description of harm	Percentage
PTSD Mental Disorder – Medium limitation in functional capacity	20%

This disability degree will remain in effect from the date of 10.1.2012, the date of the claim submission, until the follow-up review scheduled for 01/2014, to which you will be summoned by us.

In the event you need medical treatment or other services, you can refer to our bureau or regional clinic.

Respectfully,
Orna Shtuzman
Compensation Officer

Why did it take them five months? And what does that even mean, twenty percent? Temporary? Wait, it's only until January. In four months it expires? I sit down at my parents' computer and try to find more information online. Twenty percent means a monthly allowance of 750 shekels (approximately 210 USD). How much are they going to pay me retroactively? From the date of sending the letter? From the date of submitting documentation? And wait a moment, what about the therapy?

The doorbell interrupts my train of thought. Dad opens it and my nephews storm in with shouts of joy. Efrat and Ofer have come. I shut down my parents' computer making sure I haven't left any incriminating clues behind. I shove the letter from Orna Shtuzman into my bag and go downstairs to say hello. What if Mom and Dad ask about the letter? What will I tell them? Fortunately, they don't.

Later that evening, I carefully read all the relevant material on the Disabled Veteran Department's website. I can't find anything about psychological therapy. All the information refers to medical treatments, transportation to the clinic, disabled vehicles, and more benefits I am not entitled to with twenty percent disability rights.

◆ ◆ ◆

The following day, I have a session with Gideon. He offers me coffee and we go into his office. Gideon shuts the door and arranges a few things on his desk. When he turns back, I wave at him with the envelope. Gideon throws himself into the therapist's chair and smiles, "Well, would you like to share?"

I hand him the envelope. He opens the letter and reads it out loud.

"I have no idea what twenty percent disability rights means," I comment without any expression. "It means someone there wants to help you. Twenty percent is the minimum that one starts receiving in allowance and significant benefits," Gideon replies and his look calms me down.

"And what about the therapy?" I ask with concern. "You will tell them you're being treated by me, and they will approve the therapy for a certain period," Gideon explains. "We'll have to prepare for another review board around January." He details the process and explains that as long as the disability rights are temporary, I will have to appear before the review board once a year.

This means that every year I will have to sit in front of people I don't know, tell my story all over again, and convince them I still need therapy. I can't focus my thoughts.

One moment I'm pleased that I passed the review board and that they'll approve the therapy. A second later, I feel like I don't even deserve this. Why do I need to receive money every month?

Gideon says he thinks I am also eligible for a few days of vacation in a hotel each year. How would I explain at work going on a vacation without taking days off? Would I tell my parents that I go to a hotel alone at the Dead Sea like Yossi?

◆ ◆ ◆

Over the next few weeks I don't tell anyone besides Gideon about the review board's decision. I focus on reading everything the Disabled Veteran Department has to offer over and over. Old documents of instructions, guidelines, guidelines' amendments, and all kinds of weird concepts like awarding electrical appliances and clothing as well as eligibility for medical treatment compensation.

I've waited so long for this reply. Every day that passed I thought about how I'd feel when it arrived and what I'd do if they didn't approve the therapy. I expected a feeling of relief with a positive answer, but now I'm mostly concerned about the additional review board in a few months.

I'm also concerned with how to hide the fact that I'm suffering from PTSD. Despite a few years having passed since I started dealing with it, I'm still at the beginning of the road — and it's not at all clear where that road leads.

TRAVEL LOG: MIKHMORET

The phone is vibrating. An incoming message from Mom. "Tomorrow we're coming on a trip up north with friends. We would love to see you while we're there." If I know her, she probably initiated the trip just to see me. Even if I told her I was in the desert, they'd still come.

I think about everything I've been through since the army. Gideon's words echo in my head. Dozens of times he asked in his gentle voice, "Did you get a chance to talk a little with your Dad?" I'd smile without saying a word. Perhaps it's about time I talk with both of my parents after years of keeping silent. They weren't the only ones I made sure to keep quiet around. I didn't dare talk about my situation with anyone who really knows me.

The entire time I felt like I was trying to exploit the system and take something that I didn't deserve. That's why I was so disgusted by the shady lawyer. All he wanted was to extort as much as possible — less for me and more for his gain. I respond to Mom in the affirmative and we make arrangements to meet the next day at noon.

◆ ◆ ◆

I watch the sun setting into the sea from inside my warm truck. After that, I distance myself from the shoreline in order to find a safe place to pass the night. I go on a gravel path that takes me in the direction of the nearby fish pools. I park next to two abandoned buildings.

Behind the trees I can barely feel the wind and there's enough room in the building for my truck and tent. I start a fire outside and sit down. Tomorrow I'll be staying at Hila's empty house in Mikhmoret and a couple days after that, I'll drive to Jerusalem for Klein's wedding.

I have known Hila, since childhood, from our neighborhood. Before I set off on the journey I looked for spots where I could stop for a shower and to freshen up. Hila had just traveled to Tel Aviv. When she heard I'd be passing through Mikhmoret, she rushed to offer her vacant home.

A light crackle from the fire interrupts my stream of thought. It causes me to jump up in panic, pops my heart out of my chest, and silences all sounds in my ears. Immediately after that, I hear another explosion from the opposite direction. I freeze in terror, once again, and go deaf.

It takes me a couple of seconds to realize that the adjacent structure echoes any noise that comes from my campfire. My first thought was that someone is sitting there, imitating the sounds of explosions to scare me. I know it doesn't make sense, but in my mind there's always someone who's searching for me, someone watching me.

Just like each of the previous nights, I beat myself up for deciding to set out on this journey in the first place. Tabenkin was right. What the hell am I doing here? What good is this trip? Why force myself to suffer?

The thick wood catches fire and the fire grows stronger, expanding the aura of light around me. It calms me down a little. I eat dinner and make myself comfortable. In a couple of hours it's supposed to rain, but I have a safe place for the night.

I put out the fire and get ready for bed. The moment I get into the tent and sleeping bag, I feel soothed. The temperature is pleasant and I feel safe inside. I give thanks for being here. And that another day has gone by without being called out to war.

♦ ♦ ♦

I wake up in panic to the sound of a bird screeching and ten single shots, right over my head. I freeze in my sleeping bag. What was that? Fireworks? Hunters? Someone trying to scare me? I can't figure out whether it is part of a nightmare or perhaps what I heard was real.

It's the middle of the night. I go nearly an hour without moving. Occasionally, I plummet into a near-sleep state, like a quick hallucination, from which I wake up to the sound of shooting. I am terrified, but after a few times, I understand that it's probably all in my head.

With the gentle light of morning, I wake up again, this time to the pleasant sound of raindrops on the building's roof. And then I fall asleep again.

♦ ♦ ♦

I wake up to a new day and the smell of rain. Yesterday's haze has dissipated and the skies are partially cloudy. The air is clean and it's possible to see into the distance. After a morning stroll along the shore and a dip in the cold water, I return to the truck and begin my drive to Mikhmoret.

When I arrive at our meeting spot in the nature reserve, my parents are already there. "My Ingale,"[i] Mom says and hugs me with teary eyes. Dad adds his typical embrace, along with a few slaps on my cheek and a "What's up?"

We continue along the path and find a grassy spot overlooking the sea. Mom takes out schnitzels

---

[i] From Yiddish, a nickname for a boy.

and salad from the cooler while Dad walks around the truck impressed. "Look! He's got everything back here."

Along with the meal comes a slew of questions.

"Is this how you sleep, alone?"

"Isn't it scary?"

"The truck isn't giving you problems?"

"Do other people sleep next to you?"

I respond with short and practical answers. Inside my head I hear Gideon's voice pressuring me to start sharing, but it doesn't work. I can't seem to muster the courage to talk about what I'm really going through. I've had first dates in which I've shared more than I do in the conversations with my parents.

Since the war, something in the discourse with my parents has gotten stuck and hasn't evolved. In recent years, perhaps, it's even deteriorated. I know they want to ask, but don't know how. And I convince myself that it's best not to talk about it.

When I was a young boy, we traveled in Israel a lot, and each trip was accompanied by my father's stories. "Here we trained with the tanks, there we prepared for the war." Since he's learned of my PTSD, he doesn't share anymore. It seems like we both want to talk, but are unable to kick off the conversation. The fact that I'm closed off to their questions and give short answers doesn't help.

After the meal and coffee, we pack up the gear and prepare to say goodbye. Mom gives me a strong hug and asks that I take care of myself. Dad gives me a few pats on the back and comments that it's okay to take a break and sleep at home for a few days. I tell them that tonight I'll be sleeping at Hila's, who they know from the neighborhood. This calms them.

I go back to the truck and start to drive in the direction of Hila's house. At the entrance to Mikhmoret the truck's battery charge light comes on. I open the glove compartment and look at the additional gauge I installed during the restoration. Eleven volts. This means there's no charge at all.

I stop in Hila's parking space, but don't turn off the engine in case the weak battery won't start again. I open the hood and go over the wires I connected myself. There isn't a wire or electrical connection that I don't know inside out.

After a few seconds I find the disconnect and succeed in fixing the fault. I'm filled with a feeling of a strong connection to the truck. It's my hero, the greatest thing I've done in my life.

It's the first time I've gone all the way with something and didn't think about money or time and didn't listen to the opinions of those who tried to discourage me from doing it. The truck was there during the difficult periods of coping with the post-traumatic stress. It never complained or expected anything in return. It taught me things in its own way and placed challenges in front of me that I enjoyed solving. When I picked it up, it was completely rusty and the body was filled with holes and now, after three years of obsessive work, everything's perfect. Down to the smallest screw, it's just as it was when it left the dealership more than thirty years ago.

During the restoration period, my day job became a side matter, and the truck became the center of my life. I didn't know it then, but in hindsight it was an escape to a protected place that was mine alone, a place to self-treat my PTSD.

Perhaps it's time to pay a little more attention to the truck. I spread the mat under the car and roll myself under. With a rag in my hand, I start checking over everything. I look for new dents in the car's undercarriage, parts that have come loose, or any sign that indicates something is wrong.

When I finish checking, I go into Hila's house and rush to get organized, even though all I can think about is sitting down after a shower and writing until nightfall. It seems like meeting with my parents and the desire to share the story with them sparks an obsession and I feel the uncontrollable urge to continue writing. Only this time, the obsession pushes me to a positive place, just like the truck's restoration.

2013-2014: TEMPORARY APPROVAL

In recent months I've adapted a new routine. Every morning I leave before the traffic jams and arrive first at the office. On Sundays and Thursdays, I start my day at the gym and on Tuesdays I run with a group.

Every few months I load up the car and go to the desert for three days with friends. Lately, I've started looking for another car I can fix myself. Working with my hands, especially dismantling and assembling, has always interested me.

My current off-road car is modern and everything in it seems complicated. I start searching for a vehicle that is simple enough for me to care for myself. After browsing forums in Israel and overseas, I come across an off-road Suzuki truck of an especially rare model.

I tell everyone that I am looking for this specific truck and after a few months, I manage to track down one of the last ones in Israel. The next day I go to the office and tell Leonid, my officemate who was also a partner in the search, that today I'm going to see the truck.

Leonid is an avid car lover. He always talks about how he used to help his dad to take apart and reassemble an engine during his childhood in Russia. He asks if he can tag along.

We leave the office early and drive to a small village in the Jerusalem Mountains. We arrive at a neglected farm, filled with dreamy junk. There's old heavy metal machinery, a cute yellow excavator in pieces, and car parts everywhere you look. The owner greets us and takes us to the back of the farm. And there it is, as if waiting just for me — a truck in a gray-rust shade, without wheels, leaning on an improvised iron beam to keep it off the ground.

I check the truck from the outside. Its windows are shattered and the roof is perforated from all the rust.

The truth of the matter is, I don't have a clue what to check when buying a car in this condition. While I stare at this magical iron creation, Leonid is already peeking under the truck with the eyes of an expert.

"What is this? It doesn't have a front driveshaft? No front-wheel drive?" he announces decisively, and with a Russian accent. He's trying to warn me that the seller is about to swindle me. I continue to go around the truck, patting and examining the dents in the sheet metal, studying the new curves, and trying to read the energy in my first encounter with the machine.

"What about the price?" I ask, knowing that I will probably pay any cost. "2,000 shekels (560 USD) and it's yours," the owner says. I check the floor of the truck that's covered with acorns and dry leaves. "Is that your final offer? Meet me halfway and we'll close the deal."

"What is this?" Leonid yells with his head under the hood. "Look at the wheel arch. It's all holes here, blyat'. You can see the ground. If you buy this you've completely lost your mind. The engine is all rusty and most of the parts are missing." His accent makes me laugh.

I continue looking at the truck. It's possible this opportunity won't come again. "Fifteen hundred and it's yours. Any less than that and I'm selling it to another buyer who should be here tomorrow," the owner responds. "Okay then, tomorrow I'm coming with a tow-truck," I say. We shake hands.

"Did you see the roof? Everything is holes like Swiss cheese. It's not even scrap." Leonid laughs, in disbelief that I'm paying money for this rusty pile of metal.

◆ ◆ ◆

The next day, I arrive with the tow-truck. We put wheels on the truck and transport it to my parents' yard. Dad is just coming home from work when we get there. He puts down his briefcase and helps me roll the truck into its new home.

After, he goes into the house, and I remain alone with my new-old purchase. I sit in the driver's seat, trying to gently move the old levers, exploring what's broken and what managed to survive the past thirty years.

Thirty years. The truck and I are exactly the same age. The year 1984. Where do I even begin? By finding a house where I can start working on the truck.

I prepare a list of requirements for my new home and start looking. First and foremost, I need a big yard with no neighbors so I can make noise and work on the truck. Second, I need to be close to work so I won't waste time and fuel in traffic.

After a couple months of searching, I stumble upon an ad with no photo and almost no details. After a short phone conversation with the landlord, we arrange for me to come and see the place. I leave work in the middle of the day and within ten minutes I arrive at the address.

Yaron, the landlord, instructs me to park on the street and go down the path behind an iron gate. To the left of the path is his well-groomed villa, and on the right, old sheds with wooden doors, their hinges grown tired from holding them in place.

Behind the semi-opened doors it's possible to see piles of junk, gardening and work tools. I continue on the path and a familiar odor fills my nostrils: the smell of my childhood in the neighborhood. Adding to the aroma is the familiar sound of clucking.

There's a chicken coop here! Parked next to the coop is the landlord's off-road car and next to it, a forklift and an old John Deere tractor. A typical farm.

Yaron is waiting for me at the end of the path. We shake hands and go on a tour around the small house. We start with the front yard — wild grass with fruit trees and around it an old bamboo fence that's falling apart.

The garden is a little neglected. The overgrown grass has pushed up the stones of the access path. Old garden furniture is scattered in all kinds of places, seemingly disused. In the back there's a large paved area adjacent to another shed that belongs to the landlord. "This is the seating area. It's great for a barbeque," says Yaron, who's trying to sell the property.

"Can I come here with my car?" I ask.

"There's a path behind the house, a little sandy and with weeds, but it's possible with a slightly lifted vehicle. What car are you driving?"

"I have a small all-terrain car, but I want to renovate an old truck I have, also a four by four," I say in an attempt to appeal to his love of all-terrain vehicles.

We enter the house — a spacious living room with a large window facing the front yard, an intimate kitchen, and a small bedroom with many windows. The toilet and shower are small, but comfortable. I don't need more than that. I give my okay to Yaron and we close on an entry date.

Later, at home, I prepare an exact sketch of the house on graph paper and cut paper models of my furniture to see if it fits. I calculate the length of the cables I'll need to install the home movie system and projector, and revise a list of electrical outlets and internet I'll want to add.

That same evening I start packing what I can. For a few days, before work I load my car with boxes and unload them at the new house.

On moving day there is hardly anything left to take over. I load the remaining boxes in the car and scan the apartment to make sure I haven't forgotten anything. All that's left is the notebooks. I've saved them for the last trip.

I take out the red plastic bag and the operational plan book from deep inside the empty closet, give the empty rooms a final look, and bid my first apartment farewell. I step out to the street, get in my car, and start the short drive to my new place.

The first thing I do upon entering is shove the notebooks and the Operational Plan Book deep into the closet, which I immediately fill with clothes. Only then do I start arranging the rest of my things. After a few hours of organization, my phone vibrates, reminding me that it's time for my session with Gideon.

◆ ◆ ◆

I immediately tell Gideon about the relocation of the notebooks. He looks at me and after a long silence, asks, "Don't you think I should read what you wrote?"

The room is quiet. I smile with embarrassment and keep silent. Every once in a while I blurt out an unclear "pfff" and divert my gaze to a spot in the middle of the room. Gideon understands and changes the subject.

After the session, I return home to continue unpacking boxes. I have zero capacity for procrastination and in just a few hours the house takes shape with everything in place.

I dedicate the weekend to working on the garden. I mow the lawn, lift the entryway's stones, pull the weeds, fix the bamboo fence, and paint the posts.

The following day, a tow-truck arrives at my parents' house and transports my truck to its new abode. I sit in the center of the lawn and gaze with satisfaction at the work I've done over the past few days. All my muscles are tight from pruning, pounding down pegs, and carrying boxes.

The combination of hard work, a visible outcome, and the scent of a mowed lawn breathe optimism into me. I fantasize about the workshop I'll build here and think of creative ideas for additions and improvements. I can sit for long hours by myself and simply look at the world — to observe, make plans, and fill out to-do lists.

It's already late and tomorrow I need to get up early. I go inside my new home and organize my clothes for work. Who knows what kind of night I'm going to have? It's best that everything be ready so if I wake up a little late, I can get dressed immediately and leave.

I go to pick out a shirt and notice the plastic bag of notebooks peeking from the back of the closet. At that moment I decide to take them to my next session with Gideon. Maybe after he reads them, he can tell me what's written in them. I take a shower and get into bed. Like every night, I'm thankful that war didn't break out today.

◆ ◆ ◆

On Thursday, a week after the move, I report for an introduction with Avital, the rehabilitation worker in charge of my case. At the gate of the Disabled Veteran Department I show my ID card and once again find myself in the dilemma of vacant handicapped parking spaces. After a security check I get in the elevator and go up to the third floor. I ask where Avital sits, and one of the girls directs me to the end of the corridor.

Avital's office door is the only one surrounded with plants — not one or two, but a veritable jungle. It seems so unrelated to the gray and depressing look of the government building.

Beyond the closed door I hear Avital speaking in a loud and hoarse voice. I can't understand whether there's someone else in the room or if she's talking on the phone. After a few minutes the door opens and Avital invites me to come in.

I enter and look around. The walls are packed with thank you letters that indicate Avital is a veteran in the division. On the table there is a large calendar and on top of it, three rounded metal boxes of hard candy. Also on the table is an old landline telephone with way too many buttons.

Avital is much older than I imagined her. Her skin is dark and her hair is pitch black. She wears many pieces of rattling silver jewelry. I sit in front of her. She opens a box of candy, puts one in her mouth saying slowly, in a didactic tone, "Shalom Omri, I'm Avital and I'm your rehabilitation case worker. The purpose of this meeting is for me to get to know you better and to see how I can help you."

Avital starts explaining about the department, but I can't get past the candy in her mouth. Then she asks me to introduce myself and, if I want to, the background for my treatment.

Once again, I present my entire history for a person I don't know: my childhood, the army, the nightmares, and my concern that the Veteran Disabled Department won't approve continued therapy with Gideon. Avital assures me, saying she will take care of everything and retroactively approve the payment for therapy.

It seems like, despite her many years in this gray place, she is still very patient and truly wants to help. When I tell her about my anxieties and the nightmares that began after release from the IDF, she seems like she'll burst into tears. There were even moments when she stopped sucking that candy. "It is so hard to hear that another generation had to go through war," she says. "We're in the peak of treating those injured in last year's operation in Gaza."

Avital's phone rings, interrupting the conversation. Her kids want to know what's for lunch. Avital tells them that there's schnitzel and baked potato. She explains to them how to warm up the food in the microwave and which dishes to use. Our conversation is interrupted three more times by these kinds of logistical questions from Avital's children. She apologizes and pops another candy into her mouth.

Toward the end of the conversation Avital explains the benefits to which I'm entitled. A discount in municipality taxes and an annual convalescence of five nights in Israeli hotels. This and all kinds of other things relevant only to married couples or those intending to purchase an apartment.

She takes me on a tour of the office and introduces me to the people who work in each room. They tell me more about the benefits for which I'm eligible. Just like Gideon said, twenty percent disability rights are the lowest grade that awards a small allowance and benefits.

I walk behind Avital through the various offices and don't ask a single question. I barely utter a word.

After meeting with Avital I get in the car and drive
through the heavy afternoon traffic in central Israel.
From here I head straight to my session with Gideon.
A strange feeling comes over me. On the one hand, I
feel a sense of relief that now it's certain, the Disabled
Veteran Department is going to pay for therapy.

And on the other, I have a strong feeling that I'm
exploiting and cheating the system. Why do I deserve
a vacation of five nights at a hotel at the expense of
the state? Perhaps I exaggerated my nightmares
before the review board. Sometimes I feel like I only
got into this because I wanted to be discharged from
reserve duty, which was happening right in the
middle of the exams period. Somehow, I got dragged
into this reality of review boards, disability rights,
and psychological therapy. Perhaps it's best if I finish
the therapy, the temporary disability benefits will
end, and I won't have to come here anymore.

I remember my first visit to the Combat PTSD
Clinic. "Were you shot at?" was the first question the
soldier who answered the phone asked. "Yes, I was
shot at," I replied. But I don't think I really was shot
at. The shots were next to me, but never really at me.

"Was there a specific event that caused this?" Guy
Shulman asked in my first evaluation at the clinic.
Although I didn't really have the answer, I told him
that Stern's injury affected me in particular.

Gideon got fixated on Stern's incident because he
read Shulman's evaluation during our first meeting. I

still don't know if Stern's injury was the most significant event, but I do remember that after it happened I felt fortunate.

We both stood in the turrets of the tanks, which were concealed behind a low mound of sand. Each of us was in our own tank, but we were extremely close to each other, perhaps thirty centimeters between the tanks. The sniper, who only saw figures and not the tanks themselves, mistakenly thought we were terrorists and needed to choose between me and Stern. I was the one who approved the shooting and he selected Stern.

With these thoughts I park my car next to my parents' house and walk to Gideon's clinic. He is outside the house, feeding the alley cats. "Hi there," says Gideon, as usual examining my body language to gauge my mood. "It looks like you have news," he says. "Come on. I'll make coffee and we'll sit and talk," Gideon continues, opening the door carefully so the cats don't come in. It's a battle Gideon always loses, and this time three make it past him and into the kitchen.

Gideon makes me a cup of coffee and pours himself a glass of flat Coke. We enter the office and he closes the door. I carefully sit in the chair, holding the coffee. Gideon throws himself on the chair, pulling his shirt away from his body to let the air in. The room is silent as we both sit having our drinks. I start the conversation.

"I've been to my rehabilitation case worker." I tell Gideon about my meeting with Avital and how I feel I don't deserve the benefits. Gideon tries to calm me. "Try to enjoy the benefits and the new pocket money. The State of Israel will survive and you deserve this." His smile implies that he doesn't really believe the benefits bother me. "I've known Avital for many years. She's not exactly known for being nice." Gideon adds.

"Really? She was so patient. I felt like, even though she's a veteran, she had patience and a great desire to help," I come to her defense. "Really? You probably captured her with your charms too," says Gideon while attempting to relax in his not-so-large chair.

"I brought you the notebooks." I reach into my backpack, take out the red plastic bag from Office Depot, and give it to him.

◆ ◆ ◆

I go to the next session on high alert, eager to hear what Gideon thinks after reading the notebooks. I start with the usual update of everything that's new from last week. Gideon's interested in the progress of my truck and the plans with my friends. I tell him we plan to sleep on the beach. Gideon asks if my nighttime visitor comes when I'm with friends at the beach.

"Even with friends I don't sleep well and I'm in a state of anxiety that someone will come," I explain.

"It wakes me up once in a while, but the moment I see my friends next to me, I relax."

"And what if you sleep during the day?"

"I'd still have trouble, but it's not actually the same thing."

"And when you imagine during the night that someone's watching you, what are you afraid he'll do to you?"

"I don't know... nothing? Do you know what's it like when someone stands in front of you and just watches?" I ask, knowing how weird it sounds.

"You must have a feeling that something is about to happen," says Gideon in an attempt to understand why I'm actually afraid.

"In my mind it's as if he'll do something to me, but it never goes past that. He's just there in front of me. At home I'm constantly afraid that I'll look out the window and see someone there looking at me. Perhaps a thief? Maybe someone who wants to murder me?"

"A thief doesn't murder people. And what, people just go around killing for no reason?" Gideon attempts to downplay the situation. "It's very difficult to see out the window when it's dark outside."

The seriousness with which he relates to the situation causes me to keep sharing. "Sometimes at night, I go out to my car park. It's very dark, and in order to drive out I need to turn the car around. When I look in the rear-view mirror, I always imagine someone suddenly appearing. Someone standing in my path. When it happens, I immediately turn my face forward so as not to see the figure. I continue driving backwards without looking, just so I don't see a figure that's not even really there."

Gideon sighs. "You must have done many bad things," he says in a moment of sarcasm. Then, with a sharp transition to reality, "You keep thinking that people are looking to harm you. You only think of Stern as someone you've wronged? Or did you hurt many other people?"

"Stern is someone I saw wounded. It's not that I did something bad to him, it's more that I'm disappointed in myself for what happened."

"And what kind of punishment do you think you deserve for it? In all of your nightmares someone comes to harm you, to murder you, to beat you up, or just to terrorize you. When this someone comes to your home at night, what does he want to do to you? The general idea of someone chasing you demands a reason. Usually, we chase someone who's done something wrong, who's hurt others." Then he tosses out, "I read your notebooks."

My body freezes. I assumed he'd read them in time for the session, but I didn't want to ask him so as not to put him in an awkward position. In fact, it's possible I was afraid to ask because I knew the question would lead us to talk about the notebooks. And now I feel half paralyzed and my heart is pounding like crazy. What is he going to say about the notebooks? I look at Gideon from my frozen body and say nothing.

"You can surely write. It was fascinating, and very different from the way you've described the war here in our sessions," says Gideon with a serious look. "It was much quicker, intensive, and packed than what you described." The truth is, it's been seven years, and I'm actually not even sure I remember all the details.

"I think you didn't hurt anyone," he continues. "On the contrary, you actually received compliments. Many people think that it was because of you that everyone pulled through. In your notebooks you mention Klein telling you this. You also compliment and note the Russians from your team as soldiers that can be counted on. From reading it, it would seem that there's something in your conduct that structured things for your soldiers." Gideon continues to analyze what I wrote in the notebooks, and I remain frozen.

"According to what you describe, you cannot be blamed for Stern's injury. You went to sleep for a little, and they weren't supposed to shoot at you." Gideon takes off his glasses and cleans them with his shirt.

"But they did shoot, and I was sleeping," I blurt.

"The fact that you went to sleep is wrong?" Gideon wonders and puts his glasses back on. "What, you're not allowed to go to sleep after not sleeping for several days? When you're barely functioning? And what were they thinking, the guys from the reconnaissance company, when they shot at your tanks? That you were Hezbollah?" he asks sarcastically, knowing Hezbollah doesn't have tanks.

I've managed to forget how tired I was in those days. I dozed off for a few minutes when my gunner woke me up to say they've called me on the radio. "I think because we were behind some dirt embankments, they didn't see the tanks," I explain to Gideon. "They could only see the upper part of our bodies or just the heads of the commanders who stood outside the tanks. Anyway, I should have made sure that everyone was inside the tanks and that we could identify the force that was supposed to join us." Again, I blame myself.

"It wasn't some instinctive shooting," Gideon reacts to my words. "They announced on the radio to receive confirmation or to report the shooting. You're not supposed to know what they are aiming at. It's the exact terror scenario that you describe in your nightmares. Someone sees something, and you don't know what he sees, but he's coming to harm you."

"They thought they knew who they were shooting at and didn't mean to strike us at all. I didn't even know that someone was looking at me," I reply in an attempt to refute the conclusion he's drawn from the notebooks.

Gideon takes a deep breath before he carefully words his answer, "War is the most unpredictable situation, no matter how much you train and prepare. Look at the case of Stern. You train, guard, do everything with the helmet on, and barely lift your head from the tank. Then comes something like that and in a second, everything breaks down. And not only did it break down everything you were holding on to, you were left with the thought they had a choice of who to shoot at, and they didn't choose you. You describe in your notebook how close your tank was to Stern's and they shot him. For your whole life before the war you had control over any situation. Could it be that this was the first time that something destroyed the mental structure on which you built yourself?"

He stops for a minute, tries to read my body language, and continues. "Today, you know they saw you. You were unaware of them, and then tragedy happened. This is exactly what you describe happening in the window of the house. There's someone out there, he sees you, looking, peeking at you, and you're scared to be caught off guard again. You mustn't move or he'll know you're there."

The session ends and I'm left with Gideon's final insight. It takes me a while to digest what he's said. There's definitely something in my night terrors that's connected to the loss of control and fear of moving. If I had been the one to move, perhaps they would have shot me and not Stern.

And I cannot ignore that with Stern's incident, as well as at night, everything begins with a startled awakening. At nights I wake up in a dark place, feeling like I'm in danger. I don't know if someone has already positioned himself with the purpose of harming me. Any second he could pull the trigger and shoot at me. At night I'm alone. There's no Stern to take the bullet. I won't be so fortunate this time. There's no one else to aim at.

Despite everything, I can't identify the feeling I have after the nightmares. Something still doesn't quite fit in Gideon's analysis.

◆ ◆ ◆

The next sessions with Gideon focus on the notebooks. More accurately, on his attempts to show me that there were many environmental conditions during the war that prevented me from performing my best. Gideon has a very good memory. Despite the fact that he's already returned the notebooks to me, he continues to pull out precise quotes to support his claim that I have no reason to blame myself.

These sessions make me look at things in a slightly different way. The conditions were really harsh and the war broke out after several days during which I had hardly slept. Each time I managed to catch a few minutes of sleep, something terrible happened.

It started when we opened the path to Bint Jbeil. When we finished, I dozed off on the commander's chair, and a few minutes later Stern was shot. Later on, after Stern's evacuation, the deputy battalion commander saw me and told me that I had to get some shut eye because I looked terrible.

I went into one of the nearby houses where IDF soldiers were staying. I sat on the floor and leaned against the wall without taking off my flak jacket, protective vest, or helmet. I fell asleep before my ass even hit the floor.

After a few minutes, the deputy battalion commander ran into the house shaking me, "Avner is wounded. It's not good. Come quick." From that moment until the war ended I didn't sleep. I only dozed off a few times without noticing — standing up, even when the tank was moving, and I was in command.

◆ ◆ ◆

Understanding that perhaps I wasn't responsible for everything, and the official approval of the Disabled Veterans Department changes something in me. Suddenly, I'm able to open the subject with more people. At first, to a few close friends. After that, I become over confident and in each conversation I want to raise the issue of the war and share the insights of my therapy.

Sila came to tell me that his girlfriend threw him out after they argued and all I wanted was to change the subject and tell him about the war. He told me about his troubles and problems in his relationship, and I interrupted him about wars until the topic switched and I was able to start venting.

After my close friends came the dates. Even on the first date the most important thing for me is to find out whether or not she also sees a therapist. Someone who's never seen a therapist instantly seems childish to me. Someone who hasn't gone through something big that shook her life isn't good enough. They will never be able to understand me.

At the height of this period, I serve as a stand-in therapist. Nearly every date I succeed in getting them to open up and tell me something big about themselves. Ronit tells me her father used to sexually abuse her. Na'ama tells me she had eating disorders. Ya'ara tells me that her mother died the year before in a car accident. At some point during the date they pull themselves together and realize they've said too much. "I can't believe I told you that on the first date. It is so pleasant to talk to you," the sentence repeats itself each time.

Immediately after that they attempt to get some information too. "What about you? Surely there's something you don't tell on the first date," they say. I pretend to evade the question, only revealing at the end that I'm coping with PTSD. And if they don't believe me, I pull out the disabled ID. After such an open conversation, with plenty of alcohol, and an entire pack of cigarettes, each date ends with a one-sided infatuation. I fall in love, and they vanish.

◆ ◆ ◆

Five years after the Taglit project and the correspondence with Klein, we finally get together for a beer. This is the first time we've met since our military service. After an exceptionally strong hug, we sit at the bar. We order beers and instantly dive into a conversation about the company and the war.

Klein reminds me of many details I've forgotten about how I ran the company and the soldiers. I confess to him that I can't explain why I was so agitated and angry all the time. We recall many common stories. Klein keeps going back to the war and says I was the only one in the company he truly relied on. We talk about the tour we did afterwards on the Lebanese border and the pizzas we used to order every night.

"Listen, you were really a jerk," Klein says to me with a big smile. "I remember my mom was sick and I asked to go see her. I opened the door to your office and asked you for leave, and you replied that there's no one to go on stakeout in my place and there's no way. But the next day, when I asked Avner, he approved my leave."

Wow. I had completely forgotten about that too. Now I remember, his mother wasn't just sick; she was dying. In the last few months of my service her condition deteriorated until she passed away. I don't remember denying Klein, but the story sounds credible to me and fitting to the person I was at that time. Klein and I say goodbye with a good feeling, despite his last confession.

TRAVEL LOG: KLEIN'S WEDDING

I owe Klein a huge apology. How could he even speak to me? How is he not angry with me? His mother was about to die, and I told him he couldn't go home to be with her. What an idiot I was. What the hell was I thinking? Why was the military so important? How could I turn off my emotions like that and blindly follow the mission?

All I wanted was to please my superiors. All that motivated me was to come off looking good in front of them. Something in my behavior became automatic. They defined for me what was allowed and what was forbidden, and from that moment on that was the law with no deviations.

Indeed, the military is built on what will happen to you if you don't follow the rules. Safety incident reports are written from the perspective of what the team didn't do. As if those were the reasons for the outcome.

"The team didn't perform an overturning exercise," it says in the investigation of the overturning incident, as if this was the cause of the tank overturning. "These instructions were written in blood," it says on the sign of the safety instructions at the shooting range.

I was constantly thinking about what to do to avoid disaster. In the end, disaster happened. The entire war was a disaster. And after it I did the forbidden — I dodged military service.

I go to bed and prepare myself for a nightmare-filled sleep after my daily burrowing into my post-trauma. To my surprise, I wake up just before noon in the cozy bed in Hila's protected room. I spend the day lying around in the garden and thinking about Klein. I have to apologize to him.

Later on, I pull the plastic bag with the buttoned shirt and nice shoes I prepared for Klein's wedding out of my truck. I go in to take a shower and get dressed in the clean clothes that feel stiff and unnatural. I leave Mikhmoret in the direction of Jerusalem and run straight into the heavy afternoon traffic.

Everyone is stressed. In the middle, myself and the blue truck, soiled by the mud from the northern streams. Envious looks from the tech people around me sitting in boring cars make me appreciate what I have. I have dreamed of going on a journey with the truck I built for such a long time.

Suddenly it hits me. The night in the abandoned structure next to the beach was my last night alone camping. I run over the plan for the rest of the trip in my head – yes! There's a chance that from now to the end of the trip there will always be people around. This thought floods me with a sense of immense relief. I've grown tired of terrifying nights. All I want is to sleep soundly.

On the other hand, a new thought already starts pecking at me. Could it be that I've shorted myself? On a journey of one month I'll only have slept alone for one week. Stop being a masochist, I respond to myself with Tabenkin's tone of voice.

I park the truck in the crowded parking lot of the venue garden and walk toward the entrance. I feel completely out of place. I have no idea if Klein invited anyone else from our military service.

In the years after my release, I've completely forgotten the names of most of the people who were with me in the military. I can't remember where they're from in Israel or in which period of the service we were together. If I stumble across someone from the military in the street, I recognize a familiar face, but can't recall any additional details.

I never forgot Klein, but since the service ended, we didn't keep in close contact. We met for the first time when I was a platoon commander in basic training and he was a new recruit in the parallel platoon.

When I was promoted to be a deputy company commander, he was a tank commander in the company. Over the service we always had a special connection. We liked and understood each other.

As a commander it's not always easy to create a balance between friendship and command. But in Klein's case, who knows exactly where the friendship ended and the command began, it worked perfectly. I, as usual, was an idiot, but he managed it extremely well.

I go in and collect the card with my table number. At the entrance hall Klein's future wife approaches me. She hugs me warmly and whispers in my ear, "Dror (Klein) was so happy to see that you RSVP'd. It was important to him." After that I greet Klein who, as usual, looks at me with a huge smile. "You're such a king for coming."

After I say hello to the bride and groom, I continue to the bar and order a gin and tonic. I have been traveling alone for eight days now and I've hardly had any alcohol. I grab the glass with one hand and a handful of sour gummy snakes in the other.

I turn around and notice Heiman's familiar walk in the distance. Heiman was a platoon commander in the company during the Second Lebanon War. He remained in the army and advanced to the rank of deputy battalion commander. I put my glass to the side and shove the sour snakes into my mouth in order to give him a strong hug with both arms. I haven't seen Heiman in several years either.

Heiman orders a beer and we settle next to a bar table in one of the garden's corners. He tells me about his new position and we immediately start talking about the war. It's impossible to meet someone who was in the war and not talk about it. It seems like people who were in the war are only able to talk about it with each other. They wait for the opportunity to see someone who was there so they can unload a little.

I give Heiman the highlights of the things I've been dealing with in recent years. Heiman confesses that he hardly gets to talk openly about the war, but he picks up the pace quickly and asks many questions. He asks me what PTSD means to me. I try to explain, but the right words don't come out and I'm embarrassed to mention details.

Heiman says no one took the lead in the period after the war and the soldiers had no one to talk to. I think about that for a moment and agree. Even before Avner's injury and the shell-shock suffered by Peri, the company commander who replaced Avner, the company wasn't united. In general, the battalion and the military didn't know how to cope with the ramifications of the war the day after it ended. They expected everything to go back to normal by itself.

During the conversation Heiman points out several times that he remembers I functioned really well. I think he says it in an attempt to ease my feelings of guilt. This prompts me to ask Heiman about my personality as the deputy. "You weren't easy," was the first sentence he lets escape instinctively. I tell him about my conversation with Klein about his dying mother and the horrible answer I gave him. Heiman responds, "I don't remember, but it sounds like an answer you could have given at that time."

In order to reinforce his words, Heiman tells me something I had completely forgotten. On one of the post-war days, when we were positioned in a grove next to the border, Heiman came to me to exchange his night vision device which was broken. He was about to go on operational activity and without the device it's impossible to navigate the tank. There was a shortage of these devices and I didn't have a replacement to give him.

Heiman says I dug through my container and finally brought him a garbage bag with a night vision device in it. Heiman opened the bag and saw that the device and the bag were covered in congealed blood and emitting a strong odor. "What is this? Stern's night vision device?" he asked. And I responded, "Yes, it's the only one we have in the company." I gave Heiman the bag and told him there was no other choice.

After he distanced himself from the container, he opened the bag again, which had been sealed for a week and a half since Stern's injury. A horrible smell of blood and decay came from inside and Heiman felt like he couldn't handle it. He put the bag on the floor and banged on it with a large rock until he heard the device shatter. Later, he brought it back and told me the device was faulty.

We continue to reminisce, but the story about the night vision device sticks with me. When I leave the venue garden and walk toward the parking lot, I remember more details. I remember how I tried to replace the night vision device after Stern's injury, but the logistics officer told me, "If it's functioning, I'm not replacing it for you." And what did I do? Instead of cleaning the blood or breaking the device myself, I chose to drop the problems in someone else's lap. What a good-for-nothing nobody I was.

◆ ◆ ◆

I start the truck and begin the night drive to the Dead Sea. The dark cabin of the truck, rolling down the frightening road from Jerusalem, is now filled with self-anger. No one wanted to be my soldier, I think, and recall the words of the Combat PTSD Clinic's commander. I remember I was agitated all the time. Angry at a commander who fell asleep on stakeout. Upset with the ordnance officer who failed our car during the weekly inspection. Angry at the battalion commander. Angry at the country for being stuck there instead of going to the beach.

I couldn't handle things that didn't go according to my plans. It gets me thinking about Lavie, the company commander from the reserve. When he didn't agree to release me from the reserve service, even when I told him that something was wrong, it was a similar answer to the one I gave Klein about his sick mom. Both Lavie and I were controlled by the fear that we would not be able to meet the task, and all out of blind loyalty to the military.

Am I like that today? I can't imagine a situation in which I'd screw over a subordinate or an employee who works with me in order to maintain loyalty to the system. In recent years I feel the need to rebel against the establishment. I always find myself on the side of the underdog. Perhaps it's a type of penance.

Around midnight I enter the hotel's parking lot at the Dead Sea and start preparing for a relaxed, comfy night. Still dressed in the clothes from the wedding, I unload some of the dirty equipment from the truck and take it with me to the reception desk.

The lobby is completely empty – a random mid-weekday in the middle of March at the Dead Sea. At the reception desk I am asked to present my disability ID card and the voucher I received from the Disabled Veterans Department. The first time I arrived at a hotel as part of these convalescence days, I didn't have my card and they didn't want to give me the room. I was ashamed to go around with the disabled ID card in my wallet all the time and didn't know they attributed so much importance to it at the hotel.

I go up to the room with all my equipment. It's big and spacious and has a balcony facing the Dead Sea. It's dark now and you can't see much. It's dead silent outside, there's no wind and the temperature is comfortable. I breathe in the hot air and feel pleasantly surprised by the calm around me.

After a good shower I go to bed, but my thoughts won't let me rest and I decide to continue writing.

2014: SECOND REVIEW BOARD

I start my master's degree studies. After a little more than three years as a software developer, I decide that I have enough money to take a little break and focus on my studies. At the same time, I meet two more entrepreneurs and we begin working on an idea for a new product. I inform the company I work for about my intention to leave. It doesn't surprise any of the managers. The ones who are most surprised are my parents. "You're leaving? Why? The salary is really good," is mom's first reaction.

"That's true," I reply, "but I have enough money and it's not interesting for me at the office. My head's filled with other ideas that are more important to me right now."

"And you won't be doing something else? What will you do all day?" Mom asks.

"I'm working on an idea for a product with a few partners and I want to invest more in my degree," I reply to soothe her. Deep inside I know that the start-up idea is mainly an excuse to not work.

Mom tries to not make a big issue out of it, but it's evident that she's concerned for my financial future. Of course, we don't talk in depth about the subject. And Dad, who adapts to every reality, immediately offers financial assistance.

◆ ◆ ◆

The truck project is moving along slowly, but working on it fills me with a sense of satisfaction I've never known before. I finish dismantling it into pieces, and while I do, the truck tells me its life story.

It served its owner faithfully as a work truck until it was abandoned somewhere in the Jerusalem Mountains. Many parts are missing, but everything that is there is original. It seems like it was important to the owners to maintain its original state as much as possible. Most of the screws have never been unscrewed and the wiring harness remains unchanged.

When I first encountered the truck there were many plastic parts that were tossed on the floor inside. Over time I found where all those parts went. The cover of the glove compartment, a small shelf for personal equipment above the passenger's legs, and the headrests, which are unique for this model and should be installed on the inside of the rear window.

Each little part that I manage to salvage fills me with pride. The original radio with the "Suzuki" label, the venting shutters, and the symbol in the center of the steering wheel. Apart from a few light dents in the front, the truck's sheet metal is completely straight. I still haven't figured out the reason for abandoning this beloved truck. The main issue right now is the rust. The ceiling is perforated, under the front wheel arch there are huge holes, and the cabin back side is almost gone.

One day Ilan comes to visit me in the workshop. Ilan, a friend of my parents, worked his entire life fixing cars. He examines all the sheet metal from every direction and bangs with his hand on the suspicious spots. When Ilan finishes examining the goods, he stands behind the truck, his hands holding the tailgate. "People like you need therapy. Do you know what you're getting yourself into?" he asks and continues to look at the truck while he feels it with his experienced mechanic's fingers.

"Listen, the situation is not as good as I imagined, but I'll learn how to fix everything," I respond with a phony smile. Ilan notices my concern and says, "Go get me a marker." He starts drawing lines on the truck. "You're going to cut out the entire roof, along with the window frames, and replace it with a roof you'll get from another car," he determines.

"How do we do that?" I ask in a frightened tone,

trying to pretend I'm not bothered by the marker lines on the rusty metal. "You weld it slowly and work very accurately. You'll succeed," Ilan tries to reassure me.

The visit ends and I remain alone facing the truck and the markings. There is no way I'm going to slice the car in half like that. Whatever it takes, I will fix one hole at a time without taking any unnecessary risks.

◆ ◆ ◆

As the date of the second review board approaches, my tension rises and with it, the nightmares increase. One night I awaken from a nightmare and remain lying in bed terrified. My mouth is completely dry, as if I've been yelling or breathing heavily all this time.

After I breathe through the fear, I look out the window to make sure no one is watching me. The tangerine tree outside the window looks like the silhouette of a man and I try to convince myself there's no one there. If he's out there, he will soon make a mistake that will give up his location.

Like every night, there is no one outside and no one is really looking at me. When my body relaxes, the details of the dream start to seep into my consciousness and assemble a story. Like always, at this stage I am certain that tomorrow I'll remember all the details and don't need to write anything down. But the truth is, most of the time I'm unable to recall the nightmare and just remain with the feeling that something bad and scary happened.

I will not give up on this dream. I have to write down what happened. In an unprecedented move I get out of bed and stand next to the bedroom door, frozen. I have to get to my laptop from the coffee table in the center of the living room. Even now someone is watching me, waiting for me to make a mistake and expose myself. I mustn't turn on the light. I can't show any sign of being up. Even the use of a small flashlight is strictly forbidden. Night discipline.

I gently open the bedroom door and peek into the living room to see if someone's there. I look at all the small indicator lights that are around the house: the projector, the computer screen and the router. What a fool I was to leave everything on like that. It's not proper operational protocol.

After a long wait, attempting to convince myself that there's no one in the living room, I count to myself – one, two, three... and then quickly leave the bedroom, walking hunched to the center of the living room. I disconnect the computer from the chargers and quickly go back to bed.

The time is 3:23 and the shadow of the tangerine tree still looks like someone watching me. Why did I have a nightmare tonight? Was it the moment Dad suggested I come with him for a memorial evening or the proximity to the date of the second review board?

It was a nightmare of pursuit. I remember trying to escape from prison with another group of people.

Good people, like me. People I know in real life. Actually, it wasn't a prison, it felt like slavery. We were working at a construction site. It was pouring rain and we received an assignment that felt endless: to bring up all the tiles of the large building to the top floor. There was an elevator and little carts to carry the tiles. Everything was extremely heavy and we were forbidden from using the carts. I need to write down what happened.

> I talk with one of the workers. He looks like a hippie, with long brownish hair, rings on his fingers, and tanned skin from being on vacation at the beach. A minute before that he was walking around with his girlfriend. They were hugging, but I got the impression that something was wrong. He seems like a quiet guy and she wants him to share more. After the hippie talks to his girlfriend he comes back, sits next to me, and starts crying.
> We start flooring the building together. All around us there are building materials. Wooden pallets loaded with blocks and large containers for mixing the concrete. I don't understand why we are flooring the building at such an early stage of the construction. It's not even time to place the tiles. From our spot, there's the beginning of a track for the small carts, exactly like those of an old coal mine.

While I talk to the hippie, he suddenly hops on one of the carts, which starts racing at top speed into the coal mine tunnel.

I get into a cart of my own and start chasing him. The cart travels on the track at a crazy speed and takes turns that are too sharp. At the beginning it's fun, but that quickly turns into panic and the feeling that it's only by pure luck I don't have an accident. The track ends unexpectedly and the hippie and I are thrown at a huge garbage shredder. I land on the side of the shredder and the hippie falls into it. The loud noise of electrical engines is heard. The gears of the shredder start to turn and I try to help the hippie get out. He manages to grab my arm and we escape at the last second. Slowly more people start falling from the track into the shredder. They're all covered in garbage juice which looks like hot chocolate or thick mud.

We attempt to get off the huge trash facility under the shredder but can't find a way that enables a safe descent. The fear of being trapped is replaced with the rush of escape. We mustn't be here. Someone is chasing us. The people who had previously worked with us up in the building are now the ones searching for us. They hold baseball bats and menacing iron chains. We are also surrounded by guards who watch us on the security cameras. I continue to search for a way out and finally manage to exploit the cameras' dead zone so everyone can escape.

I run at the front, not as a leader, but like someone who wants to get the hell out first, at the expense of the others.

I cross the fence line and look back. The moment I turn my head, a shot is fired. The Russian guy running behind me falls at my feet. He lies there without moving, face down, but it seems like he's still breathing. I grab his shoulder and turn him to face me, revealing a horrific sight. Most of his mouth is gone and in the center of his face, there's a gaping hole through which I can see the ground beneath him.

I let go of him and continue running. His body once again hits the ground.

I try to run as fast as I can, but it's no use. I'm running so slow. Almost in place.

Somehow, I manage to escape.

Others don't.

My surroundings change into a construction site with densely built villas. One of the contractors instantly understands what's going on and tries to block me at the front. I go into one of the parking spots and hide until a woman in a truck yells at me that I cannot be here and I have to get out. She claims to own the house I am hiding in and tells me I have no permission to be here. When the woman realizes she's looking at an escaped prisoner she gets even more frightened and tries to get back into her truck, which has sunk into a pile of dirt in the meantime. I attempt to steal her truck while explaining to her that we're innocent. I reassure her that I won't do anything to her. Later, the hippie shows up and tries to help me get the truck out. He pushes it from the rear while I sit at the wheel. The wheels spin fast, raising a thick cloud of dust, but the truck doesn't move.

This is when I woke up, feeling the presence of someone looking at me. The details of the nightmare assemble images in my mind while I put them into writing.

The image of the villas construction site reminds me of the outskirts of Bint Jbeil after the bombing. The convoy of people who escaped after me from the factory probably symbolize the big retreat after the running over incident.

And the Russian guy who was shot next to me is Stern's story exactly. The next morning, before I even brush my teeth, I cover all the indicator lights in the living room with black tape.

♦ ♦ ♦

My temporary approval from the Disabled Veterans

Department is about to expire. I have quickly grown accustomed to receiving the allowance and my weekly sessions with Gideon. The concern that they'll revoke my rights to therapy raises my anxiety to new heights. Gideon tries to assure me saying that, in his opinion, they will award me another year. Avital, from rehabilitation, also says she'll do everything she can to help me get at least another year.

In our last session, Gideon gave me a letter to present to the review board. He began with the description of Stern's incident and my fears of another entry into Lebanon after the war. Further on, he stated my current fears focus around the reserve service orders, despite my new role as a training officer. He summarized my childhood in the shadow of my dad and uncle, who were wounded in the Yom Kippur War. He also mentioned my family's expectation to follow the glorious combat soldier tradition after Ofer chose to not serve in a combat unit.

Gideon signed off the letter with the words, "In my assessment, Omri requires a permanent, reassuring recognition as a person with post-traumatic stress disorder. Only this will allow him to reduce the feeling of terror over reserve service. Only then will he be able to strengthen his sense of normalcy. Only this way will he feel that someone in a position of authority understands him and what he went through in the war. Your approval gives him legitimacy and the chance to have a proper life."

In anticipation of the second review board, I go over all the materials: the copy of the claim, Gideon's letter, the protocols, and the evaluation. I prepare a page of messages I want to pass on to the members of the review board. I also print out the description of the escape dream I wrote a few nights ago.

On the day of the review board, I once again enter the menacing building on Shaul Ha'melech Street in Tel Aviv — a little nervous but much more experienced than the last time. I go up the elevator and follow the signs for "review boards."

The hearings are usually held in the evenings, when the building is empty and all the offices are closed. I take a seat in the waiting room and after a few minutes I'm called in. I sit in front of the review board and notice they aren't the same people from last time. They open the meeting and ask if there's any change in my condition.

"A year ago I gained recognition and it provided me with temporary relief. I was very nervous about the process, which took more than a year. I received the letter with the review board's decision and couldn't believe that my problem was actually recognized. Until I received the disabled card, I kept worrying that someone would change their mind at the last minute." I thank the system that approved my claim and continue. "My condition hasn't changed very much. It's only been a few months and I go to therapy once a week. The last two weeks, in anticipation of this second review board date, were not too good." This is a huge hint that the period between review boards is too short. "I'm doing my master's degree in business administration while working full time. A few months ago, the cumulative stress of studying and working took me to unpleasant places and I decided to slow down, take a little vacation, and concentrate on my studies."

I specify the reasons for my decision to leave my job. "Security tensions in Israel or assignments at work can easily stress me out. These are immediately followed by nights with very little sleep and a lot of nightmares. In general, if something small bothers me during the day, I can expect hours of nightmares after which I can't fall back asleep. I had a very good period after I stopped working. I woke up easily in the morning and went to bed relaxed. Life was more balanced and I managed to concentrate on my studies. However, in the past few weeks, I've had harrowing nights. I live in fear that my temporary approval will end — and mainly the therapy I'm getting."

"You're still in the reserve service, right? How are you doing there?" one of the board members asks. "When I was a platoon commander, everything manifested for the first time and I was on the verge of leaving the reserve service. The Combat PTSD Clinic exempted me from reserve service for a year, but it was hard for me to see others go while I didn't.

"Currently, I'm a training officer in reserve, which means I've returned to the reserve service without going on tanks and without taking part in operational deployment. My dream is to establish my own business after I finish my studies or to integrate back into another company, but I have concerns about the pressures and the framework." I'm attempting to illustrate how post-traumatic stress affects my life and my future.

"My therapy is advancing. In the beginning I would wake up from a nightmare, soaking wet, scared to death there were people in the house. The day after, I wouldn't even be able to remember any details from the dream. As the therapy advanced, I learned to understand what happened while I was sleeping, and this way I have a little control over the fears that I wake up to.

"I still wake up in the same condition, but I somehow manage to tell myself there's no one out there. After many times in which I'd completely forgotten the dream, I've succeeded in regaining my composure and write the dream down. The little control I've managed to obtain doesn't prevent the nightmares or effect their frequency, but it greatly improves my ability to cope when I'm awake alone in bed."

"Thank you Omri. Is there anything else you would like to add?" asks the chairman of the committee. "Yes, I would like to share something I wrote during one of my recent nights. Perhaps it will succeed in expressing the feelings I experience at night." I hand the chairman of the committee the dream that I printed in advance. He carefully reads what I've written, and his body language says it all. He nods his head heavily, his lips are tight. The other guy quickly reads the letter and says, "Thank you very much Omri." I leave the old building with the same terrible feeling that I'm attempting to exploit the system. I don't deserve all this.

After the second review board, something changes in me again. I no longer feel the urge to tell people about my PTSD, the nightmares, and about what happened during the war. When someone asks me about something related to the war, I immediately feel as if I've been hanged in the main square and everyone's looking at me.

In Israel, there's no way to escape stories about wars and soldiers. News reports on television, stories of heroism, and memorial days are an integral part of life. When the topic comes up in conversation, even if I am not part of it, I immediately move my eyes to nowhere so I don't make eye contact. I pretend to be engaged in something else and simply pray that no one will mention me or ask me any questions.

If they do ask, I shrink in the chair and respond with a short and decisive answer that makes the questioner feel uncomfortable. If, for example, someone were to say, "Omri, you were also in Bint Jbeil, weren't you?" I would answer, "Yes, it was horrible." After that, there would be silence until someone changes the subject.

◆ ◆ ◆

After a few months I receive the reply:

> I am hereby honored to inform you that the medical review board has determined in its meeting that there has been no change in your condition. Your rate of disability therefore remains at 20%.
>
> The disability rights will remain temporary until the next review scheduled for the date 01/2016, to which you will be summoned by us.

Two years with no review boards. I rush to call Avital and tell her about the decision. Avital doesn't hide her joy. She starts telling me about a grant program for my master's degree, but I express reluctance. "You deserve this. Don't be so hard on yourself," she says. This is also what Gideon keeps saying. I'm finally convinced.

Later on, I tell Gideon about the conversation. He laughs and says that I'm the first person to touch Avital's heart. A few weeks after that, Avital calls to tell me the grant was approved and I've been partially reimbursed for tuition.

The truth is that the news comes at a slightly

critical economic juncture. It's been almost a year since I quit my job and from that moment on, I've mainly spent money on rent and parts for the truck.

The approval for two more years provides me with a little peace of mind. This year I've even allowed myself to use the convalescence days and went to a hotel in Eilat.

I'd never been on a vacation by myself. The deal includes full board, and not a moment went by without my stomach bursting with food. Five nights is enough time to get to know the hotel employees in all of the shifts. And mainly to spend a lot of time by yourself, time for thoughts to scatter in every direction.

During the vacation I decided to step down from the start-up idea and start looking for a full-time job. With perfect timing, literally on my return from Eilat, I receive a job offer.

Even though I have no experience in managing products, a small company offers me a position as product manager. The job interview goes well and the next day they get back to me with an offer. The salary is so good that I don't need to bargain, and surely I can't refuse.

TRAVEL LOG: DEAD SEA

It's 3 am. I shut down the computer, cuddle into the sea of pillows scattered on the bed, and instantly fall asleep. When I wake up, the room is already illuminated by the rays of sun that are emerging over the Edom Mountains. I make coffee and go out to the balcony in my underwear. The sun bathes my body and I feel every cell come alive at its own pace.

I go down to breakfast. After two weeks of making coffee on the camp burner next to a slice of bread with tahini, I am overwhelmed by the abundance and colorfulness of the hotel's dining room.

From there I go back up to change into a bathing suit, then down to the pool. After a few hours, I go back to bed for an afternoon nap. When I wake up, I go for a run along the seashore.

After dinner, I pass through the lobby on my way to the room. There are a few couples scattered around, all with their heads in their phones and no one communicating with the person in front of them. This world is so weird, I think to myself, and go upstairs to write about the beginning of my relationship with Noya.

2014: NOYA

A new routine in my life begins. After nearly a year of fun with the truck under the guise of a start-up entrepreneur, I start working as a product manager for a small company. I start early in the morning and go to the office, where I spend the rest of the day. In the evenings, I try to catch up on some little assignment in the restoration project, or go on a date.

This week I went on a first date with Noya, who brought with her a great deal of presence, gumption, and a captivating smile. We spent the evening in a pub and then I took her back to her mom's home. I felt a serious click and it seemed to be mutual.

At the end of the week I suggest to Noya that we go to the beach. After spending a few hours in the sun, we head back to the parking lot. On our way, I ask her if she wants to come visit me at home and see the truck. Noya says yes. When we get there, I give her the tour. We walk around the yard and Noya is excited by the workshop and my truck. Eventually we go into the house and have a beer in the comfort of the air conditioning.

We sit close to each other on the couch with music playing on the radio in the background. Every once in a while, Noya puts her hand on my leg, which makes me tremble all over. We laugh and at the end of the night, we also kiss. I take Noya home and ask if she wants me to host an evening of angelitas for her. Noya says yes. I'm surprised she even knows what this is.

On the third date I make us a rolled melawach[i] with hummus, tomato paste, and hard-boiled egg. Even after a long debate we can't agree whether the angelita was invented in Kfar Saba or in Herzliya, but we open up enough to talk about more profound things. Noya tells me about the phobia she has of vomiting, her fear of flying, and her parents' divorce.

And I, after a long time of avoiding the issue, reveal to Noya my PTSD. I tell her I have nightmares, but can't bring myself to tell her about my fear of the dark and of someone watching me.

Noya asks with sensitivity about the events of the war and my relationship with my parents. "The truth is, they barely know anything. Only that I'm seeing a

---

[i] Board-like bread, a Yemenite pastry.

therapist and that I requested to be approved as a Disabled Veteran to cover my therapy costs," I say and look down.

"Wow, that's not good. You have to talk with them," Noya implores. She shares how her relationship with her parents changed after she had an in-depth talk with them during their divorce. "Don't you want to tell them?" she asks.

"I want to but can't. It's like I don't have the guts to tell them the things they're afraid to ask," I conclude. I notice that she doesn't ask what I feel at night either. Perhaps she's afraid too. And I don't have the courage to tell.

♦ ♦ ♦

A little after I meet Noya, Operation Protective Edge breaks out in Gaza. This mini war leads to harsh weeks of nightmares on the front lines of my personal coping. Recently it's become something of a routine.

I go to bed and debate sleeping with the air conditioner on or the window open. On the one hand it's July and the heat and humidity are nearly at their highest. On the other, I'm afraid I won't hear the siren warning from the missiles flying from Gaza.

My house is made of drywall. I call it a house made of cardboard. It's not safe to stay inside when the siren goes off and the missiles are on their way. According to the instructions for my area, I have 90 seconds to reach a secured space. This is the time it takes the missile to fly from Gaza to my village.

In these 90 seconds, I'm supposed to get it together, get dressed, put on shoes, and cross the neighbors' garden to reach the street where the public bomb shelter is located.

So far, there've been three alarms while I've been home. The first time, I was already outside, so the trip to the shelter was short. The second woke me up from a Friday afternoon nap, and the last was early Saturday morning, while I slept with the window open.

I try to be as prepared as possible. I organize a pair of shorts I can quickly pull over my boxers, a white V-neck shirt hanging on a hanger, and shoes that I can put on quickly without socks. Everything is arranged next to the door. In times like these I make sure to keep my phone charged throughout the day, and next to the bed I have two flashlights prepared, a headlamp and a large flashlight which shines a great distance and is battery efficient.

Even after all the preparations I don't go to sleep relaxed, and that is probably the reason for the nightmares I have every night. Most of the dreams are characterized by pursuits. Sometimes I'm being chased and sometimes I am the one doing the chasing. Even when I'm the chaser I'm certain that justice is on my side. It's only toward the end of the dream that I realize I've made a big mistake.

Today the news reports the escalation down south and the expansion of the Gaza operation. They start talking about recruiting the reserve. During the night

I wake up in panic without remembering what I've dreamt about. I only have one thing in my head: I have to get away from here.

I try to go back to sleep, but I can't stop thinking and planning. Is it really possible to escape? I can fly to the United States and crash with friends. Just like that, with a small bag. Just to fly away from here never to return.

I plan in detail what I would take with me. Perhaps I'll even write a heartfelt letter to the Jewish Agency, in which I will tell them about my problems and ask for assistance in moving permanently to the United States.

No, that would take too long. I need to do something immediately. How much time do I need from the moment I make this decision until departure? Can I buy a ticket right now and fly in a couple of hours? How close to departure can I buy a plane ticket online? I wonder how much it'll cost.

I open the computer next to the bed and start searching for a flight. Good, the next flight is leaving in a few hours and there are still a few seats left. I stare at the screen and let my thoughts wander, planning how I'll get to the airport and what I'll write to Mom.

"I left the country. Don't worry, everything's fine. I will call you when I land in a few hours."

I'll send the message at the last second before takeoff, so she doesn't have time to call and convince me to stay. When I'll land in Seattle, I'll send Amy, from the Taglit Project, a message saying I'm on my way to her and need help. I even plan the emotional reunion with Amy: how she'll pick me up and I'll hold her tight and start crying.

The more I allow my imagination to work, the more disturbed I become as I discover unresolved issues related to leaving Israel. Where would I leave the car so it wouldn't disturb the neighbors? I'd want it to be shady enough, so the paint doesn't get damaged.

I select the area under the mulberry tree but remember that in a few months it will be fruit season and that could damage the sheet metal. I debate whether to take the new laptop I got from work or my old one. If I leave the work laptop, I'll have to ask Dad to go to the office and return it. Indeed, they'll fire me the moment they hear I've escaped without giving notice. But if they fire me, how would I finance my stay in the United States?

This prompts me to imagine a phone call with Dad after I land. I explain to him which items in the house he can sell and how much to ask for them. The couch from Ikea is stain-free and in great condition, I note to myself. I look around the room and notice the closet. What about the notebooks? I don't want to take them with me, but I can't think of a safe place to put them where no one will stumble upon them by accident.

This is how more than two hours pass until the birds begin to chirp and the bedroom starts to fill with a gentle morning light. I slept for just three hours and I still can't fall back asleep. At some point my obsession to flee the country is replaced by self-pity about my office job in modern slavery. Why does a person need to work ten hours a day? What kind of life is that?

On days like this I have no reason to be thankful for war not breaking out as it has already happened. All I can pray for now is that they don't call me up for reserve service. Right now, there's a fifty-fifty chance that they'll recruit my battalion with an emergency mobilization order.

The operation in Gaza comes right before my planned trip to a music festival in Belgium next week. Bad timing, but this is a small problem.

On Saturday before my trip to the festival I meet my cousin, Yuval. Many of his friends are still serving in key positions in the military. Yuval tells me about two of the brigade's vehicles that were on patrol close to the Gaza border fence. They entered an ambush of a Hamas[i] squad that infiltrated Israel through an improvised tunnel.

One of the vehicles got hit by a missile. Driving in the vehicles were Peri and another good friend of Yuval's. Their condition remains unclear. I know Peri from the Second Lebanon War. A few days after Avner was injured, Peri arrived as his replacement. A few hours after Peri entered Lebanon with us, a

---

[i] A Palestinian Sunni-Islamic organization founded in 1987 and in control of the Gaza Strip since 2006.

horrible incident left him shell-shocked. But after a few hours he returned to combat duty and later advanced in the military.

From the moment I hear about Peri's injury I'm not able to function. In the afternoon the rumors start. One moment they tell me that Peri's been severely wounded, and shortly after that he's slightly injured from shrapnel. Only toward the evening do I receive a definite answer that he's doing well, but an officer and a soldier were killed in the incident.

Evening. I'm alone in the house and don't know what to do about my flight to the festival in a few days. Should I cancel it or go anyway? I can't bring myself to go dancing at a festival given the current situation in Israel.

My wild imagination instantly drifts to a scenario where they call me to reserve service just as I get to the festival. I can already imagine how Lavie would arrange a seat on the first flight back when I'm actually trying to escape. I'm also afraid that if they don't call me to the reserve service, I'll constantly be glued to the news flashes from Israel.

In the three days that follow, I'm unable to concentrate at work. I sit for long hours waiting for the phone to ring, calling me to the reserve. I feel like I've been recruited from the first day of the operation, even without the order. Do they know that each time they set out on some operation in Gaza, every PTSD sufferer like me reluctantly reports as well?

I've already told everyone at work about my debate over canceling the trip. Maybe I'm looking to get their approval to go, or maybe I wanted to show everyone that it's hard for me to go. As far as they are concerned, there's no question, "Of course you have to go."

A day before the festival all the airlines announce the cancellation of flights to and from Israel due to the situation. Only El-Al, the national airline, is continuing to fly as usual. I feel sadness mixed with joy. On one hand, my ticket is with El-Al so I can fly. On the other hand, if my flight was to be canceled, it would solve my dilemma.

◆ ◆ ◆

On Wednesday night I complete all my preparations for the flight and take a cab to the airport, where I meet with the group I'm joining for the trip. I met them through Gilad, who's studying for a master's degree with me, and invited me to take the trip.

The plane is filled with Israelis, mostly traveling to the festival. The fatigue of the last few nights and the knowledge there will be no siren in the airplane overpowers me and I sink into a deep sleep. I wake up close to landing and all I want is to reconnect my phone and make sure nothing terrible happened while I was asleep. A news report about three paratroopers killed in Khan Yunis[i] brings me back to reality.

---

[i] The second largest Palestinian city in the Gaza District.

We get into a cab that takes us from the airport to the festival. On the way we stop for shopping: alcohol, ice, cheeses, and snacks. The guys take care of everything and I just drag along with them from one stop to the next, feeling like half a person. I'm exhausted and don't want to see anyone. They talk about the evening's lineup and all I want is to go back home and watch the news.

The cab drops us off at the festival entrance. Tens of thousands of people are carrying camping equipment, bags with alcohol, and food for the coming days. We organize our equipment and start the walk to the festival's camping area. There we put up the shade canopy, lay out a big mat, and set the tents.

The festival lasts for four days. Meaning, three nights of parties that start at noon and end at one o'clock in the morning. We arrive a day ahead of the festival opening to enjoy another party at the camping area. As if one really needs another party prior to the three days ahead. I wish it was over already.

Toward evening we sit in the compound we've set up and start drinking. When the pre-festival party starts, I already feel a little drunk and dizzy. Around us are an insane number of happy people.

Very quickly, I ditch my group and settle somewhere in the back, behind the crowd, far away from the stage — just me and my disturbing thoughts, completely detached from what's going on around me.

At some point I decide to go back to our compound, climb deep into the sleeping bag with my phone, and catch up on what's happening in Israel. The IDF shot at a school from which missiles were fired. Fifteen Palestinians were killed and dozens were injured.

◆ ◆ ◆

The second day of the festival starts badly. The morning news flashes about the wounded and casualties put me in a foul mood. We spend the day under the canopy, on top of a mat.

Toward the evening, we start preparations for the big party. I have no other choice but to drink like a madman. Maybe it will loosen me up a little. When everyone's ready, we start the long walk toward the main stage.

The gang's all wrapped in Israeli flags, except me. I walk to the side and a little behind in an attempt to distance myself from this display of Zionism. Even on a normal day it looks excessive to me, and definitely in such a sensitive time, when a crushing operation is taking place in Gaza.

This display of the flags isn't unusual. Part of the festival's thing is to represent your country and celebrate international diversity. The problem is, our flag evokes so much antagonism and is so controversial that I want no part in it. In these moments I'm even a little ashamed of the flag. I envy all the other party goers that love their flag so much and are proud of it, as I used to be.

It reminds me that several years ago I had a dream: to buy a big truck and drive it on Independence Day with a big Israeli flag displayed. As a teenager, I was the one who suggested we hang the Israeli flag over a camp we sat at on the beach. I was also the one who thought it was important to come back early from my post-military trip straight to Israel's 60th Independence Day celebrations. My friends tried to talk me out of it.

These thoughts make me realize something in me has changed.

◆ ◆ ◆

After a superficial and sloppy security check we enter the festival. A guy approaches our group and asks to take a photo with us and all the flags. As someone who isn't wearing a flag, I assume the role of photographer.

When I return the camera to him, he blurts out to his friend, "these cute little Jews." After they leave, someone approaches us. He tells us that the guy who asked to take a photo gave an upside-down Nazi salute[i] when we weren't looking.

That is all I need to split my emotions even more. There's a war going on in Israel, missiles are flying

---

[i] Known as The Quenelle. An alternative way to perform the Nazi salute, which is forbidden in Europe.

into our homes, friends who were called to the reserve service are in mortal danger. And in the meantime, I'm at the best festival in the world, trying to escape the Israeli flags while being exposed to anti-Semitism, which recalibrates me to the values I was raised on. What a mess of conflicting thoughts happening in my head.

We're walking toward the main stage. Soon Avicii is up. Suddenly I feel the intense urge to urinate. I stop for a moment looking for a toilet sign. I tell the last person in the group that I'm going to take a leak.

"Avicii is starting in a moment and if we keep stopping, we won't get a good spot," he answers. At this point I've completely lost my patience with this organized tour. The last thing I need right now is a commitment. I don't want schedules.

"Go. I'll find you," I respond with a smile. It's obvious to me that I won't be able to find them among the hundred thousand people dancing at the main stage. To some degree, it pleases me. I go into the portable toilets, a little drunk and wobbly. I feel a momentary relief by the fact that I'm not in the vicinity of the flag bearers.

On the way back from the bathroom I see the main stage for the first time — a huge amphitheater with a stage in the center and towers of speakers. The stage is full of moving elements — waterfalls and secret doors for the dancers who emerge each time from a different corner. It's so impressive, for a few moments my sour face is replaced by a smile.

I settle down on one of the grass slopes surrounding the main stage, still feeling quite upset. From time to time, girls who see that I'm alone approach me and attempt to strike up a conversation.

Where are you from? First time at the festival? For how many days did you come? Where do you sleep? A little about the situation in Israel and all kinds of opening questions. Each time I'm asked about the operation in Gaza I explain that it's very difficult and complex.

As for me, I'm just looking for peace and love. "Peace and Love" is the combination of words I use the most when apologizing on behalf of the State of Israel. This brings a smile to the other person, who's trying to not go deeper with questions.

When one guy asks me for more details and does a quick calculation of my age, he realizes I served during the Second Lebanon War. I tell him a little about Lebanon and he salutes me, saying "well done," before vanishing immediately. I understand it's the alcohol speaking. What an idiot I am. They came to a music festival. Why would they even care about the situation in Israel? I have to stop talking about it.

I try to dance and focus on the impressive stage with the tens of thousands of people who are worshiping the Swedish D.J., but I'm not very successful. All that's on my mind are the frightened soldiers sitting in a tank in Gaza right now. I feel guilty for being here, celebrating at everyone's expense. The thoughts are relentless, and after I realized I'm talking nonsense, I try to not communicate with anyone around me. It works pretty well until Janneke arrives.

◆ ◆ ◆

Janneke introduces herself and the others, "I'm Janneke, this is Niki, and my husband, Joost." Niki comes to plant a kiss on my cheek and Joost shakes my hand with a big smile, then gives me a manly hug.

"Niki I've heard before. What did you say your name and your husband's name were?" I ask awkwardly, and after a few attempts to say Janneke and Joost, I get a look of "not quite, but good enough" from Janneke.

They came to the festival from the Netherlands. Janneke is a really tall woman and very strong, with loads of presence. It seems like she's the one making the decisions.

Niki, a friend of the couple, is a petite blond with big breasts and tattoos that peek out from every possible direction. The truth is, she doesn't look Dutch. She looks like she came here to have fun and therefore didn't skimp on any party accessories.

Joost, Janneke's husband, seems like a quiet and likable guy, but his connection to the trio is a little odd. He's short, almost like Niki, but chiseled like a German. Niki and Joost dance together on one side and I dance with Janneke on the other, a little confused by the fact her husband is right here next to us.

While we're dancing Janneke, asks me many questions about the situation in Israel and it appears she isn't startled by what I tell her. I try to only talk a little, but a lot comes out.

Janneke tells me this is their fourth year at this festival, and that every month they go to a different festival in Europe. That's insane, I think.

Over the past year I've seen videos from this festival hundreds of times, from every possible angle, full sets of all the most reputable D.J.s in the world. I've waited so long for this moment, and now I'm finally standing here with a hundred thousand people around me, and all I can think about is the military and war.

Janneke sees that I'm troubled and suggests I take a little walk to get some air. "Breathe a little, maybe when you come back you'll feel better," she says and softly strokes my face. "Good idea, I'll go get us some beers," I say and start climbing the hill toward the bar.

Janneke was right. Distancing myself from the main stage manages to calm me down. On the way to the bar I take deep breaths and look at all the people. They seem happy, relaxed, and trouble-free. They probably go to festivals once a month too. And they don't have wars.

I return with a tray full of beer and shots and see Janneke rummaging through her shoulder bag.

After handing the drinks out to everyone, I stand next to Janneke. Her right hand is still deep inside the bag, and with her left hand she holds the beer I gave her. Janneke calls me to come closer and asks if I want a pill.

"What do you mean, a pill?" I reply.

"Ecstasy," she says and smiles.

"I've never taken it," I admit and ask naively, "are you also taking one?"

"I've already taken one and a half, my husband two, and Niki is supplementing now with another half. Do you want one? Maybe it will loosen you up a little."

I smile. I don't know what to say. I've never done drugs. The closest I've come was a small drag from a friend's joint. Today doesn't really seem like a good day to start. I start making a risk management table in my head, most likely with an idiotic smile on my face.

Janneke pulls her hand out of the bag and shakes mine, slipping me half a pill. "I gave you half because this is your first time and this is a turbo pill, not some party trash," she clarifies. I put my closed hand in my pocket and with my fingers feel the rough edge of the halved pill.

Thoughts fly in all directions and in three seconds the risk management table turns into thoughts about mental breakdowns, delusions and people thrown in the gutters in the first light of morning after a rainy night.

"Take it and drink all your beer. Only good things. I promise you," Janneke says with a convincing look. In a very uncharacteristic decision, I say to myself three, two, one – and pop the halved pill into my mouth.

I taste bitterness that fizzles on my tongue and immediately rinse it back with a big gulp of beer. I look at Janneke with an embarrassed smile and confess, "I have a tendency to be anxious."

Janneke gives me a kiss on the cheek with a motherly pat on the head. "I know sweetie, it wasn't difficult to notice. Don't worry. You're going to fly." I smile at her apprehensively, give her a strong hug as I plant a kiss on her cheek and then say, "Peace and Love." Janneke bursts out laughing and makes the shape of a heart with her fingers while making a cute puppy face.

"Drink lots of orange juice tomorrow, if you can find any. Make sure it's natural. The pill depletes your vitamins," Janneke advises. "No problem," I answer. I start smiling much more than I had been before.

"How does it go with alcohol? Because I drank quite a lot," I continue to question. "It goes great," Janneke replies.

We all continue dancing. As time passes, happy moments start to pop up more and push aside the thoughts about advanced weapons and battle readiness. I can't stop smiling. The stage continues to surprise at just the right moments. Song after song I set off on an imaginary voyage that fills me with positive thoughts. The lighting is insane. How come I haven't noticed until now?

Lasers sweep the stage in all directions in perfect sync with the music. I feel the bass in all my internal organs. Fireworks in all shapes and colors light the sky at just the right timing. Following the fireworks, lasers once again come down from the sky and caress my body from the tips of each hair on my head to the soles of my feet.

My cheeks hurt from smiling. With every familiar song I get chills throughout my body from excitement that makes me want to hold on to this moment.

"Are you starting to feel something?" Janneke breaks my train of thought. "I'm so freakin' hot," I reply and notice my face is wet from sweat. "Then all is good, relax and enjoy. More than you can even imagine is possible." Janneke winks at me and plants another kiss on my cheek. "And no coffee tomorrow! Caffeine is not good in the morning after a pill," she adds another 99 cent tip.

Out of the corner of my eye I see a girl dressed as a fairy. She has pink paint in her hand and she's painting people. When she passes me, she stops and says, "You! You are the type that has a big heart."

I turn my cheek to the fairy and give in to her. She starts drawing something, holding my face with one hand and drawing with the other. Lines, circles, and smears with her finger create magical moments of a soft and pleasant caress, which sends endless chills throughout my body.

I focus on the tips of her fingers grabbing my chin and her wrist leaning against my ear like a soft pillow — such a pleasant sensation from a touch I've never felt before.

I close my eyes to enjoy every second, surprised by the abnormal duration of this moment, until I finally get a kiss from the fairy on the other cheek. When I open my eyes I see the fairy waving goodbye and disappearing in the direction of the main stage.

I turn to Niki and ask her how it turned out. "It's really beautiful," says Niki with a mischievous smile. "She didn't paint a dick and balls?" I ask. Niki rolls in laughter, then shares the joke with Janneke and Joost.

I feel like I can do anything and I finally manage to forget all the troubles. I dance in a frenzy, overflowing with endless energy. I'm familiar with every track. I sing, I yell, I whistle and joke with Janneke.

The optimistic thoughts are released with the combination of alcohol and the music until I am overwhelmed with excitement and joy. What wonderful things the world has to offer. How much fun it is to look at everyone around me: beautiful, young, and happy. No one can beat me. I can fulfill any dream I want, go wherever I want, travel all over the world, and visit all my new friends from the festival. I have to come back every year!

Niki comes closer and asks how I'm feeling. I scan my body and mind and arrive at the unequivocal conclusion: I'm flying. "I couldn't be better," I answer without removing the smile from my face.

"Janneke gave you a quarter of a pill because it's your first time. She will get you another quarter pill for tomorrow," says Niki. I turn around and approach Janneke, feeling a little deceived but smiling.

"Don't believe Niki," she says. "I felt bad telling them that I gave you half because it's very strong. It was half. And here's the other half for tomorrow. Put it in your pocket and don't tell Niki. And remember Omri, lots and lots of juice, no coffee. We're going to be leaving soon. Write down my phone number and update me on how it's going," Janneke finished her instructions in a responsible adult tone.

She reaches into her bag of gifts, rummaging through it while I dance behind her. Finally, she hands me half a pill wrapped in a sealed bag. "Take, for tomorrow. Take it after you drink a little, and have fun kiddo," she smiles at me.

"I simply can't stop sweating and my cheeks ache a little," I say in concern.

"Enjoy it, slowly you will learn to control it," she says, finding it a little difficult to construct the sentence in English.

"Janneke, you're my angel," I say.

I continue to dance until one o'clock in the morning when the last performance ends with a crazy fireworks show. I could stay for another whole day in the same spot and just dance and enjoy myself to the moon and back.

The festival, for that evening, ends abruptly, and a swarm of 200,000 people flows from the various stages to the exit gates. When I get to the camping area, everyone's already asleep. I pull myself together with a bottle of water and throw myself into the sleeping bag, unable to stop thinking about the amazing experience.

♦ ♦ ♦

In the morning we wake up relatively early and start exchanging experiences. "Where were you the entire night?" everyone asks. I answer modestly, "Here and there, mainly hung around the main stage."

Some of the flag bearers currently serve in the standing military and it's better to not tell them about Janneke and the pills. We spend the morning mainly recuperating from the night before. Eventually, we're able to recover and get to the showers.

It's the third night of the festival. After we drink, we walk excitedly to the performance arena. On the way I plan how to cut myself loose from the group and take Janneke's pill. When we start walking down the lawn, I turn around and climb to the usual place. After a few hours, night falls and the stage comes to life. Armin van Buuren, my favorite D.J. is starting his set. This is my sign to reach into my pocket.

The next morning I'm already starting to feel the fatigue. Recovery is difficult. While the gang is telling how they lifted a few girls on their shoulders and danced in the middle of the arena, I sit on the sidelines thinking to myself what a pity it is I can't tell them where the real party was.

There is a whole dimension they are unfamiliar with, a parallel world that's entirely energetic tenderness. There's one more night of festival and Janneke isn't here. After a brief conversation with our British neighbors, I'm all set with another pill for the evening.

◆ ◆ ◆

In the morning we begin our journey home. I return to Israel feeling like my life is divided into two periods: before and after the festival. What an insane party — the vast amount of people, such investments in the set, the lighting, the fireworks. And the D.J.s, coming onto the stage one after the other, the best in the world. The feeling that I can do anything is still with me, and with it, the intense need to be free and happy. Who needs a relationship when you're about to conquer the world?

Two days after I return to Israel, I end my relationship with Noya and feel great about it. This feeling lasts for three days until heavy depression comes, together with a military operation in Gaza that doesn't seem to end.

The transition from fairytale-land to war-land is extreme and difficult for me. The nightmares return with an intensity I've never known before. The days don't allow me to relax either. This week four people were killed by a mortar bomb.

When I hear about it on the news, I'm filled with anger at my country. It doesn't make sense to me that I should live in this place just because I was born here. It doesn't make sense that one moment should determine my entire future. The world is so big and filled with so many possibilities. There's no reason for me to stay and waste my life fighting for the most controversial piece of land in the world.

I wait impatiently for my next session with Gideon, hoping he'll be able to calm me down a little. In front of Gideon, I can't keep it bottled up and I quickly tell him about my experiences at the festival, including the drugs. I can see on his face that he's slightly alarmed. He even blurts out "don't make me angry," with a kind of paternal concern, very different from Janneke's maternal calm.

◆ ◆ ◆

Going back to work is impossible for me. I spend two weeks sitting in front of the computer at work doing nothing, but checking news websites. In the evenings, I watch the news, and every night I come up with new nightmares.

The operation in Gaza lasts until the end of August. A few days later, my manager calls me in for a talk, tells me that it's not working out, and I'm fired.

In a desperate attempt to save my job I tell them I'm suffering from combat PTSD and that's why I've been unable to function during the operation in Gaza. They are taken by surprise at this revelation, but it doesn't make them change their decision.

After all, what start-up company with four employees would want one of them to be dysfunctional each time missiles fall from Gaza? I worked for the company for three months, two of which I glared at news websites. And in the middle, I disappeared to go to a festival in Belgium.

Being laid-off deepens my depression. The thoughts that I can fulfill any dream are vanishing. I can't do anything. I'm incapable of even holding down a full-time job like everyone else. How can I succeed in life when I can't even go to work like a normal person?

• • •

The depression and free time bring me back to working on the truck full time, perhaps the only job I can handle. Here, no one can tell me what to do. I'm the one making all the decisions.

From morning til night, I spend my time in my workshop continuing with the endless body work. The challenge is big, but with a great deal of creativity and thought I manage to advance with the project.

Working on the truck brings back my motivation and the will to wake up as early as I can to get as much done as possible. Along with the motivation, my desire for a relationship comes back.

I send Noya a message and invite her for another evening of angelitas at my house. Fortunately, she says yes and arrives the same night. From the moment she comes in, I'm flooded with all the feelings I had for her prior to the festival. I apologize and tell her about the festival, the pills, and the days that followed.

We continue to date steadily. A few weeks later I duplicate a key to my place for her, and a remote to the parking gate. That means she's moving in. This is the first time I'll be living with a partner and according to my friends' and Gideon's reactions, everyone's expecting me to become stressed.

But something in my relationship with Noya turns living together into something natural and flowing. While Noya is at work I dedicate my time to making room in the closet and finding additional storage spaces in our small home. Noya doesn't come alone. I also make room for the bed and water bowl of little Shushu, her dog.

My relationship with Noya develops quickly. The chemistry between us is great and we talk a lot about the post-traumatic stress. Noya's questions make me think differently about many things. She's 29, grew up in Herzliya, works in a bank, and has a black belt in karate.

Noya is sharp, a pusher, a go-getter and independent. This is the first time I feel like my relationship is the work of a winning team; the first time I'm with someone who challenges me and teaches me a great deal.

The moments that Noya succeeds in seeing the world through my eyes are the ones that make me fall more and more in love with her. One day, we sit at a coffee shop for breakfast while two tractors are working vigorously outside.

I, as usual, am mesmerized by the sight of the lengthening and shrinking pistons and enchanted by the professionalism of the operators. Noya keeps silent with a smile on her face while I stare at what's happening outside. Finally she says, "It's like a dance for you. The dance of the tractors." A sentence that so accurately describes what's going through my mind in the moment.

♦ ♦ ♦

The frequency of the nightmares decreases significantly and Noya's presence next to me in bed soothes me. Despite this, one night I wake up with a completely dry mouth and the feeling that someone is watching me.

When Noya's here I manage to overcome the paralysis, but still sense the existential danger from what's going on outside the room.

I reach out to the other side of the bed to figure out if Noya's still here or if she's already left for work. Even before I make this determination, I'm filled with anger that Noya gets out of bed in complete silence and when I wake up in panic she's not here. What's wrong with letting me know when you get out of bed?

I feel Noya on the other side of the bed and hear Shushu wake up, take a few steps, and sit down in the center of the bedroom. Where is she going in the middle of the night? Why is she being so quiet too?

I reach out to my water bottle that I regularly place by the bed and finish it with one gulp. If a stranger wants to know how bad a night I've had, all he needs to do is check the water level in my bottle. In calmer times I finish half a liter during the night, and in not so good periods I finish off the entire liter.

I turn to Noya, still a little upset for not informing me when she leaves the bed in the morning. Shushu's stomach makes noises. I'm full of concerns that there's someone outside the room. What the hell brought on the nightmare tonight?

I continue to lie in bed facing Noya's back, reaching out, bringing my body close to hers and holding her tight. She doesn't know that each strong hug in the middle of the night is the result of waking up in great fear. Thoughts start to flow and I recall the nightmare, which was about escaping and failure as usual.

Shushu leaves for the living room and scratches the entry door to the house once. Noya wakes up immediately out of some maternal instinct. I close my eyes and pretend to be asleep. Why does Shushu want to go out? Doesn't she know she can't go out right now, while someone is watching, waiting for us to make a mistake?

This is the first time I haven't been alone after waking up from a nightmare. How did both of them become part of my private coping?

Shushu scratches the door once again and Noya turns on her phone screen to check the time. I hide behind her, peeking to see how much longer we have to sleep. The time is 05:21. If I manage to fall asleep, there's enough time to catch a few good hours until the morning comes. Noya turns to me and says, "Shushu wants something." No, this isn't happening. It's forbidden to get out of bed.

"She only scratched the door once, it's all good," I try to assure Noya. I don't tell her that Shushu's stomach has been making noises for several minutes now. How can I explain that I don't have the courage to open the door for Shushu myself?

Noya leaps out of bed and leaves the room. God, what if there's someone there? Noya doesn't stop in the kitchen. She continues toward the living room and opens the main door. Shushu leaves the house and Noya goes after her. It's so dark out there — a fucking black hole as far as I'm concerned. I've never stepped outside like that. That door has never been opened while he was out there.

I'm frozen in bed, completely paralyzed. What will I do if Noya doesn't come back? How will I be able to go outside and help her?

The house is completely quiet. I'm still in bed, trying to listen to what's happening outside. Maybe she's crying for help. God, this has never happened to me. I've never left the room in the middle of the night, except for the time I stealth crawled to the living room to fetch the computer and write down the nightmare I submitted to the review board.

What's going to become of Noya? Why is it so quiet in the house? I imagine Noya's in mortal danger and instead of helping her I'm lying here like an idiot, motionless.

Noya returns to the room with Shushu behind. I'm afraid to look at Noya out of concern that something happened to her. She curls up in bed and goes back to sleep. Shushu lies down in her bed and in a few minutes goes back to snoring. Only I remain awake with my thoughts about yet another failure.

The hens in the neighboring coop are already gossiping before another day of laying eggs. Noya's alarm will ring in a moment and she'll jump out of bed, leave the room and put on the clothes she prepared yesterday. She will do all of that in perfect silence, without preparing me for the moment I wake up and find her not next to me.

◆ ◆ ◆

Memorial Day is coming, and like every year it brings with it a bag full of surprises. In recent years I've tried to ignore this day as much as possible. During childhood, it was nearly impossible to not be exposed to the Memorial Day events at my parents' house.

To be honest, it wasn't possible to evade any news at our home. When I got up in the morning, the first thing I would hear was the beeping of the news from Dad's transistor. Even when we flew to England and France for my Bar Mitzvah trip, Dad brought the transistor radio. He made sure to turn it on every day and listen to the news on an Israeli radio station.

"It's transmitted in short waves," he would be amazed every time anew. "You can hear the news of Israel from anywhere in the world." He would say it proudly, as if it was an Israeli invention.

News wasn't just on in the morning. The radio in our kitchen was on all day. Every hour in Israel, all radio stations broadcast five minutes of a live news break.

Toward the evening my parents would turn off the radio and turn on the television in the living room — to watch the news. And if, God forbid, we were on the road and were late for the evening news on television, Dad would turn on the radio broadcast of the same program in the car. The truth is, it impressed me each time that we could hear the television in the car.

In Israel it's impossible to not know bereaved families, and occasionally I would hear from Dad about his friends who were killed in the war. Over the years people I knew from the military and from childhood were also killed, but none of them were from my immediate family.

So, at our house, apart from the television and the radio, Memorial Day was another normal day, much more serious and sadder than usual, but not really a day of mourning.

After my release from the IDF something changed. When I teared up during one of the Memorial Day ceremonies I told myself that I've probably become a little more sensitive since the war, like my father who cries occasionally when he sees something on television.

In the years that followed I threw big parties on Independence Day that starts the same day Memorial Day ends. The planning and organization of a party for hundreds of friends created enough distraction that I wouldn't have a spare moment to sit in front of the television or go to a ceremony. Instead, Memorial Day would be filled with endless tasks of gathering gear and preparing the compound for the party.

When we stopped organizing parties on Independence Day, I already lived alone. That's when

Memorial Day became even more meaningful to me. During Memorial Day, all TV stations broadcast only content relevant to the observance. Comedy and lifestyle channels stop broadcasting for 24 hours.

It would all begin when I started exposing myself to this content. It could be a report on television or a radio program. It might be just for a few minutes, but I would enter a state of existential anxiety that would close me off and send me to bed for an entire day. The vast majority of people around me didn't serve in combat and couldn't have guessed how I felt on Memorial Day. I would become agitated and have little patience for anything. All I wanted was to be left alone and to withdraw inside myself on this day.

At some point I started to fear that if someone close was to be killed in battle or a terrorist attack, we would become a bereaved family and I would no longer have this day to dedicate to my self-pity.

♦ ♦ ♦

Noya's mother lost her first husband, who was a combat pilot. From our first encounter a deep connection was created between us. We didn't need too many words to understand there's something between us that is far beyond. Sometimes she was the only one who understood my reactions and tried to support me every chance she got, even when Noya herself couldn't see what my fears were based on. The only time we didn't succeed in understanding each other was on Memorial Day.

A week before, Noya's mother informed me, "It's clear that now you're a part of the family and you're coming to the memorial ceremony." I nodded in agreement when inside fears awakened. How will I react at the cemetery?

That same night I woke up with a completely dry mouth and remembered I dreamed about missiles falling everywhere. Everyone was outside, only I was in the shelter. When the bombardment subsided, I went outside and started to search for survivors among the ruins, but couldn't find anyone. I ran between houses, moved rocks, looked in every corner and yelled non-stop, but no one answered. While I was running through the rubble, I woke up.

On the eve of Memorial Day, I sit down for dinner with Noya in the living room. We turn on the television. News reports and documentaries about heroic soldiers and bereaved families are broadcast on all the channels.

A few seconds of a random soldier's childhood photos, who was killed in the line of duty, is enough to completely overpower me. In one moment, a barrel of explosive thoughts is ignited and I start thinking about people who've remained nineteen while life itself goes on. It was by pure luck that I didn't become a Memorial Day photo myself. I didn't do anything particularly good in the war, on the contrary, I made mistakes. People who were injured near me weren't any better than me. They hadn't made decisions that were any worse either. They were just unlucky.

These thoughts undermine my sense of control over reality, and after a few seconds I burst into uncontrollable sobbing. Just like that, without any warning, I sit next to Noya with dinner on the table and cry like I've never cried before. I feel my throat constricting and my entire body tighten.

Noya immediately comes to her senses. She turns off the television, lays me on my side with my head on her knees, and starts stroking my head. I don't dare look her in the eyes. I cover my face with my hand while my body shakes and trembles from crying. A flood of tears into a sea of self-pity.

When I wake up in the morning there's a note waiting for me next to the bed:

> I don't know what to say. There are probably no comforting words either. It's yours, completely yours. I want to hold you tight and say that everything will be alright. I wish I could understand what you're feeling and what happened to you there. I can only promise to be next to you in silence. I hope that a day will come when you want to share. In the meantime, I settle for your tears and have faith that our love strengthens you, even if only a little.

The Memorial Day incident brings us even closer. Noya succeeds in containing a large part of my idiosyncrasies. More than anything, she's learned to not become offended when I forget things, can't concentrate, or stare at the walls. We continue to talk openly about my crises, about events from the military, and about the difficulties regarding the reserve service. We develop a habit — get into bed at night, cuddle together, and talk till the early morning hours with our lips almost kissing.

One night I tell Noya about the notebooks and how I can't bring myself to read them. Noya says she would be happy to read them and find out what I went through during the war. "But only when you feel comfortable. No pressure, Mami," she adds with her lips nearly touching mine.

I tell her about Shira Nelson, who fell asleep while reading and the devastation I felt. Noya promises there's no chance in the world that she'd fall asleep from something that is so important to me. She says that she's sure I described my experiences well. It's hard for me to argue, I don't really remember what's written aside from the fact that the writing is very technical. All I wrote was where we went and what we did, without too much detailing. Just to remember.

♦ ♦ ♦

I go back to work part-time and truly enjoy the new balance in my life. Three days I work at the office in

Tel Aviv and four days I spend in the workshop with the truck. The only things that get me out of the workshop are off-road trips.

Once every few weeks, Noya and I load the car and head out with our group of friends for three days. Noya gets along with my friends famously despite the fact that a large part of the time we talk about car upgrades. Not many girls come on these trips but she's something else. She is able to spend nights in the forest in the middle of winter and to get everyone to open up about their problems.

When Noya moved in with me, we bought a closet at Ikea. The next day I came home and found the closet assembled with Noya being in the last stages of arranging the tools back in the box. "Are you still surprised? Haven't you figured out yet that I'm not your typical girl?" She said when she saw my look. I smiled and hugged her tightly.

♦ ♦ ♦

My spare time is well spent. Now I wake up every morning with Noya. When she goes to work I take Shushu for a walk outside, make coffee, and step out to the workshop.

There, I work almost non-stop until the afternoon, when I find myself overcome with hunger. Most days are invested in the truck, but I have time for other important things too. Noya keeps saying she wants to get back to her karate training, but she doesn't have a punching bag.

Once I asked her to teach me how to kick. She demonstrated a few times in the air and then she moved to my shin. "I'll be gentle, don't be afraid," she said and two seconds later she almost broke my shin bone with a sharp and precise kick.

To not become Noya's punching bag, I installed one for her. I welded a few metal rods and created a hanging device that connects to the mulberry tree. Noya invited her little sister, also a black belt, and they both kicked the bag excitedly.

The truck project continues to generate many challenges and alternately, provide hope as well. Most days something gets stuck, or I discover more rust and broken components.

There are very few days that everything goes as planned. I solve the problems with yet another video on YouTube, reading a chapter in the car manual, or by making a desperate phone call to a friend.

When I run out of ideas, I leave everything and go out on a ten-kilometer run through the fields. After ten seconds of running, new solutions start to come up. Throughout the run I plan in detail what I'll do when I get back. Sometimes I become so focused on it, that by the time I pick up my head, I see that five kilometers have passed. I can barely remember where I've run.

One of the goals I made at the beginning of the truck project was learning to do things with my hands. So far I've done everything by myself, but for the final body and chassis paint, I decide to go with a professional who specializes in classic cars.

To save costs, I plan to transport the truck's body myself. In the evening, when Noya comes home from work, she finds me struggling with the body, partially loaded on the trailer. Noya puts down her bag, takes off her heels, and lifts one of the corners of the truck.

Thanks to Noya's help, in a few minutes the body is placed in the center of the trailer, and all that remains is securing it with ratchet tie straps. Noya and I step back and smile to each other at the strange sight of half a truck, like it was taken off a factory's assembly line. It's not every day that you see the body of an old vehicle intact and clean, but without any essential parts like wheels, windows or doors.

Early the next morning we load Shushu in the car and head to the painter. I love driving with a trailer. Even as a child I dreamed of being the driver of a huge truck that transports large cargo from place to place, required to perform complicated maneuvers.

The painter at the shop opens a color guide for us, and together we narrow down the possibilities. Another dream coming true. I always wanted Dad to buy a new car so we could pick its color. At some point I realized Dad was not going to replace his old van and that Mom would never buy a new car. I never imagined my first opportunity to choose a color would be after I restored an old car.

When you choose a color for a new car, there's usually a limited number of possibilities for each model. Here, I have to make a choice out of all the colors and shades in the world. My favorite color is blue, but I find it hard to give up the truck's original gray color. Finally, Noya finds a shade that combines blue and gray, and together we select a matte finish.

We drive back home with an empty trailer bouncing behind us on the highway.

TRAVEL LOG: TZUKIM (PART 1)

I remember Noya and my heart is flooded with yearning. A little more than six months have passed since the breakup. The direct connection between us is completely severed. Noya unfriended me on Facebook and we both removed the "following" status on Instagram. This doesn't prevent us from visiting each other's Instagram account without leaving any trace though.

Her page is filled with photos of beaches in Greece and off-road trips in Israel. She never reveals who she's traveled with, just leaves endless thick hints that she's still there, waiting for me to come around.

At first, I thought I was the only one continuing to visit her account, but when I uploaded a photo from our trip to Spain, and the following day she uploaded a photo I took on that same trip, I no longer had any doubt. Since then, I've become addicted to looking through her Instagram in anticipation of another post, more proof that Noya is also thinking about me.

I go into Noya's Instagram to keep up to date, but this time there's nothing new on her profile. I close the computer and curl up in a pile of pillows on the bed.

In the morning I pack up my gear, put on my dirty travel clothes, and go to the hotel's parking lot. I check the oil and coolant level and start up the truck to heat the engine.

The anticipation of getting back to nature fills me with a sense of freedom and energy. I get into the truck and start driving. The truck's windows are open and the desert air blows in all directions.

Occasionally, cars overtake me. The drivers slow down next to the truck and signal "well done" to me with their hand. Every few cars, I also see a hand with a phone aiming its camera at the truck. I smile back and sometimes add a pleasant honk.

Close to the entrance to Ein Yahav, I turn right to the Nekarot valley. This allows the convoy of cars that have formed behind me to continue at a normal speed. I drive slowly on the path in the center of the valley and enjoy the desert landscape.

The rare amount of green vegetation is a pleasant surprise for me. I can't remember the last time everything was blooming like this. The lower part of the valley is a wide ravine, but as I advance west, the valley walls become cliffs that border its two sides. The path winds right and left in between the valley walls, and I slow down even more to listen to the sound of the wheels on the pebbles.

At some point I decide to stop and enjoy my solitude even more. I get off the path's grooves and park to the side of the trail, under a big acacia tree. I turn off the engine, fire up the stove, and sit down on one of the rocks.

The truck's engine makes gentle ticking noises. These are the cooling fins of the radiator settling down from the drive. The black tires are coated with white dust and the sheet metal's color has changed from matte blue to grayish. From the low rock I'm sitting on, the truck looks monstrous and sexy. I scan the side closest to me and think, "I fucking assembled a car!" The coffee nearly overflows, but I manage to take the pot off the fire in time and turn off the stove.

The absolute silence of the desert. Just the sound of coffee being poured into a small glass. And every once in a while, a gust of wind in the distance. What serenity.

♦ ♦ ♦

Further on, I connect to the ancient Spice Route and drive back east to the road. When my phone regains reception, I have a message from the Tzukim Project with instructions on how to get to the cabin.

I heard about the Hikers' Cabin Project in Tzukim a little before I went on this journey. I searched for communities and various forms of living that I could visit.

A family that has guest rooms in the community village of Tzukim, close to the Israel National Trail, decided to build a free cabin for hikers. They were looking for volunteers to help with the construction.

Building a cabin in the desert sounded interesting to me. The project began a couple of months ago, and from the few photos I've seen, most of the volunteers are much younger than me. I hope that won't stop me from connecting. My original plan was to stay here for a week and a half. Now that I'm about to start, I'm concerned I may not be able to hang on that long.

I leave the truck in the guest parking and continue on foot toward the logistics area of the complex. Three shipping containers create a three-sided square with a kitchen and a large dining table in the center. Over the kitchen there's a canopy tied to the containers, waving intensely in the hot desert wind. In the distance, on a small hill between the guest rooms and the logistics complex, part of the new Hikers' Cabin is already standing.

I climb the hill and examine the cabin up close. It's divided into two areas: one large and open, the other small and closed off. The roof is made of bamboo covered with corrugated plastic to keep the rain out. From the top of the hill, a spectacular view of the Ashosh Valley can be seen.

I enter the large room and meet a guy sitting on a tall pile of mattresses playing guitar. He introduces himself. His name is Noam and he's a veteran soldier walking the Israel National Trail. Noam isn't very familiar with the building plans, but he assumes that the small room will serve as a bedroom and the large room will host workshops. He joins me and we go on a tour of the complex, finishing with a coffee facing the view.

The following day, six more volunteers taking a break from walking the Israel National Trail arrive at the complex. Raz, who coordinates the projects, calls everyone to the big room of the cabin where he explains the tasks for the upcoming week.

"The work will be centered on building a stone terrace around the entire cabin," he says and goes over to mark where the terrace will begin on the ground. "It's not complicated. You dig a little in the ground to form a ditch that will serve as a barrier for the stones. The ditch will be filled with concrete and on top of it we will place the first layer of stones." Raz confesses this is the first time he's building a terrace, so we're all going to learn on the fly.

We're divided into teams and start working. No one in the group has any experience building, and very soon I find myself explaining to the others how to work with the tools and concrete. The guys talk a lot about the trail and their plans for the continued hike. The fact that I've already done the Israel

National Trail makes me a kind of authority with the young guys. Even the story of the truck and the journey intrigues them. For the first time in my life, I feel like an experienced adult.

The group unites quickly and a pleasant routine begins. Every day there are people on duty making meals and washing dishes. Those on duty get up before everyone else and prepare a light meal and coffee. Later, they organize another ten o'clock coffee break, and to finish they cook a big lunch.

Every day a few more people are added, and the group grows. Despite the lack of experience, the construction of the terrace is advancing at an impressive rate. I enjoy the physical work and relish the feeling of every muscle in my body working. It reminds me of the days I used to work on the truck or in the garden.

During the day I look at the people around me, listen to conversation, and imagine how they will view this experience when they're my age. A little more than a decade separates me from the rest of the volunteers. The question, "what do you do?" isn't relevant here. They've all just finished their mandatory military service and they're not doing much. This encounter makes me appreciate everything I've have done since my release. I've been through quite a bit. Yesterday a debate arose about plans for the future, careers, and children. The guys shared my views and for the first time, I felt closer to them.

In the afternoons, I go on hikes in the desert or take the truck for a ride. One night, just before sunset, we climb a hill overlooking the stream, and one of the girls gives a yoga class for everyone. At the end of it we meditate to the sounds of a HAPI drum that Raz brought.

The sun has already set behind the distant mountains. We lie on our backs and my thoughts race to the sounds of music. And then, I sink into something that feels like a scene of a movie.

I see, in my mind's eye, thick smoke that is reminiscent of a serious bombing. I shut down that picture with one sweep and attempt to think about good things. But the images resurface again and again until I decide to give up and let my thoughts return to the smoke.

I see the images from the perspective of a small child. Everything is in slow motion. The people fleeing the blast zone are running for their lives. I see their faces for a split second before they run by. I'm the only one not running anywhere. I stand in place without moving while they implore me to escape with them.

The meditation ends and we return to the kitchen to start cooking. A conversation develops about the yoga session and the meditation that followed. Everyone is describing an enchanted meditation and total relaxation. "I was in fantasy land," says one of the girls. Why am I the only one who experiences war every time I close my eyes?

Later in the week, when everyone has gained experience working on the terraces, I decide to look for another project to focus on. I hang around the cabin and see Raz struggling to weld an old iron pipe. I approach and try to help with what little knowledge I have about electrode welding. Raz suggests I take on the chimney project for the hikers' room. He shows me the old pipes he's collected at the landfill and the old fireplace he received as a donation.

I agree to take the assignment. I find a piece of paper and a pencil and draw a plan for the chimney. Then, I bring the few tools I found in the shed and start cutting the pipes and adjusting the angles. The farther I get with the work, the more my welding improves.

It's been a while since I experienced the feeling of learning a new skill. I can only compare it to the feeling I got during the restoration of the truck. I continue working and in the process I discover more ideas for upgrades, such as connectors that will make it easier to replace parts of the chimney in the future. It's so much fun to work once again on a project that is entirely mine.

◆ ◆ ◆

The next day, everyone resumes working on the terrace and I continue with the fireplace project. On one of our coffee breaks I open Instagram, go into Noya's profile, and start scrolling through the photos.

My hands are dirty and the touch screen isn't reacting properly. I am battling to scroll, trying the back arrow, a few more random taps until I accidentally like a photo on Noya's profile. Oh, no. I've broken all the unwritten rules that prohibit me from leaving a trace. I hurry to undo the like and close my phone. What an idiot.

A minute later Noya sends me a message with a screenshot documenting the notification she received. "What am I supposed to do with this?" she asks. "It was by mistake, but yes, I was snooping," I confess.

I feel my heart rate increase and the heat spreading through my cheeks. Noya sends a winking smiley and we continue to text as if we never stopped. I update Noya on my journey with the truck and tell her I'm volunteering for a project in the Tzukim.

"What a coincidence, tomorrow Liat and I are going down to Eilat for a festival," she writes, and without too much thinking I ask her over to see the project. Noya agrees.

In the afternoon I head into the desert with my computer to write about the breakup.

2015: THE BREAKUP

My relationship with Noya is progressing and lately the issue of having kids comes up at every opportunity. The first time I told Noya that I think I don't want children, she calmly responded that at some point I'd change my mind.

It's come up several times now, and each time we have the chance to talk I feel like I'm failing to tell Noya the whole truth. I tell her that it's not for me, and she reacts with understanding and empathy. She says it's not the time and that she doesn't want any at the moment either.

She always ends the conversations with a word that gives my reluctance temporary validation, while deep inside I know that I'm not into it at all. For the first time after years of dealing with PTSD, I enjoy my routine. Work is not the main thing in my life and I have a lot of free time that I fill with trips and working on the truck.

If we have kids, would I still be able to afford to work only three days a week? Would I still find time to travel in the desert and build things in the workshop? I have yet to encounter a couple with children that manages to live like that. And besides, I don't have that spark that people have in their eyes when they talk about their wish to become parents and raise the next generation.

This week Liat, Noya's best friend, came to visit us. Noya maintains a million social circles. Out of all her girl friends, Liat and I have the best connection. Liat is three years older than us, and when we get together she always makes us laugh with stories about the single life of a girl in Tel Aviv. Her stories are filled with small and unimportant details and somehow the men always have weird names.

During her visit, we talk a little about the future and Liat asks when we are going to have kids. I respond that I don't think I'm up to it. Liat is surprised. She turns to Noya and says, "But you always wanted children, didn't you?" Noya smiles, as usual, and tries to lighten the mood. "Well, fine, we'll find a solution for that," she says.

We continue the conversation like nothing happened, but something inside me becomes unsettled again. We are deceiving ourselves. How can we go on like this when each of us sees our future together in a completely different way? It feels like Noya doesn't understand how it's possible to not want children.

A few days later I'm sitting with Noya on the couch in the living room and we're watching a television interview with someone who introduces herself as "child-free." This is the first time I've encountered this concept. I listen to what she's saying with interest.

"Not everyone has to have children. I don't feel the need for it. People trying to convince me to have kids tell me that I'm selfish and at the same time say I won't have anyone to take care of me when I grow old. So who's the selfish one here? Me or them?" She explains calmly and continues, "I enjoy my freedom, the spontaneity, and can't understand why they all expect me to want to have children. There are other ways to live."

Wow. Every word of the child-free woman penetrates deep into my heart, describing perfectly what I feel but don't dare say.

"What is this, I think that I am child-free!" I toss into the air. Noya hurries to respond, "What are you talking about, child-free. Mami, what's wrong with you?" I repeat the sentences of the child-free woman from the television in my head and say, "It's exactly me. I've never heard anyone talk like this, I thought I was the only one." Noya keeps silent for a moment, smirks and continues, "But you don't want kids right now. It's not that you don't want them at all. It's not the same thing."

Once again the conversation ends with Noya saying that my reluctance is temporary, but this time it affects the relationship, and in the days that follow we're distanced. After that interview I know that it's completely okay for me to think like that, that there are other people like this, and there's even a name for it: child-free.

◆ ◆ ◆

One day, a surprise guest lands in our house. Noya's dad arrives from Mexico and stays over for the night. Noya's parents got divorced several years earlier and since then he's been living in Mexico. He is sick and insists on not taking care of himself. He barely lifts his legs, just drags himself and his pipe slowly from place to place.

Toward the evening, we sit together in the garden for a warm glass of water with mint. Noya's dad asks many questions about our life together and I cooperate patiently. At some point the million-dollar question comes. "And what about the future? What's next?" he asks with his hoarse voice, lights up the pipe, and takes a puff.

"Next? We'll save money, go for a trip around the world, and live life," I reply. Noya's dad keeps quiet for a moment and says, "And when will you have children?"

I smile and look at Noya. "Less our thing," I respond. Noya looks at her dad and reinforces what I've said. "We want to have fun. We love our quiet time," she says with confidence that doesn't convince anyone and explains that right now it doesn't work for us. Noya's dad reminds her that she always wanted children and that it's something that probably isn't going to change. After that there's silence around the table.

Noya's dad takes a few more puffs from the pipe until finally he blurts out his assessment of the situation. "Well, Noya, what we have here is an egocentric guy who's afraid of life and doesn't want a family. I suggest that you cut this off as soon as possible and get it over with." He gives me a tired, yet determined look and continues, "This man will never want children."

Noya tries to calm him down, "You can't determine things like that without knowing him." In this moment, I feel it's Noya who doesn't actually know me.

I sit without saying a word. After a few seconds, Noya's dad tries to lift himself from the bench without success. After the second attempt, Noya helps him up and he drags himself inside.

The two of us remain sitting in the yard, silent. Neither of us know what to say. There's a storm raging in my head. On one hand, I feel like shouting at him. On the other, I wasn't really offended by what he said. The truth is, he's right. I really don't want children.

At noon the following day Noya's mom calls me. "I'm so sorry you had to hear that. I'm ashamed he said that to you," she apologizes. I can hear she's trying not to cry. "I'm proud of you for not paying attention to him, because you shouldn't. Noya loves you and you love her, you're great together, and you'll find your own way. Don't listen to anyone." Her words are touching, but the train has already left the station.

◆ ◆ ◆

In the days after the incident with Noya's dad, I'm troubled – until a decision is made. That evening we meet up with friends in Tel Aviv. I'm completely disconnected from everything, trying to build up the right words to tell her.

In the car, on the way home, Noya asks what's wrong. "I can't do this anymore," I reply. "We're deceiving ourselves. There's no future here." This is a big surprise to Noya. She's probably tried to ignore the elephant in the room for some time now. Maybe she thought things would work out by themselves.

"I don't want kids, and I won't want them in the future," I continue, "and each time I say something about it, you don't believe me and somehow interpret it as if one day I will want them."

We arrive home and Noya heads straight into the bedroom, with me behind her. She packs a suitcase with clothes from the closet, collects Shushu's bed, takes the dog, gets into the car, and drives away without saying a word. I remain alone in the silence of the house, in the complete darkness of the countryside. A moment later I sit on the bed, look around at all of Noya's things – and burst out crying. "Oh God, what have I done?" I say out loud. I just removed the person closest to me in this world from my life. That's it, I'm alone again.

◆ ◆ ◆

The following day, when I get back from work, the house is half empty and totally void of life. The days after the breakup are hard, especially dealing with the people around me that seek an explanation.

On top of it all, the third review board of the Disabled Veterans Department is already around the corner. I've been going to weekly sessions with Gideon for four years now, and in our last session he hinted that we'll need to reduce the frequency toward the end of treatment. He guesses the upcoming review board will determine whether I receive permanent disability or have my disability rights revoked.

My concern that the temporary recognition is about to end causes an increase in the frequency and intensity of nightmares. Many nights I wake up with the feeling that someone is out there. I lie in bed terrified of someone waiting for me to make a mistake.

Now that I'm alone, going out of the house is scary every time. Yesterday, I ordered a pizza and when the delivery guy called, I was afraid to cross the dark path leading to the street. It wasn't until he began honking that I ran up without looking to the sides. When I reached him, I was like a bomb about to go off. And when he complained about waiting I burst out at him yelling. I returned home with the pizza and immediately realized that I was a complete idiot.

◆ ◆ ◆

After the breakup with Noya, I try to understand the real reason I don't want children. But even with Gideon's help, I'm having trouble fully understanding the decision. Indeed, it comes from fear, and the obvious connection is to the war.

The war completely changed the way I look at life, and since then I live in constant fear that war will break out again. When you think about it, since the military, I've run away from every commitment or responsibility. I'm in constant pursuit of a life without constraints. A child is the complete opposite of all that. You can't run from him and he slows down the pace of progress. But is this the real reason? I'm not so sure.

TRAVEL LOG: TZUKIM (PART 2)

Upon finishing dinner, we all sit around the campfire. After a week together, we share many funny memories and deep conversations. Soon, everyone will continue on their journey. Some of the volunteers are continuing their trip on the Israel National Trail, and I will continue south with the truck. A bittersweet feeling is shared as the time in our newly built cabin comes to an end.

Thursday morning is the last working day of the week. The chimney is ready, and all that's left to do is to connect it from the inside of the room to the roof of the cabin. Just as we sit down to lunch, Noya texts me that she'll be arriving in a few minutes.

I grab half a pita with hummus and go out toward the parking lot. In the distance I see Noya's car approaching. She parks next to the truck and steps out of the car in jean shorts, a loose black top, cool sneakers, and a necklace with a big silver pendant. Liat is wearing a black dress, flip-flops and huge sunglasses.

Noya looks at me and starts laughing. I'm dressed in a work shirt covered in dust, and my favorite jeans that I've had since restoring the truck. I smile at Noya. She approaches me, gives me a kiss on the mouth, and hugs me warmly.

"You haven't changed your pants since the restoration project?" she asks and pushes the clump of dirt, that is me, away from her. Liat shoves in, moving Noya to the side. "Give a hug here, I don't care. I miss you," says Liat and squishes me to her.

I take Noya and Liat on a tour of the cabin and the guest room complex. Liat doesn't quite understand what I'm doing here with all these kids, but Noya comes to my defense.

Noya tells her that not everyone is like her, sitting in an office all day. We finish the tour and sit down for coffee facing the desert view. Noya tells me that they're going to the festival in Eilat. "You have to drop by, we'll get you tickets," she says.

We finish the coffee and return to the parking lot. Noya stands next to the truck, patting its sides. "You're crazy! This is perfect!" she says. Liat's phone rings and she answers it, pulling away from us.

Noya seizes the chance and asks me how the journey is going. In one moment, we're both thrown back to the time we used to talk about everything. I briefly tell Noya about the difficulties I have at night in contrast to the ultimate freedom during the day.

And then, I open the truck's door, reach into the narrow gap behind the seat, and pull out the red bag. "I brought the notebooks with me," I reveal to her. "Still not looking in them?" Noya asks in a soft and soothing voice. "I've been driving around for three weeks and still don't have the nerve to take them out of the bag," I admit.

I turn on the computer to show Noya the first page I saved at the beginning of this journey. An empty page with the title "2006: The War." The cursor blinks, taunting me.

"Don't worry Mami, the right moment will come," she says confidently, pulling the front of my pants to bring me closer. I say goodbye to Noya and Liat who are continuing their way to Eilat.

The clean-up after the meal has already started in the kitchen. "We saved you some food," says Noam and hands me a plate filled with goodies. I sit down to eat and watch Noam washing the dishes. After that, we have coffee.

Later on, we go up to the cabin where we find an exhausted group of people. In every corner there's people who've fallen asleep on half-laid out sleeping bags. We've worked hard over the week and the fatigue is obvious. Noam and I look at each other and immediately join in the relaxing snooze.

Toward the evening I receive another message from Noya, "So, what... are you coming to visit us?" I ponder how to respond. The drive to Eilat at the speed of my truck will take at least an hour and I won't be able to drink because I need to drive back. "I'm trying to get you a ticket for the festival. It will be great," Noya continues to convince me. That's it, stop being afraid. I'm going.

I load all my equipment on the truck and inform the guys that I'll be back later tonight. Of course, the drive lasts longer than planned, and after two hours I finally get to the hotel. I send Noya a message, and at the entrance to the hotel I see her talking to the guard. She holds a lit cigarette in one hand, a packet of Marlboro Lights, and her mobile in the other — typical Noya.

Noya notices my truck and signals me to approach the parking lot. The guard opens the gate and says, "Park here, next to the gate. I'll keep a special eye on it." Knowing Noya, she's already made sure that I would have a safe parking space. She knows I'd be concerned otherwise.

I pull up next to the guard's station and get out. I'm wearing a filthy pair of jeans and a black T-shirt, the only one I have that's stain free. My black work boots are covered in dust. Noya looks at me and laughs. She grabs my hand and leads me toward the concert area.

We sit outside the compound, and I continue to tell Noya about all I've been through on the trip, from the monument at Mount Adir to volunteering at Tzukim. Noya is riveted by the stories and asks a ton of questions. She knows me so well and the natural manner in which she behaves reminds me of how close we once were. She's been the only one sensitive enough to my pain.

Ivri Lider's performance ends and people start to exit toward the hotel. The sharp transition from complete disconnect to behaving like we never broke up stresses me out. Very soon, I regret coming.

"I think I'm going back," I say to Noya. "What do you mean go?" she protests, pulling me toward the hotel. "There's no way you're driving two hours back right now. You're spending the night here with us."

I walk behind her to the elevators in the lobby, and from there to the hotel room. Liat is already in the room, and when we walk in she says, "Welcome. Not everyone gets to sleep with the two blondies."

The vibe is weird. Liat is in her pajamas, attempting to understand her place, Noya is all festive and excited, and I'm a bag of filth trying to not soil the furniture. Liat saves the day when she announces, "Well, I have a long phone call I need to make with some Efraim guy. I'm going outside for a smoke." Noya and I laugh at another weird name.

Liat steps out onto the balcony, closing the drapes and window behind her. Noya and I remain standing in the center of the room for a few seconds and then start hugging intensely. The hug immediately leads to a kiss accompanied by the feeling that we're doing something wrong. We look at each other for a second, then resume kissing with excessive savagery, along with heavy caressing.

A few minutes later, we lie in embrace under the covers, a little in love and quite embarrassed about Liat, who's still out on the balcony. After a few minutes, she enters the room and asks, "Are you kids done? Can we go to sleep?" We laugh and huddle to make room for her.

Noya and I spend the night in each other's arms on the edge of the bed. Noya's touch and smell bring back fond memories of home and family.

◆ ◆ ◆

In the morning I'm first to wake up. I say goodbye to Noya and set off back to the cabin in Tzukim. Two hours of quiet and time to think about yesterday. What do I do now? I feel like disappearing into the desert so I don't have to deal with this.

I park the truck at the entrance to the guest room complex and start my preparation for the last leg of the journey. I crawl under the truck and look for any issues.

Spots that are too clean on the dusty driveshaft indicate that something has come loose. I open the screws, cleaning them well and adding special Loctite glue that will prevent them from coming loose again. Then I re-tighten them according to the car's manual torque. I clean the residue of oil and dust from under the engine with a rag. Where are the days when everything was polished clean?

From under the truck I move on to the cabin, trying to locate noises. To my surprise, I discover more and more screws that have come loose from the jolts of the drive: the closing mechanism of the glove compartment, the balancing screws of the passenger door, and the dashboard screws. I patiently go over each one and make sure they are tightened well. Finally, I pull out a package of wet-wipes and start cleaning the dust from the dashboard.

♦ ♦ ♦

Saturday morning, noises of packing in the cabin wake me up. The guys are busy with their final preparation for continuing the Israel National Trail. The temperature in my sleeping bag is perfect and I try to snooze for as much time as possible before starting the day.

While I struggle with myself inside the sleeping bag, one of the guys comes over to wake me up and say goodbye. Most mornings I'm cranky and impatient, but some paternal sentiment makes me get out of the sleeping bag. They're ready to go and some already have their backpacks on. The farewell is emotional. It's obvious to everyone that a special chapter in our journeys has ended. We also know it's most likely we will never meet again.

After the morning preparations I also continue with my journey. I sit in the cabin, open the windows, and start the engine. It's just you and me again, I think patting the steering wheel. I leave Tzukim and drive the Arava Road for a short trip up to the Faran valley.

It's early in the morning and I have the whole day ahead of me. My body is relaxed and feels entirely charged with good feelings. The spaces spread out before me and the scattered acacia trees in the distance remind me of the savannas in Africa. I drive slowly and easily through the path that winds the wide ravine, breathing in the desert around me, and thinking about how much freedom there is here, only five minutes from the main road to Eilat.

I arrive at the confluence with the Zihor valley that takes me to Route 40. I'm very familiar with the areas on the sides of the road from my tank commanders' course training. To my left is the entrance to kibbutz Shitim, which always served as the starting point for night navigation training.

After that, a facility for pumping water that served as landmarks for us. And finally, the entrance to the Shizafon base. How I hated that moment the bus would turn onto the Shizafon access road on Sunday mornings when I'd just come back from a weekend off.

After the turn into the base, the training firing zones begin. On the east side of the road are the famous M areas. Next to one of the observation towers a company of eleven tanks is parked, probably waiting for crewmembers to come back tomorrow from weekend leave. In the distance I recognize that they're Merkava Mark 4 tanks, a newer model than the ones I served on.

I continue driving on the straight road with my gaze pinned on the tanks spread to the left. The tanks recede into the distance behind me, but my thoughts are still stuck on my history as a tank crewman. There's no way I'm passing through here without stopping.

A photo of the truck next to a tank is a complex image that represents most of the thoughts that have gone through my mind in recent years. I take a quick glance in the rearview mirror before I cut to the left and descend to the side of the road. The area is grooved from the deep tracks of the tank's heavy chains. The truck jumps and rocks in all directions when I try to make a straight line toward the parked tanks.

I stop the truck next to one of the tanks and step out with my camera to capture the moment. "Bro, you can't be here." A soldier with a tattered flack-jacket standing on the dirt mound behind the tanks shouts at me.

He jumps off the mound and advances toward me to stop me before I move away from the truck. Behind him, the commander arrives holding a military radio in his hand. "Is it possible to take a picture of the tank with the truck?" I ask. "Sorry, you can't. I'm not allowed to let you," says the commander calmly after realizing I'm not the type to try and steal weapons from the tank.

The soldier with the vest examines the truck and says, "Man, what a cool truck. I've never seen a Suzuki pickup-truck before." I smile in satisfaction. "Thanks. Are these the tanks for the commanders' course?" I ask him. "Yes, of the 196th brigade," the commander replies. "I was in the 188th," I say, placing my hand on the ruler rail that holds the protective bazooka plates. "Really? In which battalion?"

"Fifty-third," I reply, "I was the deputy company commander of the A company when it transitioned into an operational company." The commander thinks for a moment and then asks in amazement, "Avner's deputy?"

In this moment I feel like the family member of a big celebrity. "Yes, Avner's deputy. How do you know Avner?" I ask. "He's our battalion commander. This is his tank," says the commander and points to the tank I'm touching.

"He moved to Mark 4? You don't say! If that's so, I'm going to take a picture of this tank even without permission. If anyone makes trouble for you, send him to Avner," I state moving backwards a little with the camera so that Avner's tank and the truck will both fit into the frame. The commander and the soldier guarding the tank don't object and even move away from the tank so as not to be in the picture. I look through the camera lens and adjust the aperture.

"You were with him in the war?" the commander asks. He probably remembers Avner's story. "Yes, bro," I reply from behind the camera, trying to not make eye contact with him. "He received the Medal of Courage in the war," the commander points out.

"He indeed received the Medal of Courage," I say and continue to fiddle with the camera. "Avner told us after he was wounded, you remained alone to command the company and led the battalion's rescue mission," the commander continues to assemble the information puzzle.

"That's also true. When he took the first rescue helicopter to the hospital, I stayed there." I move the lens away from my eye and smile to lighten the mood and end the conversation.

On the way back to the truck I put the camera in the bag. Another soldier from the guard team joins us from the direction of the dirt mound. "Bro, he was Avner's deputy during the war!" the soldier with the vest shouts to his friend who's just arrived.

"Really? Wow, he's a king," says the other. After a few more questions about the truck renovation, I bid the guard team farewell and continue the drive toward Shaharut.

My encounter with Avner's tank raises the emotional bar and the significance of this day. I haven't spoken to Avner for at least a year and I didn't even know he was the brigade commander at Shizafon. How could it be that of all the tanks in Shizafon, I chose to stop right next to his? What a crazy coincidence.

◆ ◆ ◆

I get into Shaharut and park next to Danny's garage. We got acquainted through a blog I wrote about the restoration of my truck, but we never actually met. "Welcome," says Danny who emerges suddenly from the bushes behind the garage. He shows me the trailer where I'll stay for the next few days. "Make yourself at home. The sheets are clean and there's hot water in the shower. I have to finish a few things in the garage."

I put my bag in the bedroom and return to the garage. Danny makes coffee and we get carried away with a conversation about the truck restoration and trips around the world. Danny has a great deal of knowledge about mechanics and all-terrain vehicles. He can't understand why I insisted on preserving the original configuration of the truck.

Over the course of the restoration many people told me I must add power steering and that it would be impossible to stay comfortable without air conditioning. The more criticism I heard about my decisions, the more firmly I stood my ground. I felt that no one understood what I was trying to do. As far as I was concerned, what was good in 1984, when I was born, would be good for me even thirty something years later. More than anything, it's a story of coming back to life, understanding that the truck is awesome just the way it is, and that there's no need for upgrades.

Danny finishes his work and invites me to join him and his wife for dinner. The conversation around the table revolves around life in Shaharut, a closed alternative lifestyle community on a secluded mountain in the middle of the desert.

Danny shares many stories, videos, and pictures from different events in the village. While we look at the photos from the Purim party, I ask Danny to tell me about one of them. In the background of the photo there's a wall full of work tools and old metal parts arranged in perfect order. "What is this cool place?" I ask.

"Erez's workshop."

"Is it here, in Shaharut?"

"Sure. Every year we have our Purim party there. We had a party there a week ago. You're one week late," Danny laughs and sips from his beer. I smile, "The truth is, I'm more interested in the workshop than the party."

♦ ♦ ♦

In the morning I go to visit Erez's workshop and find him standing outside, staring at a pile of steel – a thin guy with straight, light brown hair, light blue eyes, and tanned skin.

"Erez? I'm Omri, a friend of Danny's," I introduce myself and shake his hand. It's rugged from hard work. I tell him about the photo of the Purim party. Erez laughs and throws another glance at the pile of metal. "I'm going to build a desert side-car for a dirt bike," he announces.

We walk into his workshop and Erez goes to boil some water. I stand in the center of the room, next to the large workbench, and look around. I've never been in such an impressive shop. The tools are meticulously arranged along the walls. Dozens of collector's items hang in every corner. There's heavy antique machines used for bending and flattening iron. And of course, the dirt bike to which the sidecar will connect. The workshop ceiling is high and part of it has a wooden gallery with a drum set in it. Is this what heaven looks like?

I sit down with Erez for coffee and we start talking about my journey and the truck project. Erez recommends that I pop over to a natural pool thirty minutes away from here. A few of the dry river beds were flooding last week after some heavy rain. In the coming weeks, fresh water will stay in the natural reservoir and create an amazing pool.

"When you go there, come by with the truck, I want to see it," says Erez. He takes his coffee to the workbench. Feel free to walk around the workshop, I have to move ahead with a few tasks." This is my dream, to be surrounded by tools all day, like him. I walk around, finish my coffee, thank Erez, and leave the workshop.

The following day I come by with the truck. Erez comes out of the workshop and immediately goes to check it out. "This is so great," he says as he walks around the car inspecting the quality of my self-made upgrades. I accompany Erez around the truck and instantly spot small flaws in the paint and mediocre welding in the equipment apparatus. A craftsman at his level probably thinks it's all very amateurish.

Erez invites me to join him for lunch. He sets the table on the balcony and we sit down facing the Edom Mountains on the Jordanian side of the border. Erez tells me about his childhood in the Arava desert and about a Suzuki truck like mine that was always the attraction of the children in the kibbutz. We drift into a long conversation about life at the pace of Shaharut and about the projects he's working on. Erez returns to the workshop and I get into the truck and drive to the pool. I hang out there until sunset.

I spend the last day in Shaharut roaming around and randomly meeting interesting people, who make me question if I could also live life in such simplicity, with the unique serenity of a remote place in the middle of the desert.

Early in the morning, I pack up everything, tie the equipment on the truck and go to watch the sunrise over the Kasuy dunes. Driving down from Shaharut, the blue hue of morning begins and is slowly painted with pink that changes into orange.

Yesterday evening there was a strong wind that reshaped the dune with gentle waves of sand. I take the coffee kit, climb to the top of the dune and sit down on the sand. I watch the sun start to rise and wait for the water to boil. When the sun comes up, the gentle sand waves create a perfect shadow, which adds to the unique look of the dune, and exposes the many tracks of rodents and mammals that celebrated here all night long.

From the Kasuy dunes I continue to stock-up for the last time at a nearby gas station. While arranging the things in the truck's fridge, I receive a message from Erez. What could I have forgotten in Shaharut?

"As someone who's already stuck his nose in quite a few irons, screws, sheet metal, and wheels, it's difficult to get me excited about these things, but your machereika[i] is truly exciting. You did an amazing job, and I'm happy you're enjoying it today. So, if you're in the area and need a hand, or a screw, I'm always here." Immediately after that message I receive another, "The world is divided into two kinds of people: those who do, and those who talk."

---

[i] From Yiddish, a machine that makes no sense.

I feel chills running up and down my spine. This is not the message I expected to get.

I sit down on the edge of the sidewalk and read Erez's message over and over. How could it be that he wrote me such a message? He's the most talented person I've met and he lives in a dream workshop, surrounded by his perfect creations. My heart pounds from excitement. How could it be that two days after we met he's still thinking about my little truck? I get into the truck and drive south on the Arava Road. Erez's message fills me with such pride that I hug the steering wheel and pin my chest to it.

I exit the Arava Road to a dirt road that leads to the entrance to the Raham valley. It is also full of vegetation: purple, white, and yellow flowers. A calm morning with the slight pleasant heat of spring. I start with a slow drive in first gear, gain a little momentum and continue to cruise slowly in second gear.

The windows are open, and my eyes roam the walls of the ravine. It's still early and the cliff shades the path. A few large white clouds form a play of light and shade on the distant mountains. I breathe in the desert in all its glory. This is the first time I'm crossing the desert all alone. The slower I drive, the more I connect with the ground and the grip of the wheels.

I get to a sharp bend in the dry river bed. This is a great spot for coffee. I step out of the truck with my coffee kit and climb onto a rock from where I can see the picturesque trail bending in between the huge boulders. I imagine the moment these boulders fell from the cliff. Next to the huge boulders are smaller rocks, evidence that on the way down part of them shattered.

I think about how long these rocks have been in the same place and wonder if they're comfortable in their new location. Between the rocks I see piles of leaves and small branches from the floods that have come through here in recent years. The desert has so much fun during a flood.

The coffee will be ready in a moment. I stand up, spread my arms to stretch, and let the desert penetrate each and every part of my body. It's time to write the last chapter.

2016-2017: THE END OF AN ERA

The date of the third review board has arrived, and again I find myself at the entrance to the horrible building on Shaul Ha'melech Street. While waiting for the review board I once again go through the pages I've prepared. When they call my name I enter the room and for the third time tell the three strangers about my biggest fears and my most intimate experiences. Next to them sits a typist who summarizes in short, emotionless sentences, the nightmare of my life.

Later, at home, I go over the meeting and as always, feel like I'm in a bad dream. Now I have to wait in suspense for the letter that will determine my fate. The same intolerable uncertainty once again.

My thoughts about the review board and the waiting time push me to spend a great deal of time in the workshop. Noya is gone, there are no projects at work, and all I do is work on the truck.

The chassis came back from the paint job and the refurbished axles and steering system were assembled on it. I managed to get the missing parts in the all-wheel drive system and assemble them too. Finally, I have a rolling chassis that you can push from place to place. Another significant milestone in the project.

I mount the engine back to the chassis and improvise a few wire connections in an attempt to start it. After several failed attempts, I go over everything in detail together with the pictures I took before the disassembly. I locate several wires I connected incorrectly and I'm finally able to start the engine.

It coughs a little and discharges a large cloud of smoke. This is the first time since I've had the truck that the engine has come to life. Who knows how long it's been since a mixture of fuel and air flowed to those combustion chambers. A mixture that, with the perfect precision of the spark plugs, causes the blast that pushes the pistons and turns the engine.

I place my finger on the throttle located on the side of the carburetor and gradually allow more air and fuel to flow to the engine. The RPM increases and a big smile spreads on my face. I continue to play with the throttle and listen to the engine. It sounds like there's life, but the patient is not doing so well.

After long days of trying to tune the engine and checking, I discover that engine oil is going into the cooling system. Could this be the reason the car was abandoned? There is no alternative but to disassemble the engine as well.

Without a lot of knowledge, I disassemble the engine and all the surrounding components. With dirty mechanic hands, a laptop, an original copy of the car manual, and a great deal of free time, I replace the head gasket and renovate the engine head.

This is how another month of hard work goes by, over the course of which I wanted to trash the project more times than I wanted to continue working on it.

Finally, I connect everything, and the engine starts with the first try. It sounds precise and reacts to every slight touch on the throttle. The engine is connected to the chassis and the wheels but it's impossible to drive anywhere because the truck's body, seats, steering wheel and brakes are not on yet. This doesn't prevent me from starting the engine every morning when I get into the workshop. I sit on a chair in front of half a car, drink my coffee, and listen to it run.

Next, I bring the body of the truck back from the painter. I connect it to the chassis and start the assembly, which includes restoring the electrical system and the interior of the car. That's it. I'm in the final stretch of the project.

On one of the visits to my parents' house, it's waiting for me on the table. The response from the review board. I go into my old room, open the letter, and sit down on my childhood bed.

Evaluation of disability – re-examination

I hereby inform you that in its meeting on the 24.12.2015, the medical review board has determined there is no change in your mental state and your disability has been permanently determined.

The degree of disability remains therefore at 20%. The disability shall remain in effect as permanent.

I can't believe it. I read the letter again and again. "Your disability has been permanently determined." Permanently is forever? Could it be that this review board nightmare is over? "The disability shall remain in effect as permanent." What is "permanent"? Is there someone in the world who could cancel or re-open the case? It seems to me that permanent is forever, no more review boards, no more trying to convince them that I'm fucked up.

I lie back on the bed, close my eyes, and take a deep and relaxing breath. For the first time in years, I feel true relief. A huge stone I've struggled to carry with me everywhere has vanished in one moment of reading those words.

My sessions with Gideon, after the review board's decision, are held in the spirit of summarizing the last four years. We recall the insights regarding the environment that I grew up in, the shadow of repressed and unspoken post-trauma. We talk about coping with the understanding that I grew up to be someone I hated so much, and my constant struggle to gain control of every situation.

I tell Gideon that the entire process I went through with the Disabled Veterans Department led me to search for a specific event as the trigger for the post-traumatic stress. Somehow everything turned out to be about Stern and I no longer know what preceded what — the nightmares about Stern's injury or my search for a specific cause of the PTSD.

Gideon asks, "Have you gathered the courage to read your notebooks yet? It could help you very much and I'm certain you'll find things in there you don't remember accurately." I stare at him for a few seconds until I finally manage to string a few words together, "I haven't read them." Gideon is silent.

"What do I do about the nightmares?" I ask him with half a smile in an attempt to lighten our last session, which is about to end. I've asked this question many times over the course of therapy.

"I suggest that you start befriending them," Gideon replies. "Turn them from nightmares into familiar events so you don't need to fear them. Don't give them the power of something that ruins your life.

The worst that could happen is you wake up for a few minutes and perhaps you'll be tired the next day. That's not so bad. If you can succeed in relating to them like that, some of them will disappear."

"Is there any reserve service coming up?" Gideon asks in an attempt to understand whether or not I'm experiencing additional triggers. "There's nothing on the horizon. Lately, I think perhaps it's time to end my duty in the reserve service," I confess to him for the first time.

"And how do you feel about it?"

"I'm coming to terms with the decision. I'm already able to admit to myself that I don't want to serve in the military. I feel I've done enough after four years in the regular army and ten years in the reserve service." Gideon seems a little surprised by my revelation. "And how is the Ginzburg family going to take this?" he asks.

I try to imagine the reaction of my parents, my brother and sister, Yuval, and uncle Yossi. "My parents will understand, Efrat will be glad, Yossi will be surprised, Ofer won't respond, and Yuval will think I'm just a cry-baby and probably won't say anything," I reply with a smile.

Gideon continues after me with humor, "It seems to me that Ofer will be glad that finally someone is joining his forces as a draft dodger."

And so, four years of sessions with Gideon come to an end. I'm at peace with the end of therapy and hold on to the knowledge that, with the permanent disability approved, I can always ask for more help if needed.

◆ ◆ ◆

The truck project is also nearing its end. The interior is ready, and once I receive the missing brake hose, I will be able to take it on its first drive. Until then, I have time to finish all the little details that will make this project perfect: new emblems ordered from Colombia and Indonesia, original rubber bands for the bed's doors that arrived from France, and light deflectors for the sides I located by miracle in Norway.

Adhering the emblems on the side of the truck takes half a day. This includes measuring and preparing a template that ensures that they'll be straight and in the same location as the original.

Finally, the brake hose arrives, and I install it. I clear all the work tools from around the car and prepare it for the first drive. I sit in the driver's seat, put the key into the switch, and turn it gently. The control lights turn on. Another quarter of a turn and the engine starts immediately. I let the engine run and wait for the temperature gauge to go up a little to signal that the truck is ready to work.

Clutch, first gear, a pat on the gas pedal, and a slow release of the clutch until the truck begins to roll toward the exit of the workshop. I increase the speed a little, then rush to push the brakes, making sure everything's fine. A few meters forward, and then a few meters backwards. I'm impressed the brakes are in working order.

The truck is ready to continue the drive on the path exiting to the street. The drive is slow and I have no confidence. I accelerate, then brake, just to be certain that everything's fine. Next, I check the lights, the signaling, steering, and the front wheel drive. It seems like everything is working smoothly.

From the village's little roads, I go out into the fields. There are no parked cars here and no pedestrians. In the fields I allow myself to press on the throttle a little more to check the performance of this old machine that's just received a new life.

Green fields, open windows, the noise of the engine in the background, a trail of dust in the mirror — just me and my new-old truck. In one moment all my insecurity is replaced with a huge smile that spreads throughout my body and extracts a promise from me in the presence of the truck. "I'm going to go on a long trip across the country."

◆ ◆ ◆

After finishing the truck I sold my other car. Later on, I packed up the house in the village and moved with the truck to Tel Aviv. Shortly after moving, I informed Lavie I would not be returning to reserve service. Then, I set off on my journey.

TRAVEL LOG: EILAT MOUNTAINS

Ten years of coping. Even after the permanent recognition and the exemption from reserve service, I'm still stuck deeply in my post-traumatic stress.

Is it even possible to overcome? Will I wake up one morning and it'll just be gone? And if it does disappear, will I still need the Disabled Veteran benefits? I can already see the letter, "It is evident there has been great improvement in your condition, no longer requiring the 20%."

And if there's no recognition, why should others serve in the reserve service and not me? And what about the one out there? Will he take advantage of the situation and come visit me again? I'll be exposed and unprotected, just like ten years ago. And then I'll have to stand in front of the review board members and convince them that something's wrong with me again and that the improvement was temporary. The fact is, my PTSD is here to stay.

Before I close the computer, I scroll to the beginning of the document to look at the empty page that waits for text from the notebooks. I left the hardest part for the end. I lift my eyes from the screen, look around me at the desert landscape, and try to let it all go.

In order to empower the moment and my connection to the desert, I decide to continue the day naked. I get into the truck, turn on the music, and put on the seat belt. The belt feels like it's taking away my freedom and I immediately take it off again. I release the clutch and continue with the trip.

The view never ceases to amaze me. I experience the desert in a way I never have before. I stop, just for a second, to take a bottle of cold water out of the fridge. I open the bottle and take a big gulp. A drop drizzles from the edge of the spout and I let it drip onto my naked body.

The path I've been driving heads toward a cliff above the valley. I stop for a moment, turn off the engine, and light up a cigarette with the entire desert spreading out in front of me. I sit on the front black bumper, and enjoy the feeling of the hot iron on my bare ass.

I get back into the driver's seat, start the engine, and shift into the lower gear in the transfer case. A steep slope is in front of me. The truck leaps forward quickly, then immediately goes back to a slow crawl toward the deep holes left by the heavy rains. The right wheel goes up in the air.

Instantly after that, the weight of the vehicle moves to the right and the wheel returns to the ground. Slow speed, a little momentum, and the truck rolls itself up without any effort. The truck advances toward the large step of rock. The front wheels go up easily. A slight fluttering of the rear section and the steep gradation is behind us. I stop the truck at the top of the cliff and step out to look at the impressive drainage basin of the valley.

I get dressed and drive toward the main road that takes me all the way to Eilat, the southern city in Israel, sharing a border with Jordan and Egypt. The red mountains of Eilat can be seen in the distance, and in between them, yellow peaks. The Red Sea is in the background. In a few moments, I'll check in to the hotel for the last three nights of my trip, a minimal compensation from the Disabled Veterans Department.

I enter the hotel's underground parking and go up to get the keys for the room. After a short time organizing the room I go downstairs for lunch. At the entrance to the dining room I'm hit by a wall of noise, people pushing, and chaos.

In the line for plates there's a guy yelling into his mobile phone. On the way to the table I bump into children throwing food everywhere and mothers yelling at them to stop. How sharp, this transition from the serenity of my trip to the commotion at the hotel. How can people live like this? The situation makes me long for a quiet meal on the camping chair next to my blue truck.

I head back up to the room and throw myself on the couch. My attempt to recover from the meal is interrupted by a message from Noya. "I'm still thinking about the notebooks in the truck," she writes.

I don't know how to respond. The notebooks are closed in the backpack right next to me, like they have been during the entire journey. I don't have the courage to pull them out now either.

"I've thought about it a lot too, but haven't done anything about it, you can probably imagine," I respond. "I was thinking all day yesterday that we should meet to talk about it." Noya answers with a slightly dazzled and frightened emoji.

"I'll be in Eilat until Friday and after that I'm flying to Barcelona. I don't know when we'll have time to meet," I write, but deep inside I hope Noya will make a suggestion I won't be able to refuse.

"So, that's the thing, I just received a promotional email at work with flight offers to Eilat. Are you returning straight to Tel Aviv on Friday?" Noya writes.

"Straight to Tel Aviv," I respond. "How about I fly over to you after work and in the morning we'll drive back together in the truck? You still owe me a ride, and I think that the drive from Eilat to Tel Aviv can make up for it."

"You're more than welcome. And don't you dare come without Shushu," I reply immediately knowing that if I think about it too much, I'll realize it's a big mistake.

In the middle of the night I wake myself up shouting. I feel like I've been shouting for several hours. This is so exhausting. How is it that I have nightmares here too?

I freeze in place and begin to recall the nightmare. I remember there was a battle and I hit someone on the head. We were throwing scrap metal at each other. Each time I was sure he was dead, he came back again and again. I failed in my attempts to kill him and woke up feeling like I can't be alone anymore. I've had enough and I want to go home.

I notice I left the sliding door that divides the room open a crack. I have no idea what's hiding behind that door. I struggle to find the light switch next to the bed, still half asleep, and think someone is hiding it from me. Is that what's happening to me?

It's clear that it's all in my head, but I continue being frightened as if it's real. Maybe he's behind the door waiting for me to fall back to sleep. Even now, being aware of the fears and dreams, a crack in the door is enough to totally undermine me. I have to look at the crack the whole time. I mustn't break eye contact for even one moment. Why did I close the curtains? Now when the sun comes up no light will enter the room. Eventually, I fall asleep again.

When I wake up, one ray of sunshine manages to penetrate the room. I feel safer, but concerned that I had a nightmare in a place that's supposed to be comfortable and sterile.

♦ ♦ ♦

Noya texts me that she'll be landing in Eilat at nine in the evening. After dinner I go to pick her up. I park in the taxi area at the exit from the airport waiting for her. The passengers start coming out and I immediately recognize Noya in her usual clothing. With her, the suitcase that will help us smuggle Shushu into the hotel. Shushu recognizes me from a distance and starts pulling on her leash. Noya releases the leash and Shushu runs to get a hug and kiss from me.

I notice all the changes in Shushu immediately. Her eyebrows have completely turned gray and she's gained a few good kilos. This is what it's like when there's no one to take her out on runs. I stand up, all covered with Shushu's kisses, and kiss Noya on the lips.

We get into the truck and drive back to the hotel. "How do you feel about a good bottle of wine?" I ask. Noya responds, "Have I ever said no to you?" We both smile and I stop at a supermarket. Noya gets out of the car and goes inside. Shushu stands close to the window following her with a worried look.

"Tiny," I say toward Shushu with a silly voice. Shushu immediately forgets that Noya left, jumps into my lap, and licks my face.

We arrive at the hotel. I stop around the corner and Noya gets out of the truck with Shushu. No dogs are allowed in the hotel, so we've decided to smuggle her in. Noya takes Shushu for a little stroll to do her business before she's closed off in the room with us until tomorrow.

I put Shushu inside the empty suitcase, pat her head and close the zipper. Shushu looks at us with a weird expression, but doesn't seem to be bothered by what is happening. This is the best dog in the world.

I go down to the underground parking lot with the truck, enter the lobby of the hotel, and walk toward the entrance from the adjacent shopping mall. From a distance I see Noya approaching the guard with big sunglasses on her head and the trolley with Shushu inside rolling behind her. Noya smiles at the guard and he smiles back, oblivious to the smuggling operation taking place right in front of him. We're in.

I approach Noya, hug her, and we step into the elevator together. Inside I open the zipper a little and Shushu sticks her head out of the trolley. "Just a little more, Tiny," I soothe her with a loving father's pat. I close the zipper again and we exit the elevator to rush to the room at the end of the corridor.

We enter the room, close the door behind us and smile the silly smiles of two kids who just pulled off a prank. We take Shushu out of the trolley and Noya hugs her tightly. Shushu doesn't stop licking Noya and wagging her tail.

I open the bottle of wine and we step out to smoke a cigarette on the balcony. Shushu sniffs the room in every direction attempting to understand where she is. Then she signals to Noya that she wants to sit on her. Noya brings her knees together, the tiny dog jumps onto her, and lies down comfortably.

Noya and I fill in the gaps of the past few months. We quickly finish the first bottle of wine and I go into the room to open the second. Noya follows me in and suddenly asks, "Mami, where are the notebooks?"

What directness. "In the black backpack," I reply with indifference, a little smile, and a look at the floor. Through the corner of my eye I see Noya approaching the bag. I keep silent. These notebooks represent my fears, but just like everything in my entire relationship with Noya, I manage to deal with it with an inexplicable ease.

Noya takes out the plastic bag with the notebooks and returns to the balcony. I freeze in the kitchen with the cork in one hand and the corkscrew in the other. I start running scenarios in my head.

What is she doing out there? Could it be that she decided to read them? Maybe the best solution is to get rid of them and that's it. She can throw them out the window, into the garden, and no one will ever know who they belonged to. And what do I do if I find Noya reading the first notebook? Sit to the side and watch? No way.

I toss the cork and the corkscrew, grab the bottle of wine, and quickly walk toward the balcony. At the exit to the balcony I stop for a second and see Noya with a cigarette in her hand, sitting on the chair with her legs on the lower bar of the rail. Shushu lies on Noya's legs, looking like she's about to fall asleep. The plastic bag with the notebooks is closed on the round table. I breathe in relief, walk out, and pour wine into the glasses, trying to ignore the elephant on the balcony.

◆ ◆ ◆

We continue to talk and drink as if nothing happened. At some point Noya goes to the bathroom and Shushu follows her. I remain alone with the notebooks and the red plastic bag that I've been carrying with me for ten years now. I light up another cigarette and take a big sip of wine, staring at the notebooks and struggling with myself.

"It's just a fucking notebook... that you wrote... get it out of the bag already and read what's written in there," the voice of the hero says.

"What do you need this for? You know what happened there and you don't need to relive the same experiences again. Once was enough. Whatever you remember, you remember. What you don't, is probably not that important," the other side of my mind says.

I hear Noya flush the toilet and Shushu pacing on the parquet inside. Shushu comes onto the balcony and hops into my lap. Noya sits down next to me smiling, not saying a word. I pass Shushu over to her and go to the bathroom.

The voices in my head continue to battle. They remind me of little wars that took place in my mind when I wanted to pick up a girl and didn't have the guts to make the first move. I go to the toilet, lift the seat up and start to pee. Thoughts about those damn notebooks don't stop. And then, from outside, I hear Noya's voice:

> Before the war I knew nothing, I saw nothing, I understood nothing, and I was excited... excited by everything. Over the course of our Maccabim tour, the war broke out. It started with the kidnapping of Gilad Shalit in Gaza. We believed we'd be deployed in the southern region. It continued with the kidnapping of two soldiers on the northern border, and then we knew we'd be heading north. The Israeli government decided to respond harshly. Air-raids on Southern Lebanon and Beirut had begun.

At first it sounds to me like Noya is reading an article about the Lebanon War to try and encourage me to open the notebooks. My naive optimism is always the first instinct. Noya continues to read decisively:

> When I read that the IDF attacked Hezbollah neighborhoods in Beirut, I couldn't believe it. After that, they attacked by sea too. I remember a weekend at Shira's (Nelson), when they announced a navy ship had been hit. Her brother was a naval officer and he didn't know the fate of his soldier who was aboard. The next day they announced that a special unit was exposed during a night activity. Shira's sister began to cry because her boyfriend was taking part in this action and we didn't know his status. Everyone's worried, everyone has friends in the war, everyone knows someone. Hezbollah is flooding the north with 300 rockets a day. There are fatalities, casualties, and a great deal of damage. The north is being abandoned, the streets are empty, the orchards are void of farmers.

Did I write this? I sit on the toilet cover and listen to Noya, who's standing on the other side of the door.

2006: THE WAR

One day I went searching for a soldier who defected. On the way, I stopped to visit my cousin at his office in Haifa (north of Israel). He showed me the abandoned parking lot outside his window and said that on a normal day there isn't even one vacant parking space. A few days later a rocket fell into the middle of that parking lot and shattered all the windows in his office.

When I returned to the battalion after my visit to Haifa, we began preparing the tanks and soldiers to enter Lebanon. The teams underwent final readiness lessons for combat — lessons on how the enemy, Hezbollah, fights. We tried to get any information available to us in order to understand what would happen and what wouldn't. Dos and don'ts.

On Wednesday, August 2nd 2006, we were replaced in Maccabim by a reserve battalion who'd received an emergency mobilization order. From Maccabim we went up to the mother base in the Golan Heights to get organized. On Thursday and Friday we were working around the clock, checking our equipment, tanks, and doing final inspections.

Noya continues to read. I sit slouched in the hotel's bathroom, leaning my head on my arm and listening.

On Saturday, August 5, 2006, we received a mission to enter Lebanese territory in the area of Manara. This is a direct entry into the Saluki valley, which is known to be filled with explosive charges. It's a very dangerous and difficult operation that guarantees casualties and wounded.

The operational preparations were hasty. The soldiers and the tanks still hadn't arrived at the entry point, but the command center was pressuring us to go in and help the units that were already in battle.

Avner, the company commander, and I went on patrol and observations of the area. I sat in the car with Avner and many maps. Great uncertainty was in the air. The only things we managed to say were jokes about it being a suicide mission, and how we were the ones to get it. I couldn't stop thinking about the fact that I might not see Shira again and in one moment I realized I love her. I called right away and told her that tonight things are heating up. A second before the end of the conversation I muttered, "I love you." She didn't respond and we ended the call. A few seconds later she called back and told me she loved me too.

I returned to the car smiling and tried not to tell Avner. We had a special bond, Avner and I, but I wanted to save the subject for critical moments.

Later in the evening, the tank transporters arrived loaded with the company's tanks. In a complete mess, we unloaded tens of tanks from the transporters and stationed them in some random order to the side of the road.

Eventually the operation in Saluki was postponed and instead, Avner and Roman entered Lebanese territory with their tanks for a short patrol.

While Avner and Roman were touring the Lebanese side of the fence, I fell asleep in the car with the radio on. The car stood on the side of the Northern Route and every once in a while a tank went by making it shake. I hadn't slept for several days and nothing disturbed me. I lifted my head for a moment, made sure

I wasn't being run over, and immediately went back to sleep. Two hours later, Avner joined me in the car. I mumbled a few questions, asking how it went, and we both fell asleep in the front seats.

Early in the morning, we received a new order to move the tanks to different gathering grounds.

Noya stops reading for a moment. The memories from that evening flood me so intensely that tears start rolling down my cheeks. This is the third time I'm crying in my adult life.

"The first day, August 6, 2006," Noya continues to read from the notebook, word for word, with the bathroom door separating us.

On Sunday night they moved the battalion to the new improvised gathering ground — not a protected area, just a random access route to a nearby orchard. There, we were closer to the border fence. The access route was blocked by a large iron gate, which I broke through with the tank's rammer. The rammer is a kind of steel lump that was installed as an extra front bumper on my tank. I insisted on installing it before the war knowing that at some point it would be useful.

At first, we were very careful and tried to not destroy the roads and infrastructures in the area. At one point, we saw a long line of armored vehicles that drove freely on the road, leaving scorched asphalt behind them. At that moment we still didn't understand that this is a war and not another operation that would end soon with things going back to normal.

On the evening of Sunday night, the ordnance officer and I unloaded all the battalion tanks and placed them in the right order for our first mission. But then they asked us to set the opposite order and we had to move all the tanks into the new setup. Reversing 36 tanks on a road the width of two cars with a safety rail on each side isn't an easy task.

The second day, August 7, 2006, 2 am.
In half an hour we'll be entering Lebanon. The battalion commander shines a headlamp on a map spread over the hood of a car. The company commanders surround him, receiving their assignments. I shove in to get information about the mission. The Golani brigade commander, who's in charge of our battalion, urges us to go in as quickly as possible. We have quite a long operation ahead of us in an unfamiliar territory. "We have to start moving!" The battalion commander shouts and asks me to rearrange the battalion's tanks, again.

I get in the tank, drive toward the Northern Route and execute a pivot — a turn in place that makes a great deal of noise, gas smell, and sparks that come up from the tracks scorching the road. I start to move between the parked tanks and the safety rail on the narrow road and receive the planned route slide from the intelligence officer. While the tank moves slowly, I stand in the commander's post and paste the overlay on a map I prepared Saturday. Fortunately, the map includes the planned route.

The tank's driver is being directed from the ground by a soldier who's nearby, I'm not even looking. Just standing at balls level[i] and arranging the operational plan book, the overlays, and my personal gear. The battalion commander continues standing outside his tank, leaning against the car, and talking on his Vered Harim.[ii]

Suddenly, a feeling that I won't be coming back from the war hits me. When I pass by the deputy battalion commander, I stop and step off to say goodbye. Many people in the

---

[i] Meaning standing high and exposed in the commander's post. Generally, you should stand as low as you can to avoid getting shot at.

[ii] IDF's encrypted mobile cell phone, used to transmit classified and sensitive information.

battalion did not get along with him, but we had a special connection. I approach the car and shout for him to bring his ass outside. We hug and I remind him that he owes me two meals at a restaurant from previous bets I won. "If we come out of this in one piece, I'm doubling my debt," he says in the dark humor that is common in these situations. I choke up a little and go back to the tank. The battalion commander also climbs up his tank. A brutal turn of the tank in place, and we begin our movement.

Complete silence on all radio systems until Grover, the operations directorate officer, breaks it and starts reading the Traveler's Prayer.[i] "May it be Your will, Lord, our God and the God of our ancestors, that You lead us toward peace, guide our footsteps toward peace, and make us reach our desired destination for life, gladness, and peace. May You rescue us from the hand of every foe, ambush along the way, and from all manner of punishments that assemble to come to earth." I never felt connected to religion, but at this stage I think it's better to play it safe.

On the internal com system of my tank there is prolonged silence. Occasionally, I correct

---

[i] A Jewish prayer for a safe journey.

Eli, the driver, with "a little right" or "a little bit to the left." We join the company commander from an infantry battalion, who's waiting at the breached border fence. He takes the lead and escorts us through the entry to Lebanon. Roman, one of my company's platoon commanders, is first in line. Behind him, Avner the company commander, followed by Stern, the battalion commander, Zohar — and I'm last in the convoy.

Every few minutes Zohar loses his way and reports on the radio, "This is 1a,[i] I've lost the tank ahead of me again." The battalion commander rushes him and responds firmly to get going already. At some point the battalion commander even turns on the tank's headlights so Zohar can identify him — a brave act by him as no one wants to mark himself a target by turning on his headlights during war. There's hardly any wind and the dust from the tanks stands still. It's very hard to identify the path. The blue of morning can be seen on the horizon, the kind you see when you walk home from a party after one of your friends was too lazy to take you all the way to your house. You walk alone, five or six in the morning, the birds

---

[i] A call sign of a non-officer, tank commander from team 'a' on the first platoon.

begin to chirp and with every step you think about the bed and blanket that are getting closer, on the way to a place that is all good. In war, daylight is your number one enemy. Driving in daylight is like asking for a disaster to happen.

We arrive at the village of Itrun in the territory of Lebanon, about two kilometers east of Bint Jbeil. There's enough light outside and there's no need to use special night vision anymore. This also means we're completely exposed. In front of me there's a little town, mostly ruined from the bombing. Here and there, there are traces of store signs in Arabic and English and a few street lamp posts that are just about to fall. Everything's hanging by a thread.

It's been decided that Avner, Roman, and Stern will cross through the village to Hill 378, a route that's considered short but dangerous. The battalion commander, Zohar and I will go to Manh'ale, a protective barrier[i] under the control of the infantry battalion.

First Contact

Avner drives first toward the protective barrier and I remain in place to cover the entrance to the village. Silence. Occasionally I can hear the screeching of Stern's tracks on the asphalt as

---

[i] A protected and hidden area, mostly by a dirt embankment.

he moves away. Suddenly a flash, a blast, another flash and two explosions. Immediately after, Avner says on the radio, "I've been shot by an anti-tank missile. I've knocked over the house they shot from."

Roman attempts to retreat and hits an electric pole. I see through my tank's sights that the electric pole has fallen on top of the turret, blocking the route behind it. Now that the route is blocked, we are forced to split the force. Avner, Roman, and Stern continue to 378 as planned. I listen to Avner's descriptions on the radio in an attempt to visualize the route. If they get hit again, I may need to go and assist them.

The battalion commander calls on the network instructing me to follow him and warning me to not miss the left turn between the houses. "Immediately after the turn, there is a booby-trapped area." says the battalion commander. I command Eli, "Driver, move forward." I lift my head to see Zohar miss the turn and continue straight. I rush to hit the radio, order him to stop, and follow the battalion commander's tank. I decide to not tell him where he was about to go.

We continue our movement toward the protective barrier — a drive through the ruined streets of the village. Crushed cars, shattered windows, and walls perforated by shells. I drive in slit mode — a steel plate protects my head from the top and I look through a small slit.

We enter the protective barrier, which is actually the backyard of two houses. Inside the barrier we meet Israeli infantry soldiers. We pass the day on our tanks carrying out basic maintenance tasks for them. We only work on tasks we can do without being exposed. A quick check is done for the track's tension and internal checks that you can perform with all the weapons loaded.

The battalion commander calls me on the radio and asks me to come to his tank. I arrive and find his team outside the tank, making coffee. The battalion commander is in the turret with half his body outside the tank. I go up on the tank, hunched, and immediately sit on top of the turret. "This is how you're sitting here, exposed?" I ask, surprised since my team has been closed off in the tank for several hours.

After we exchange experiences from the previous night, Grover, the operations directorate officer gives me my first mission. Upon first darkness, I need to open a new path from Avner's protective barrier, 378, up to the village of Aynata. Opening a path means to lead a mission with armored bulldozers. They will drive ahead of me, with the blade of the bulldozer half in the ground. This way, they'll reveal charges hidden in the soil. In the Gaza sector, I opened up old routes, but I've never created a completely new one. In order to carry out the task, I receive a team on a D-9 armored bulldozer that will drive ahead of my tank. Grover shows me the planned route on the map and marks the spots where there are probably underground charges.

I join the team that operates the bulldozer. Gigi, the platoon commander in charge of the bulldozer, was recruited to the reserve service three days ago. I find him sleeping in a parked tank and update him about the mission. Gigi informs me that he doesn't have night vision equipment and that we'll need to work with lights on. He also wants to move with his head outside the bulldozer. Wow, I've stumbled on an idiot. Where the hell do you think you are? Do you want to die? Lights on? Head out? If you drive at four and a half km/h with lights on in Lebanese territory, not a second will pass before all the anti-tank missiles in the sector are shot at you.

I arrange a night vision device for him and finish the preliminary briefing for the mission. I then join an officer from the 7th Regiment named Nadav. I know him from officers' school. "You need to go down from here to the north through the forest, a clear path that was driven on yesterday. Then you'll cross an open field, reach the main road and turn south," Nadav explains to me.

"On the road? Without a D-9 ahead of me that scrapes it?" I ask. From my experience in the Gaza sector and my theoretical knowledge of military tactics this sounds crazy.

"It's been driven on a million times. There's nothing to be afraid of. A tank from my company is going to 378. It can lead you there," Nadav replies. It reassures me a little.

"And what about you?" I ask.

"My tank has no fuel. There are another two tanks in my company that are stuck. To tell you the truth, only the platoon commander's tank is in working order."

I remember Dad's stories from war. He used to say that as an officer in command, he kept moving from one tank to another when he had mechanical issues. There was never a situation when he was the one who got stuck without a tank. It seems that Nadav has given up the fight or that he's simply afraid to go on.

Then there's Avner, who reports that he had a chance to see a missile up close after it literally went over his head at the protective barrier.

As soon as it turns dark we set out on the mission. We reach Avner's protective barrier easily.

My crying intensifies and Noya can hear me sobbing from the other side of the door. "Mami? Why don't you come out to me?" Noya asks gently.

I open the door and head straight through the living room to the balcony. I grab the pack of cigarettes and ashtray from the table and go back to the living room. Noya looks a little startled. In one hand she is holding the first notebook with her finger marking her spot. In her other hand she's holding the crumpled plastic bag with the other notebook in it.

I sit on the big couch in the center of the living room, put my legs up on the table, and take out a cigarette from the pack. Noya notices the lighter is outside and rushes to bring it to me. She sits on the other edge of the couch. I stare at the wall in front of me, not saying a word. I can tell that Noya is attempting to understand how I'm handling it. Perhaps she's waiting for a signal to confirm that she can continue.

I lie on my back and place my head in Noya's lap. Shushu, the princess, instantly realizes how troubled I am and sits on my legs. I pat her, take a deep breath into my lungs, and remember that the hard part is still ahead of us. Noya continues to read out loud.

I continue driving uphill toward Avner's 378 protective barrier. Avner and I drive to an observation lookout and locate the starting point of my mission. I begin the mission and drive behind the bulldozer that displaces the sand in front of us, creating a path wide enough for the tanks. We reach a grove and decide to cross to the south side of a nearby road. It seems that the soil over there will be easier to dig and we can advance faster. After we move to the southern side, we stop immediately. The bulldozer driver complains of back pain and says he can't go any further. Only after his platoon commander yells at him do we continue our movement.

On the north side of the road, an infantry brigade begins to move. We stop for a few minutes and wait to coordinate with the infantry forces. We need to make sure they know where we're heading. At some point we continue our movement and run into a few houses that would take a long time to demolish. This forces us to cross the road back to the north side. The northern side isn't clean either, and we need to knock over entire trees that block our path. I'm afraid the trees will fall on the walking soldiers, so I instruct the bulldozer to stop until we coordinate the movement with certainty.

I try to call on the battalion radio several times, but they couldn't get hold of the infantry forces' com frequency. I'm tired of waiting. I turn off the tank's engine and yell toward the soldiers, but they don't respond. I whistle to them with my fingers but they still don't answer. It's an endless convoy of soldiers and I'm with the tank ten meters away.

Eventually, I jump off the tank and grab a soldier with a military radio system on his back. I tell him to inform the commanders that they need to move thirty meters to the north, otherwise someone will be run over. Within a few seconds they start moving a little to the north from their original path, walking like a procession of ants. It makes me laugh to see them walking quietly so they won't be heard or identified. Guys, I just got here with a 64-ton tank, the enemy knows we're here.

We continue with our mission until we arrive at our final destination – the outskirts of Aynata.

The third day, **August 8, 2006, Stern's injury**. Avner accompanies Stern along the new path I've opened so I won't be left alone on the outskirts of the village. In the meantime, the D-9 has constructed a minimal protective barrier, an open-sided box of dirt embankments that protects us from missiles coming from the direction of Bint Jbeil and Aynata.

My new assignment is to wait for company C from our battalion. They'll pass me on their way into Aynata. They're supposed to enter the village and set up a gathering area in the school's basketball court.

Stern and I park our tanks next to each other in the small protective barrier, facing Aynata. We start a sleeping rotation in an ambush drill. Two crew members sleep in their posts and the other two secure the area and respond to calls on the radio system. I fall asleep very quickly. When I wake up, Commander Benda's tank, from company C, has already stopped behind me. Company commander M calls me on the com system to report that the Reconnaissance Company of the 7th brigade are performing a single shooting at a suspicious point. A single shot is heard. Several seconds later Alex, Stern's loader, calls me on the radio and tells me that Stern is wounded. "From what?" I ask surprised, and Alex continues to report, in complete apathy, that Stern's bleeding from his face. When I ask for his condition, Alex explains that he's hardly talking and he's bleeding profusely.

I send Aviad, the gunner and Eyal, the loader, to evacuate Stern into my tank. A paramedic from the Reconnaissance Company joins us, and as we put Stern, who weighs 120 kilograms (265 pounds), in the rear corridor of the tank, I report his condition on the battalion's radio network. The battalion commander requests that I go back toward 378, where there's a landing zone set for the evacuation helicopter.

In the meantime, inside the tank, Aviad is trying to talk to Stern and keep him awake.

The tanks of company C park behind us, in front of the protective barrier. The company commander's tank blocks my way. I can't even move one centimeter backwards. From the rear of my tank, I hear Stern moaning and screaming in pain. The paramedic yells at me that we must evacuate quickly. Aviad looks at me from below and shows me that his hands are covered in blood. This whole time I can't seem to move Benda's tank from behind me. I shout at him several times on the com to clear the way until I realize I'm yelling on the wrong frequency. He can't even hear me. I don't wait another second and I shout to Eli: "Driver, back-up quickly!" He does, and we hit Benda's tank. Benda is parked at a lower point than me and my tank's tracks manage to climb the front fenders of his tank. I drive backwards, forward, backwards, and again forward, and manage to push his tank to make enough room to maneuver. I go up the dirt embankment. Another little kick to Benda, and I'm out.

I navigate with great difficulty between the tanks of company C and begin a rapid movement to 378 while reporting Stern's condition to the battalion commander and to Avner on the radio. Despite the shouts of pain that come from the rear, I try to sound as calm as possible.

On the way to 378, company M commander calls me on the radio again and asks me to help him out with a task. I tell him that the last time he asked me for something, they shot my tank commander in the face. To this day he's never contacted me on the radio system again. At this point I already understand that Stern's been shot by friendly fire. I don't know from who or where, but it's clear to me that this is the case.

I race with the tank as I yell to Eli, the driver, that Stern is bleeding in the corridor. It appears to me that Eli has been asleep the entire time we were in the protective barrier. He didn't even know Stern was wounded in the rear corridor of our tank. It's not until we started driving that Eli woke up and asked what's going on.

The smell in the tank is horrible, the smell of burnt skin and a great deal of blood. For the first time in my life, I learn that a large amount of blood smells differently than blood oozing from a small wound.

I continue racing on the path I opened a few hours ago. At some point I deviate and can't recognize it anymore. I know the area I'm in is loaded with charges. Driving outside the path constitutes real mortal danger. While the tank races forward, I try to remember whether the path is close to the road or far from it, whether it's to the north or the south. I start to sway north and south until I recognize it from afar. "Hard left," I order Eli. Sixty-four tons of tank throws our body weight to the right and we drive fast in the open field toward the path. I raise the night vision device and recognize a piece of land that looks like it doesn't belong in front of us — a spot in the middle of the field that looks like it was dug up and covered again a few days ago.

I imagine a huge underground charge Hezbollah has inserted in the ground at that spot. I no longer have the option to escape — not to the left and not to the right. The tank is racing at a top speed of forty something km/h (24 mph). Without options, I drive over the covered hole. Time stops. I imagine how I'll hit the charge and fly straight to high heaven.

I close my eyes, pray for half a second, lower my head, and wait for the boom. In this split second I manage to think about how they'll say that the deputy company commander made a mistake navigating the path that he, himself, created just a few hours earlier.

We pass the over hole, I look back with the night vision device, and smile for a split second. I turn to look forward and continue directing the tank.

The battalion commander calls me on the radio and directs me to the landing point of the evacuation helicopter. We're racing against time, competing against the daylight that's starting to come up.

We make it to the landing area with the first rays of sunlight. We step off the tank and I open the foldable gurney with Aviad. We try to take Stern out of the rear corridor. It's not easy. Kobi, the driver from the battalion commander's crew, comes to help us. A few minutes later, Avner also joins us.

Stern lies outside on a gurney with blood-soaked bandages covering his mouth. We try to talk to him and once again, the smell of blood hits me strongly in the face. When I change his bandage, I manage to see the wound. There's no upper lip and half of the lower one is also gone. There aren't any teeth either. There's literally a hole in the middle of his face. Stern moans in pain and tries to ask what it looks like, but cannot make the words. Aviad continues to calm him down and tell him that it's not too bad.

Stern lifts his arm and signals with his finger, small circles in the air, in an attempt to ask where the helicopter is. It'll be here in a moment, we say.

Where the fuck is that helicopter?

A few minutes later the helicopter lands several meters from us. We lift Stern with the gurney as he continues gesticulating the helicopter's propeller with his finger. Six people carry the gurney, nearly falling several times. Grover and Aviad can't handle Stern's weight and keep stumbling on the large rocks. All this time Stern signals with his finger in the air. We put Stern on the helicopter and it takes off, heading back to Israel. We run back to the tanks in full daylight and drive to hide in protective barrier 378. As soon as we enter the protective barrier, we turn off the engines.

Everyone is quiet. The silence of war.

The sun comes up behind the protective barrier embankment and I cannot stop smelling Stern's blood, nor the smell of dust raised by the helicopter — a strange combination of morning dew and blood.

We take off our AFV helmets[i] without saying a word. I look to my right at Avner, who seems more frightened than ever. I still have a little smile, probably because I'm unable to digest everything.

From Avner's tank, we hear someone calling on the radio speaker asking for accompaniment to company B from Manh'ale up to Aynata. I look

---

[i] A tank crewmember helmet that connects to the tank's radio system and is soundproof.

at Avner and keep silent. He looks back at me.
"Suicide mission number 2," I say to him.
"You go. You know the way. Bring them here, and from here I'll take them to Aynata," Avner says.
After Stern was wounded, I left Eyal, my loader, to command Stern's tank and I was one team member short. "I'm missing a loader. I'm going up to take Alex from Stern's team," I say. Alex takes his gear and moves to my crew.
I can't get my mind off the fact that they're sending me on this escort mission in full daylight. I barely beat the dawn to get where I am now. I start driving down from the protective barrier in the road toward Manh'ale. I take a left at the gas station and hit a street sign that stands in my way. Smoke bombs from our artillery corps are coming down everywhere in an attempt to protect me. Out of the thick smoke I recognize the battalion commander's tank. How could I miss it? I'm in a slit position, hiding inside the tank, and he has half his body outside, balls level. It makes me feel like he's in control.
I join Friedman, the commander of company B. The battalion commander rushes me on the radio, "Deputy, come on, you're holding everyone up." We start heading back up to 378. I call Avner to let him know that from

here on, he takes the lead. I look ahead in the direction of the barrier and see that one of the armored vehicles is stuck at the exit, blocking the passage. Avner can't get out. I instantly make the decision that I'm escorting them the entire way. I continue moving to 378 and tell Avner that I will continue the escort all the way to Aynata.

"Negative. Stop where you are and let everyone overtake you. I promised some blonde girl I'm bringing you back in one piece," Avner says on the company's radio.

Before the war, people always said that I have the face of someone who stays alive. As for Avner's face, how shall I put it mildly? They foretold a slightly different future. I stop on the side and let everyone overtake me. On the battalion radio system I hear the commander asking why we've stopped. Avner replies that he'll be taking the lead from here. When the battalion commander asks why, Avner answers, "Because I promised Nelson." Despite the intense pressure on the battalion at that moment, Avner's words seem logical to the battalion commander and he says nothing. It's a little weird when the entire battalion knows your girlfriend because she was the observation officer in the previous tour.

I watch the tanks of company B pass by me in the direction of Aynata before I return to the 378 protective barrier with the hope that I'll be able to rest a little. I'm exhausted and haven't slept for more than an hour straight in the last five days. The tank stops and again everyone is silent.

Not five minutes passes before I hear on the radio about a D-9 that was hit. As it turns out, the D-9 with Gigi, who opened the path with me during the night, was hit by an anti-tank missile. Gigi was evacuated from the bulldozer to a tank, and the bulldozer's driver had to run after the bulldozer, which kept on rolling down the street without a driver. Grover also joined in the pursuit because he thought someone was still in the bulldozer.

Heavy fire opened on them as they both ran through the middle of the village after it. Grover caught up to the driver and asked him if there was anyone else inside. The driver said no. It's still hard for everyone to understand that we are at war and the rules have changed. It's better to let the bulldozer hit something than to die. They were directed to hide in a house under the control of the IDF just to the left of them. Grover ran and opened the door while shouting, "IDF, IDF," so they wouldn't get shot at. In front of him, in the middle of the room, stood a huge anti-tank missile launcher belonging to Hezbollah. It was the wrong house. Grover continued to run to the neighboring house and placed the driver in a safe place.

Next, I was informed on the radio network that I need to take Gigi, who's been wounded back to Manh'ale. Again, I find myself hopping between the protective barriers, in full daylight, this time without the cover of smoke that was promised.

We arrive at Manh'ale and I see the deputy battalion commander for the first time since we entered Lebanon. It makes me really happy. Even Eran, who led the battalion rescue unit, and Zuckerman, the deputy company commander C, are here. We're good friends and it reassures me to be in the protective barrier with them.

I still smell Stern's blood. It doesn't leave me alone. At some point, I realize what I'm smelling is the dust mixed with the humidity and dew of a Lebanese morning that reminds me of that moment.

I remember writing a paper about Dad's experience in the Yom Kippur War. I recall what he told me about the soldiers during the war — how hard it is for them, much more than for us, the commanders. While we occupy ourselves with many distractions, they're left with thoughts about what they've seen. I'm thinking about Aviad, my gunner, who evacuated Stern with all the blood and his blown-up face. I continue to occupy myself with the navigation, the three radio networks, and the problems of the entire company. Meanwhile, he goes into the tank to cope with himself and what he's seen. I don't have time to digest it, and he has too much time to think about it.

When the deputy battalion commander sees me, he forces me to go sleep in a nearby house. "You look terrible," he says. I enter the structure where I find many soldiers, and fall asleep in the hallway without taking off my vest or flak jacket. I actually like leaning against a wall with the flak jacket for rest. It gives good support and the shoulder straps rise up so you can rest your head on them like inflatable neck-pillows for flights.

After about half an hour, the deputy battalion commander wakes me up. Looking at his face I immediately imagine that everyone has died. He tells me what Avner's team went through, and I realize that from now on, I'm in command of the company. I get angry at myself for going to sleep, that I wasn't there for him. He took the mission upon himself and didn't let me go because he promised Shira.

Avner's battle

After Avner took the lead and guided the forces to Aynata, he stopped at Benda's protective barrier in the school's basketball court. Avner heard a report on the radio about one casualty and one severely wounded from the paratroopers' company. They were under heavy fire and no one succeeded in getting them to a safe point where the helicopter could land. The rescue unit couldn't send forces because of the heavy fire, so Avner volunteered. He drove alone inside Bint Jbeil without a map of the area. He only had the direction of a UAV[i] watching him from above. Avner's team quickly pulled the dead body, the wounded, and the doctor into his tank and began moving toward the extraction point. Avner's team managed to make it to the landing point and transferred the injured into the helicopter. Everything got complicated from there. On the way back, the tank was hit by a mortar bomb on the turret and the radio system was incapacitated. Avner could no longer hear the directions of the battalion or the UAV and didn't know how to return to the protective barrier. Avner continued to shout on the radio, "Battalion Commander from

[i] Unmanned Aerial Vehicle.

Avner, Battalion Commander from Avner,"
but he wasn't able to hear the battalion
commander answering him the whole time.

With a great deal of resourcefulness, the
loader pulled out the emergency wire system,
which serves as an alternate antenna, and the
radio resumed working. Avner continued to
search for the way out, but while driving
through the village two more missiles hit the
tank. One of them penetrated the shielding to
the left of the loader's post. It grazed the
loader's main artery and spread shrapnel that
injured the entire team. The loader was
critically injured and lost a lot of blood. Avner
was wounded by shrapnel in his neck and face,
and the gunner got shrapnel all over his left
side. This time the internal radio system was
harmed and the team couldn't even
communicate between themselves.

The driver continued driving without
direction in the streets of Bint Jbeil in order to
make another missile impact more difficult.
After the war the driver told me that before the
start of the mission Avner told him, "If we're
hit and you can't hear me, you have to continue
driving." From the intensity of the blast, Avner
saw shadows and spots that made him think
terrorists were getting on his tank. He took his
rifle and began shooting everywhere.

Benda, the commander of company C, heard the yelling on the radio and left to search for Avner. Benda drove alone in the streets of Bint Jbeil, crisscrossing the village while shooting in every direction, until he saw Avner's tank. He drove up to the tank, pulled the entire team out, and loaded them onto the turret while they held onto everything possible. The team was transferred to a helicopter that evacuated them to the hospital. Avner's tank remained standing in the middle of the village until the end of the war.

The fourth day, August 9, 2006

Toward the morning we start making our way out of Lebanon for the first time. I really need it. Back on Israeli soil everyone is waiting for us. We start working vigorously on the tanks. Our troops, who have just finished four days of combat, don't take even one minute to rest before beginning the tanks' maintenance routine. We load the tanks with ammunition, food, and drink, and get ready to go back into Lebanon that very same night. At some point I force everyone to freshen up and rest.

I meet Amit Perry for the first time. Perry, a former officer in the battalion, was taking time off to finish his bachelor's degree when he got the call up to replace Avner. We instantly click.

I'm afraid to go back in. I want so much for someone to postpone the entry — and then it happens. They postpone the re-entry by a day. The new assignment we get is to open a path to the Shaqif A-Nimmel ridge, the northernmost point in the sector tanks are planned to reach. Before Perry presents me the new assignment he starts laughing. "You're not going to believe what I'm about to describe to you," he says with his childish smile. I open Perry's operational plan book and attempt to copy the arrows drawn on his map showing our mission. What a mess. Perry explains it to me briefly. When I start drawing the arrows on my map, I discover that the place we're supposed to reach is not even on the map I'm holding.

The fifth day, August 10, 2006

I wake up at 11:00 after a long sleep in the rear corridor of the tank. In the afternoon a group of people arrive from a well-known restaurant in the area. They light up a huge grill and make hamburgers for us. After that, we go into our briefing with Perry, the new company commander. To celebrate the end of the briefing, I shove another hamburger in my mouth — who knows when the next time I'll get a chance to eat a fatty and juicy burger will be?

Before we set off, I call Shira. A brief conversation follows with clear and sharp messages, so if something happens, we will remember the things said in our last conversation.

That's it. This time it's happening. We start our movement at first dark. The order of tanks in the convoy is: Kidron, Heiman, Klein, Golan, and Perry. Almost all of them are crossing the border for the first time. I'm the experienced one, so my task is to lead the convoy together with Roman and his tank. We arrive safely at the basketball court of the Aynata school. We stay there for the rest of the night.

Toward morning, Perry shows me where company B is supposed to be and where we'll be passing through — a path crossing valleys, mountains, and villages. I barely manage to copy the arrows on my old, out-of-date map.

The first entry into the urban area of Bint Jbeil was exciting. I heard so much about it on the news before we joined the war. It feels so weird to drive a tank inside a city. I cannot stop thinking about how people lived here until a few days ago. Around me are a grocery store, a playground, and an old market. Earlier this morning, a herd of sheep came to us accompanied by dogs guiding them. Even the war doesn't ruin their routine.

Like every day, I speak with the tank commanders on the radio, asking them about the condition of their teams, the diesel level, ammunition, mechanical issues, food and water.

My team
On most days we eat one meal. During the night we're in movement. After that, in the morning we sleep a little. Then we eat two pieces of bread with tuna, corn, and ketchup. We're all unshaven. I brush my teeth almost every day and even floss. I call it the "string of sanity."
Alex, the loader, cleans the machine guns and cares for the preparedness of the tank at every stop. Eli, the driver, arranges the equipment and performs checks on the tank's tracks. I met Alex and Eli for the first time when I was a platoon commander in their boot camp. They were new recruits in my platoon and until the end of the tour I couldn't tell them apart. I would call Eli, Alex and vice versa. They'd correct me and a second later I'd get confused again. They're both Russian, tall, and blonde. Only one of them wears glasses, but I could never remember which. It's been two years since their basic training and today I know both of them well.

Eli, the driver, is the one with the glasses, and he's a brilliant guy. In the company, people didn't think that he was a skilled tank driver, but during the war I discovered he was one of the best. The truth is he's awesome. He's independent and gives me a sense of peace in the command post.

Alex, the loader is a strong and thorough machine. He's a classic loader with a great deal of strength who never complains. He works with indifference, but never stops. It's easy for me to command people who were soldiers of mine in the past. They already appreciate me, and I don't have to prove myself. Alex and Eli are used to having me as their superior, so it's hard for them to regard me as a friend as well.

Aviad, the gunner, doesn't look well. After I update the team about the assignment for tonight, Aviad asks me to dismiss him from the combat zone and return to Israel. "I want to go home and never come back here again," he says, and the tears start rolling down his dusty cheeks. "I'm sorry for letting you down, but I'm scared and I don't want to die," Aviad continues in a choked voice. Stern's evacuation has clearly affected him to a great extent.

I respond decisively that I need him and I can't do it without him. We're all having a shitty time and it's hard on everyone. I tell him that I, too, want to go back to Nelson, once again exploiting the fact that I have something in common with him. I tell Aviad that there is no other soldier in the company I can trust the way I trust him and that's the reason he's in the deputy crew and not with one of the tank commanders.

"You know better than anyone else in the company how many things I'm dealing with during combat. You're the only one who can command the team while I command the rest of the company," I try to engage Aviad back into the assignment. I promise that I'll bring him out in one piece. He doesn't seem convinced, but he understands there's no choice.

Aviad is someone you can count on. He's nearly a commander and before we entered Lebanon, he managed the team while they prepared the tank for combat. Even after Stern's injury, he didn't hesitate for a moment and managed the operation inside the tank while I coordinated the arrival of the evacuation helicopter.

Aviad is quite a talker. He's the most talkative person I know, and each story of his starts with one topic and sails to places that are completely unrelated. But from the moment we entered Lebanon, something changed in him and he's stopped talking — complete silence up to the moment we came back to Israel. Only orders and reports.

The sixth day, August 11, 2006

We are about to start our new mission to open a path from Aynata to the Shaqif A-Nimmel ridge. Perry and I deliver a brief to the platoon commanders, and they copy the information to their operational book before instructing their teams.

We begin moving to the valley north of Bint Jbeil and Aynata. It's completely dark and I'm not the leading tank. I have no clue where we're going or if the first tank is even heading in the right direction. Over the course of the drive the Laser Warning System[i] doesn't stop beeping, showing indications from every direction. The alarm breaks into the internal radio connected to the headset. Most indications received are incorrect and come from one of our nearby tanks that's preparing to fire. Most tank commanders elect to turn off the system. It's really disturbing to hear these beeps in the helmet all the time when the radio network is busy with people talking.

I choose to keep it on. It's a reminder for me to put my head down and keep my profile low

---

[i] Sensors that trigger an alarm when someone measure a distance using a laser beam as a preparation to shoot at you.

in my post. As a deputy company commander, I listen to three radio networks simultaneously: terrible noise, incessant talking, and on top of it all, alarms from the Laser Warning System. The more time passes, the more I'm able to separate the beeping of the device in order to successfully understand what is being said over the radio.

The leading tank of Kidron, the platoon commander, continues scouting for the right route. We drive on a narrow road that reminds me of an enchanting European village. We drive a steep and narrow descent on a rural road not even the width of a tank. I need to decide whether to destroy the terrace on my left or the house fence on my right. Above the terrace on the left there's a tree grove, and beyond the fence on the right there's a drop of a few meters into the backyards of houses on the parallel street.

A slight steer to the left and the tank scrapes the stone terrace, a little steer to the right and the lamppost falls to the side of the road. Perry's driver veers too far to the right, falls a few meters into one of the yards, and gets stuck on a dangerous slope. Perry gets off his tank and switches to another.

Once in a while we need to take a long stop to close the gaps between the tanks. The night will eventually end and fortune won't be on our side.

The full moon has already set. It's even darker and we continue without lights. We go down to the road at the bottom of the valley and look for a cross point to pass to the other bank. To the left of the road there's a drop of a few meters and we struggle to find a comfortable place to cross. The live alerts from the intelligence begin to arrive. Bad news, the anti-tank squads are on their way.

What a strange sight. A company of nine tanks driving a narrow road, looking for the right route, while around us are crushed cars, demolished houses, and cultivated agricultural areas. Perry continues moving up to the point where the path turns sharply to the right, a kind of U-turn that even a small car would have trouble executing. Each direction is a steep drop off of a few meters. If a tank was to get stuck on the turn, it would strand the company in place, exposed to enemy fire. There's no room for mistakes.

On the corner there's a European style stop sign, just like the one I had in my Playmobil kit when I was a child. When I get to the turn I warn everyone on the radio about the difficult maneuver. "Watch out. If someone throws a track[i] here, it will jam the entire movement of the battalion."

I continue my descent and turn carefully. If I throw a track now, it would be an embarrassing moment and a dangerous one.

Everyone passes through the turn safely. We continue driving along the valley looking for a crossing point. After several minutes of searching, and out of an intense desire to continue, we become less meticulous about securing ourselves from the enemy. We drive in a convoy between houses and trees. We lose eye contact with each other. Perry continues alone, and I let him know on the radio that I'm stepping off the tank to examine a descent point. It looks a little steep to me, but perhaps still possible.

I get off the tank with my AFV helmet on. I hear nothing since the helmet covers my ears with noise protection. I see flashes of bombs and missiles in the sky at a distance. This is a normal thing in war. There are always flashes in the sky. I jump off the front of the tank and take a few steps to look at the descent to the valley. It's so dark outside. There could be someone here, literally next to me in the

---

[i] When the tank's tracks break or come off. Mainly occurs from the pressure on the tracks while turning.

bushes, and I wouldn't hear him approaching because of my headset. I feel like he's already here, watching me.

I decide to take off the helmet so I can hear the noises of my surroundings. When I do, I can hear endless blasts from every direction. The flashes I saw earlier gain the sound of war. Shells, artillery, anti-tank missile fire, it all sounds so close. I immediately put the AFV helmet back on my head and tie it as tightly as possible. I prefer to remain in my helmet bubble. There, everything is much less frightening. This is just an off-road trip and we're looking for a convenient way to pass, I say to myself in an attempt to calm down.

The seventh day, August 12, 2006
Perry finds a convenient passage and the convoy continues. We cross the valley and drive on the northern bank to reach the village of At-Tiri. We drive through fields and orchards with clusters of houses around us.
Boom!
"A missile was fired at me," Perry yells on the radio. I immediately respond by firing shells at the houses the shooting came from. After a few seconds, I drive back and use the Smoke Launchers. The system launches grenades that explode in front of the tank using phosphorus, which leaves a dense wall of smoke that

significantly reduces the danger of enemy hits. The explosions happen at great distance and nearly hit Roman's tank, which just came up to the position. I didn't think they would fly so far.

We quickly get organized and carry out a coordinated firing at the first line of houses in the village. We gradually ascend to firing position, release a quick shell and go back down. Perry drives backwards and joins us without harm. In a single moment the whole village goes up in flames.

We continue driving north in the picturesque village. Again, we search for a convenient crossing spot into the next valley and again we struggle to find one. This time Perry and the battalion commander improvise a descent. The maneuverability of the tank is difficult to describe. I've driven down stone gradations several meters high with it. I've climbed steep and high terraces. As the days pass in this war, my confidence in the tank's potential grows, and with it, the confidence to take it to the limits of its capabilities.

We regroup and continue our movement according to plan.

At-Tiri

We drive next to the road that leads to At-Tiri and again we find it difficult to locate a comfortable descent to go around the village. Having no other choice, we enter the village. This is the first one that isn't destroyed and looks like people are still living in it. Cars that are not crushed are parked on the street or in a garage and the street lamps are lit.

The entrance to the village is decorated with Hezbollah flags and billboards with Nasrallah's[i] picture. The entry gate to the village is decorated with colorful lighting and in the middle of the roundabout stands a Soviet T-55 model tank with the barrel pointed at us, an old monument. Perry sounds pleased with himself for identifying the type of the tank, knowing that Hezbollah has no tanks.

The D-9 is in the lead, Perry's tank follows and I'm following them. Tactically, an incorrect order of movement caused by the conditions of the road which doesn't allow for overtaking. We enter the village. To my left a car is parked with all four turn signals flashing. Why did the owner leave their hazard signals on during a war? We cross the roundabout and continue to the center of the village on a very narrow street. In the distance, I can still identify the D-9 and Perry's tank right behind him.

Boom!

---

[i] Hassan Nasrallah the secretary-general of Hezbollah since 1992.

The D-9 goes over a charge and fire opens from every direction. Perry tries to extract to the back and another charge explodes, timed with an anti-tank missile fired from the front. I drive backwards to give them maneuvering room, while launching smoke grenades that once again surprise me with the distance they reach. Perry yells on the radio that the charge was mixed with phosphorus. It's definitely not the time to tell him that it's my fault.

Because of the intensity of the blast, a huge transformer falls from an electric pole straight onto Perry's turret, just twenty centimeters behind his head. A huge lump of steel, filled with some type of battery fluid, spills onto his tank and catches fire. It was probably the phosphorus I launched that ignited it.

I continue moving backwards firing shells, one to the left and one to the right. The tank behind me fires over my head.

While driving backwards, I feel someone touching my neck, pulling my helmet, and bending my head. The tank continues to drive slowly backwards, and I try to bend inwards to reach the box of grenades. I feel my head being pulled out of the tank and my hand being pulled away from the grenades box. In one fell swoop, I break free and fall back into the tank with a string of lights and Hezbollah flags tangled around my head. As it turns out, that string was the thing pulling my head. I was sure there was someone trying to pull me out of the tank.

I continue to fire and run over a car that stands in my way. In seconds the quiet street becomes one big bonfire, as if we're in hell. Only then do I realize that the vehicle with hazards flashing was, in fact, a car with its alarm on, I just couldn't hear the sound. That's life on mute with my helmet on. I spray that car with my machine gun just because it annoys me.

Perry evacuates the wounded from the D-9 and starts driving backwards. I clear a passage for him and continue generating fire to cover his movement. This isn't according to the book, but it's also a way.

"Aviad, can you identify a house 150 meters quarter right?" I ask.

"Identified!" Aviad responds immediately and I quickly command: "Fire!"

Boom!

"Three buildings to the left of the previous house, fire!"

Boom!

We leave the D-9 on the narrow street and evacuate the team for medical treatment at the battalion aid station. One slightly wounded and the other lost his toes. There is no way to land a helicopter here because of our remote location.

"The evacuation is not urgent," says the doctor on the radio network. On the way out I consider shooting the Soviet tank, but I let it go at the last second to fire a shell at another house that looks too intact to me.

We look for a way to bypass At-Tiri and find a crossing spot with an insane slope.

"Drive close to each other. There are soldiers here. You need to drive on the tracks of the tank ahead with as little distance as possible," someone says on the radio.

We enter the valley, which goes up to the Shaqif A-Nimmel ridge. According to the original plan we were supposed to continue up to the valley's northern edge, but the area is filled with high agricultural terraces which makes it hard to pass.

Perry orders us to stop while he and the battalion commander go up the western side of the valley with their tanks to look for a more convenient way.

It's five in the morning. Soon there will be daylight. While we wait at a hidden spot inside the valley, I hear the battalion commander shout to Perry on the radio network, "Stop, stop, stop, you're running over them!"

And then silence on the battalion radio.

A few minutes later, the call for help arrives. "Two fatalities and two wounded," the deputy battalion commander reports. He requests an urgent helicopter for extraction, but the pilot doesn't agree to land because it's already full daylight and the area is threatened.

We scatter smoke grenades at every corner in the direction of the wind in an attempt to hide in the exposed valley. We unload the wounded from At-Tiri from the tankbulance[i] and load the new wounded that Perry's tank just ran over.

Perry's and the battalion commander's tanks come back down to the valley. Perry stands in the loader's post and stares into the air, his bright and clear eyes not responding to anything. I call him, but he's unresponsive. Golan, who drove Perry's tank, passes by me carrying one of the bodies and hisses, "There's no point. He's not here right now." I head back to the deputy battalion commander and signal him "Perry's done" with my hand. Once again, I'm in command.

We load the fatalities on top of Klein's and Heiman's tanks, wrap them and tie them on the turret. One of the wounded cannot stop

---

[i] A tank that's fitted with full medical and ambulance abilities while retaining the tank armament.

shouting, but he speaks coherently. He's lying on his side with a leg twisted and completely shattered. His pelvis has popped out of place and looks as if it doesn't belong to his body. The other wounded is silent, only occasionally asking us to not show the ruined machine gun to his friend. He's unaware how badly he's injured and afraid we'll upset him further.

We place the wounded in the tankbulance with great difficulty to the sound of horrid screams of pain, the likes of which I've never heard in my life. I climb onto Perry's tank to try and talk to him again, but he doesn't respond. He keeps looking at nothing. Then he mumbles a few times, "I ran them over."

I go see Golan who drove Perry's tank and ask him if he's okay. Golan, a big, muscular guy and one of my favorite commanders in the company, instantly says that everything's fine. The following day, Golan comes to me and says when he told me everything was fine, he didn't even know the tank he drove was the one that ran over the soldiers.

We keep waiting for the helicopter, but the pilot insists that it's too dangerous to land in our location. The deputy battalion commander calls me on the radio and asks me to extract the wounded. I keep silent for a few seconds, then look into my crewmembers' eyes and see an ocean of fear. We need to go back, in full daylight, the entire way we did during the night – all the way to the basketball court where the evacuation helicopter will land.

The time is eight in the morning, and I can't find the words to explain this assignment to my team. But they understand without my words, as if I've given them a one-hour briefing detailing exactly what needs to be done.

I inform the deputy battalion commander that I'm taking three tanks with me: Heiman, Klein and Eran. We are ready to set off, and waiting for final approval.

The team is quiet. Only Aviad asks me what I intend to do and how we will come through this alive. The implications are clear: driving in the open, in urban areas, on the same path we encountered the enemy a few hours ago. It's the first time I feel like it would be better to get slightly wounded and get out of here with an extraction helicopter. I would be in a hospital for a few days and then the war would be over. The probability of a four-tank convoy making it the entire way back without harm is close to zero.

The tanks organize at the entrance to the valley and secure it. The deputy battalion commander calls me again with some happy news, "We're all going back to Bint Jbeil. You lead the movement."

We start our movement, a shell in the barrel, all weapons loaded and ready to fire. I shoot short bursts from the machine gun at every bush and suspicious spot, so no fool will even think of surprising me. The shooting gives me confidence to keep going. It makes me feel like I'm scaring the enemy – that he won't be able to generate fire.

I ask Klein, who's in the rear, to inform me about every critical point he passes so I know whether to slow down or speed up. Roman is driving behind me. We divide the sectors for security and begin to drive as fast as possible.

"This is the deputy. Each tank is responsible for the tank behind it. Don't lose eye contact. Over."

The machine gun jams. I move to shells – a shell to the house on the right and a shell to the one on the left. The shells make the ground shake. I want to see who sticks their head out the window when my tank is firing like this. We identify a large fuel truck in the distance. I put the sights on target and give the okay to fire. A moment before the shell leaves the barrel, I feel Roman's shell over me. It hits the fuel truck and lifts it several meters in the air in a huge mushroom cloud.

At this point, Klein reports crossing the access road to At-Tiri. Each time the laser warning system goes off, I shoot a shell in that direction and launch smoke grenades. While Alex loads the shells, I fire my machine gun at every possible hideout. I urge everyone on the radio to do the same. "Fire at suspicious areas," I order. From a range of 300 meters I identify a truck with missile launchers. One shell and the truck blows up to pieces. We don't stop for a moment, only slowing down occasionally to close the gaps between tanks.

"All teams, shoot at everything. Shells in all directions. Over!"

Roman's shells whistle over my tank. I can see his hits and urge Eli to put the pedal to the metal. It's the same route from last night, and only now does it become clear to me where we drove, which slopes we passed, and where they fired at us from.

A warning light from the engine comes on in Klein's tank. He has to stop to cool the engine down. We continue at moderate speed until Klein reports that he's on the move again.

I go down to the valley before the sharp turn with the stop sign and instantly the laser warning goes off. I launch another pair of smoke grenades and shoot a shell at the nearby house. I feel unstoppable. It's impossible to come near me. I am racing with 64 tons of armored fire power that never ends. The whole time I'm praying that no tank gets stuck.

"All teams, lasing[i] from the left before the descent to the valley. Every second tank, use your smoke grenades. Please Confirm 2, 3, 3b, 1a, 3a, over."

We go into the U-turn in reverse. My head is under the commander's hatch that I closed at first light. And then I hear two whistles rapidly approaching the tank. I turn my head and see two missiles fly over us. I identify the smoke trail, grab the commander's control, and fire a shell in that direction. I also launch the smoke grenades.

The sound of shelling can be heard from every direction. The company functions superbly, without any nonsense on the radio, only commands and reports.

I continue on the narrow road above the valley. To my left, a slope, and to my right, a terrace and a grove. I fire short bursts from the machine gun in the direction of the grove. In between the trees I identify rocket launchers and ammunition in bulk, placed on the ground.

"All teams, shoot at the launchers to the right, on the terrace. Over."

I hear Roman's machine gun on my right. We drive as fast as we can until I identify them.

---

[i] A laser beam sent to find the target range before shooting.

In between the trees, five meters from my tank, two people with a launcher, looking straight at me.

"Two people on the right," I report while going into the tank and quickly drawing a grenade. I pull out the safety.

"Deputy, grenade!"

I throw the grenade and count inside.

Twenty-one.

Twenty-two.

Twenty-three.

Boom!

One after the other, everyone begins dispatching grenades. "1, grenade," "1b, grenade," they report on the radio.

I continue on the road that goes up the edge of the valley. There should be a right turn that leaves the road, a steep ascent that I vaguely remember from the night before. Where's the turn? I search in every direction and when I look back, I realize that I've missed it.

I immediately stop everyone, and instruct them to drive ten meters backwards. We're fifteen tanks. Luckily, no one needs to turn around.

We continue moving and finally reach Aynata. This area looks familiar. When we enter the village, I fire another shell at one of the houses. Five seconds later, out of a cloud of dust that rises from the shattered road, I see Benda's tank in front of my cannon. Fortunately for me and him, the shell passed next to him.

Benda smiles and salutes. It looks like he's happy to see me. His tank turns hard right, and I continue into the basketball court of the demolished school. Company C's tanks are parked in the court. I start turning my tank around and reverse slowly until I touch Zuckerman's tank gently. Zuckerman peeks out from his tank and smiles at me. In different times I would go to prison for scratching a tank.

One after another, all the tanks get into the crowded protective barrier.

The battalion commander calls me on the radio, "Drive to the open area at the entrance to the village. The helicopter will land there."

The time is ten in the morning. I have to cross Aynata to the point where Stern was injured, and wait there. God help us.

Infantry soldiers wait for us there and will secure the landing area. We get to the spot behind the embankments we built several days earlier.

The soldiers take the wounded from the tankbulance and the fatalities from Klein and Heiman's tanks. The helicopter calls me on the radio and asks for accurate directions to our location. I can't hear or see it. I shut down the engine and remove my AFV helmet. After a few seconds it appears from the valley and lands close to the tanks.

The pilot asks us to not delay and after just two minutes the wounded and dead are on the helicopter. He takes off and leaves us in complete silence for thirty seconds, until we turn on the engines and start moving back to the basketball courts.

I get into the protective barrier and park the tank next to Perry. I go down to talk to Perry who is still in complete shock. Golan says that Perry stood in the loader's post the whole way without moving, even when missiles went over his head. I try to talk to Perry, but he only repeats again and again that he can't understand how it happened. After a few minutes, Perry turns to me and says, "You were a hero in At-Tiri. The way you shot above me and then led the company and the battalion." I still don't feel like it's the right time to tell him I launched the smoke grenades at him.

Noon at the basketball court. I have no clue what the next assignment will be. Silence on the radio system. All of the teams are in their tanks, left with the thoughts that follow the running over incident. I don't know how Perry will be able to continue functioning with thoughts of the dead and wounded soldiers' families about to get the news. It would have happened to any tank that drove first on this convoy, and no one blames Perry. The infantry unit reported that the area was clear. We should have come up from the northern part of the valley, like we planned. But who could have predicted everything that happened between the first anti-tank missile and the second, between Klein's steering malfunction and the 2a that got stuck in a dangerous side slope?

I prepare a tuna-corn-ketchup sandwich, brush my teeth and floss with my string of sanity. When I reached the basketball court after this fast and prolonged drive, I had a short conversation with the tank's engine. I heard the ticks of the heat sink cooling down, passed a caressing hand over the shielding, and we both sighed in relief. How much more luck can I have? How many times will the missiles pass over my head and not harm me? How many more times will I be able to drive during daylight and arrive at my destination safely?

The battalion commander summons the senior command staff to come to his tank. "At 1800 hours we start our movement on the same path we cleared last night. We need to get to Shaqif A-Nimmel," the battalion commander says. "Ginzburg, you're in the lead, Benda behind."

There's no way we're doing this again, I say to myself. This is not real. "Why not two hours later, in complete darkness?" I ask.

"There's no time and we were supposed to be there yesterday. These are the final achievements in all the sectors. Soon a cease-fire will come into effect," the battalion commander replies purposefully. We'll need all the good luck with this one.

I deliver the orders on the company radio network to the platoon commanders. Perry isn't relevant. The battalion commander asks to not take any tanks with mechanical issues, no matter how small. He wants to carry out a swift movement and avoid delays. I call on the radio and update Klein and Zohar that they're staying here. Klein responds immediately on the radio, "You're not going without me, forget it!"

This is what Klein is like. Just like Aviad is much more than a gunner, Klein is much more than a tank commander. I met Klein when I was a commander of new recruits and he was in one of the parallel platoons. After he completed a commanders' course he arrived at the company and we instantly connected. Other commanders would have been happy to stay here. Who wants to put himself on this mission anyway? If all the tank commanders were like Klein, we wouldn't need platoon commanders. He has a can-do attitude. He's courageous, responsible and I can always count on him. I want Klein with me so I head over to the battalion commander's tank and ask for permission for him to join. The battalion commander approves and I inform Klein he can join us. Later, I think if something happens to him, I won't be able to forgive myself.

At 17:00 Perry calls me and says that he's taking back the command of the company. "Just make sure that I'm not taking too many risks," he says. "Right now I feel like I have nothing to lose. I'm prepared to do anything, at any risk level, and at any cost. Keep an eye on me."

I promise Perry we'll make it back safely.

We get on the tanks and warm up the engines. To get the blood and adrenaline pumping, I drive through a large tree that stood behind Perry's tank. I ask Eli to advance slowly until the rammer bumps the rear section of Perry's tank. Perry turns around with a big smile.

The fuel situation in the tanks is bad, between 400 and 600 liters in each tank. When not in war, it's forbidden to start the engine with such a low level of diesel. We've been promised that later they'll drop diesel barrels and we will be able to refuel from them.

Company C positions itself behind us. We are ready for the attack of our lives, part two.

At 18:20 we start moving. It's full daylight. I start descending toward the valley north of Aynata. Roman is leading and Kidron is last. We drive down to the U-turn.

Boom! A missile flies over Roman's tank. I receive an indication of lasing in the U-turn and launch the smoke grenades in that direction. Everyone passes through the U-turn. On the radio I hear that tank 3a of company C has been hit by a missile. The tank commander, Dvir, was my soldier in basic training.

We continue down to the second valley. On the radio I hear another tank of company C has been hit badly and they've lost contact with the team. The deputy battalion commander goes to look for him. Finally it starts to grow dark. Klein identifies a squad of launchers and fires a shell with a burst from the machine gun, killing two terrorists.

We regroup the convoy before the last descent to the valley. On the radio I hear the deputy battalion commander saying he's found company C's tank. "The turret is severed from the hull. Probably an underground charge," he determines. Zuckerman joins the deputy battalion commander and reports that the entire tank is burnt and bodies are in it. The commander, who had the hatch open, flew out of the tank and they can't find him.

The call sign for abduction procedure is sounded through the radio. Zuckerman and the deputy battalion commander identify the entry point of a missile directly under the cannon, precisely in the direction of the ammunition cases. The intensity of the blast detached the tracks and turret from their place. The deputy battalion commander requests a search for the tank commander in the area but receives a negative response out of concern for a multi-charge area.

I'm already at the entry to the last valley before the Shaqif, imagining how it all looks inside the sooty tank. The deputy battalion commander reports he's found the commander ten meters from the tank. The commander and the loader were soldiers of mine. The truth is, it doesn't matter. I know everyone in the battalion, and most of the soldiers passed by me at some stage or another.

I stop under a building to take cover. It's almost completely dark. Perry asks me to close the commander's hatch. When I report "shut," he throws a grenade straight into the window of the building above me. "Just so we won't get any surprises," he says, and I see the smile on his face.

We receive approval to carry on. I commanded Eli, "Driver, forward quick," without noticing that we're taking apart the entire corner of the building I was hiding behind. The bricks from the building's wall remain on the hull despite my many attempts to get them off with the cannon.

We continue moving north and enter the "run over" valley that goes up to Shaqif again. This time we're close together and slower than ever in order to prevent another running over. We climb to the Shaqif ridge through insane terraces. From a distance I start to see the parachutes of diesel barrels that have been caught in the trees. We get out of the valley and enter the protective barrier of company B. They came here the morning after the running over incident. To my left I see a Ferris wheel and carousels. This is the Shaqif's amusement park. Low steel barriers mark the entrance. Among the steel fences are Golani soldiers, ready for action as if they're waiting for the park to open so they can go in. An utterly surreal sight.

Before I ask Eli to shut down the engine, I take off my helmet and start a short conversation with the tank's engine, having just put it through a long and difficult drive. I listen to every sound, making sure it plays in tune. The

RPM settle and only then do I ask Eli to shut it down. A little bit of quiet, a moment of rest. The night is still young. Later on, we'll need to cover the movement of company B.

The eighth day, August 13, 2006

After a light twenty-minute nap in the commander's post, Perry calls me to his tank and informs me that we need to evacuate a casualty from the amusement park. "Evacuate where?" I ask in surprise. "Bint Jbeil," Perry replies with a look of despair. "We just got here, back already?" I say with a fake smile. I ask Perry for an escort on the mission and we decide on Kidron and the tankbulance. The soldiers from the amusement park carry the body on a gurney and we place it into the tankbulance.

We begin moving. Three in the morning and we're in a race against time, against daylight. I start feeling like a vampire. We need to get to the evacuation point and somehow return to the basketball court before sunrise. I know the way very well by now and it all goes smoothly. We arrive at a reasonable time and I can see the deputy battalion commander from a distance. He informs me that the evacuation will be carried out in 378, where I started with my first mission on the second night of the war. We arrive at 378 and again, the blue appearing in

413

the sky, which I used to love, gets mixed with the smell of Stern's blood. We move the casualty to a tank of the 7th brigade and race back. By the time we reach the basketball court it is full daylight. Again, I give thanks to some kind of a God, and mainly to the tank's engine. Zuckerman tells me about the horrors he experienced when he collected the body parts from the tank that exploded yesterday evening. I watch the deputy battalion commander take a shower with water bottles and change his jumpsuit out of disgust from the previous night. Benda, who just lost four soldiers, has a frightened look. The battalion commander sits in his usual pose on the tank watching everyone, one cigarette after the other from his stock of Marlboro lights. Packs are thrown everywhere on the tank's turret.

The company and the battalion have serious fuel problems. Some of the tanks are down to 300 liters of diesel. I have 200. Friedman, company B's commander, refueled last night from the barrels of diesel that came down from the sky. For more than an hour he transferred 500 liters into the fuel tanks using an emergency manual pump. When he finished refueling, he noticed a big hole left during the battle by a missile that crossed one of the fuel tanks from one side to the other. All of the fuel was pouring onto the ground next to the tank while he refueled.

I walk around the tanks, pumping diesel from the damaged ones. We leave those with a minimal amount of diesel, enough for the return to Israel. One of the tanks I steal diesel from belongs to team 2 of company C. I go into the gunner's compartment to traverse the turret so I can insert the manual fuel pump. I'm instantly hit by the pungent smell of burnt blood from the tank commander's injury.

When I get back to the basketball court, Eran makes fun of me for not taking off the flak jacket inside the barrier. "You're probably covered in sores under there," he says and starts laughing. Only then do I realize that since we've entered Lebanon for the second time, I haven't taken off my flak jacket. I remove it along with my uniform's shirt. My belly button becomes red and burns the second it's exposed to the air. Later on, I settle in a pastoral spot between the blade of a D-9 and the embankment of the protective barrier. And I take a dump for the first time since the re-entry.

I work with the team on the tracks and we replace one of the links. The atmosphere in the protective barrier is special in light of the rumors about the coming cease-fire, and despite the fatalities from company C and the running over incident.

Toward the evening we receive a report from the Disaster Victims' Identification Unit. They have collected the bodies in Israel and believe there should be additional body parts in the tank of company C. The horrible task is given to poor Zuckerman. During the night he goes back to the damaged tank and searches for more body parts.

On the last night of the war, the IDF suffers 24 casualties when troops try to cross the Saluky valley, the same deadly assignment we received on our first evening in the war, which was eventually postponed.

The battalion commander summons the commanders and announces, "Tomorrow morning a cease-fire will come into effect. Everyone is going back to Israel." We give the news to all the teams.

The ninth day, August 14, 2006

My company returns from the Shaqif and I begin leading the battalion out. We drive out the same path we came in, finding it hard to hide our joy in anticipation of the return to Israel. We join company C and together we approach the fence. It's still dark. We begin driving along the border. The morning begins to come up and the skies are painted blue.

Here, in Israeli territory, it doesn't mean anything. But the smell of blood remains in my head.

We enter the parking area. Roman, who drives in after me, reports on the radio that his fuel gauge is showing zero. After a few minutes he asks me to turn around and look. I turn and see his tank wobbling and choking, driving on the last fumes of fuel.

After we park the tanks, I gather everyone for a company photo. A great deal of news and television photographers walk around us. We are dusty, dirty, and smelly.

Later on, everyone goes to sleep at the battalion base in the Golan Heights. I, on the other hand, drive from the far north to Ze'elim in the south to visit Shira. I enter the base and wait for her in the office. From sheer surprise, she doesn't know what to do when she sees me. She only looks at me and asks what I'm doing here. She doesn't move until I stand up and hold her.

The next day I return to the company. Toward the end of the week we erect a large shade canopy in the grove near the border and we begin to execute nightly excursions into Lebanon.

I enter Lebanon again. The minute I cross the fence my right leg begins to shake. I drive behind the D-9 and the first thing I notice is the smell of Stern's injury — the smell of the Lebanese dust combined with the humidity of summer. It's all quiet in this sector. Not one shot has been fired for a month, but I'm still scared and do everything I can to avoid being the one to cross the fence.

After a few weeks I go home for the first time. On the way I hear a radio interview with a D-9 driver from the reserve who's in the hospital. He gives his regards to his family and thanks the tank team that extracted him after the injury. It was the driver who was injured with us in At-Tiri. We rescued him. When I hear his words, I get chills all over my body. My eyes become watery and a tear rolls down, followed by another one, and another one. I sit at a traffic light in the military truck, wearing my uniform, looking straight ahead with a serious expression, and trying my best not to break down in tears.

I was excited to go home and share my experiences. When I look at the photos online, or read the newspaper, I think, "That was me." I was part of everything. I know people who were wounded there.

But I also feel like no one is really interested in what happened. It reminds me of the "Letter to Jane Doe," that's remained in my pocket since I joined the military. "When I come home and tell of an encounter with the enemy and about the fear and excitement, you nod your heads, as if you understand, and then talk about the new car you just bought."

TRAVEL LOG: THE WAY HOME

Noya puts the second notebook on the table, lifts my tear-soaked head from her knees, and lays it gently on the couch. She gets up and goes into the bedroom to get a pillow and blanket. Shushu, who's lying next to me, just starts to snore.

Noya gently puts the pillow under my head and wraps us both in a blanket. She then adorably shoves herself between me and the back of the couch, spooning me from behind. I'm exhausted from all the thoughts racing through my mind. I close my eyes and in seconds escape into a deep sleep.

♦ ♦ ♦

I'm participating in a dark reality show and my team is making a fatal mistake that will cause us to lose. The rules of the show don't detail what the punishment will be. We will only discover it later on.

We stand in a circle in a place that is reminiscent of a television studio, but everything is dark. Dinner is served and each of us receives a piece of juicy steak. We look at each other, not understanding why we deserve this reward.

One of the team members starts eating the steak in front of him. Then we all join in as if we haven't eaten in several days. Our mouths are stuffed with meat and everyone's chewing vigorously.

When I ask, "Which cut is this?" one of the contenders standing next to me answers naturally, "Stern's cut," and continues to chew vigorously. The rest of the contenders freeze in place holding the bite in their mouths. It's not a reward, we understand. It's the punishment. Time stands still. The contenders hold the steaks in their hands and everyone's mouths begin to slowly vanish, replaced with a gaping hole in the middle of their faces that opens, as if they were infected by Stern's injury.

I panic when I see everyone's mouth disappearing. There isn't much time left and the game show is about to end. The more time passes, the more the infection and the holes in the center of their faces grow. There's a million pairs of eyes around. Is that the audience?

I try to control my thoughts. As I concentrate, the mouths of the contestants begin to return. The holes start to close. When I relax the thoughts a little, the contestants try to bring the piece of meat to their mouths again — and their mouths start vanishing again. I fight them with all my might so they won't eat the meat. The harder I concentrate, the farther they push it away, until they finally place it on the table.

I attempt to muster all of my mental power for one last push, like an arm-wrestling match that gets stuck at a crucial moment and just needs one final surge. When I see that nearly all the steaks are placed on the plate, a dim light comes up on the audience around. As the light intensifies I can see endless pairs of eyes staring at me from every direction, but just the whites of the eyes, without faces.

The show participants are no longer relevant, I think to myself. Now my mind is controlling the intensity of the light over everything. I can hardly increase my concentration any more. My body is trembling and with the rest of my strength I try to turn up the light to see the faces of the gaping eyes. Suddenly there's a strong flash.

I lose my concentration, and everything goes black again. I try to refocus my thoughts, but feel like all the muscles in my body are about to implode. There's a flash again and this time I manage to see what's around their eyes a little more. But it's still unclear. I'm tight all over and feel like another flash is coming. The light turns on and I try to hold on to it for a little while longer.

Around me there are millions of soldier heads painted in black camouflage paint. It's just possible to see the whites of their eyes and a little of the head shape. I have to figure out who they are. I try hard for a final push, squeeze as hard as I can and... I wake up in panic on the hotel's couch.

Noya is asleep, Shushu is snoring, and I'm frozen. Motionless. The blue of morning is coming in through the bare windows of the hotel in Eilat. My body is aching, exhausted, and my temperature soars. I'm covered in sweat — not moving, just trying to calm down from the nightmare.

The second notebook sits on the living room table. I reach out gently to not wake up Noya, open the notebook, and search for what I wrote about the valley's point of crossing.

"I get off the tank with my AFV helmet on. I hear nothing since the helmet covers my ears with noise protection. I see flashes of bombs and missiles in the sky at a distance."

When I read the word "flashes" I'm instantly thrown back into the game show nightmare and see the eyes looking at me.

"It's so dark outside. There could be someone here, literally next to me in the bushes, and I wouldn't hear him approaching because of my headset. I feel like he's already there, watching me."

Holy shit, this is so real.

> "I decide to take off the helmet so I can hear
> the noises of my surroundings. When I do, I
> can hear endless blasts from every direction.
> The flashes I saw earlier gain the sound of war.
> Shells, artillery, anti-tank missile fire, it all
> sounds so close."

Again I'm thrown back into the nightmare, only this
time the flashes are accompanied by the loud sounds
of explosions.

> "I immediately put the AFV helmet back on
> my head and tie it as tightly as possible."

As I read this line, the sound of a theatre's huge
electrical switch being thrown for the last time is
sounded, and the dim lights are turned off.

I close the notebook and again cling to Noya,
who's awake now. "Are you okay? Do you want to go
home?" she asks. I nod without saying a word.

We pack the equipment and get ready to leave.
Noya returns the notebooks to the plastic bag. We
return the key to reception and Noya leaves the lobby
with Shushu on a leash. On the grass outside the hotel
I see Noya with a cigarette in one hand and Shushu's
leash in the other. Noya puts the cigarette in my
mouth and lights another one for herself.

We wait a few minutes for Shushu to finish her
morning business and walk to the underground

parking lot. We tie up Noya's suitcase over the dusty equipment in the truck's bed and put Shushu inside the small cabin. Noya stands on the passenger's side, and I on the driver's side.

"We go?" I ask.

"We go," she replies with a smile.

I toss the key to her and say, "You're the driver. I'm with Shushu." I explain how to start the truck with the manual choke, and it starts with a slight touch. It sounds like the engine is happy that Noya is here with us too. We wait patiently for the engine temperature gauge to display forty degrees and we set off. Noya rolls the truck out of the parking lot. In one second she understands how it all works with the old truck. She operates the gear and the stiff steering wheel with ease.

We leave Eilat on the Arava Road. The windows are open and Noya's hair blows perfectly. Shushu sits on my lap with her head outside the window, absorbing a little of the hot desert wind. Her long ears pull to the back and her big eyes shrink to small slits of vision. This is what Shushu looks like when she feels at home.

We light up another cigarette and don't say a word. There's a long way ahead of us. I look out the window and pat Shushu while we both take in the last moments of the desert and enjoy the soothing slow pace of the truck. The feeling of a complete family fills the cramped cabin. Noya sees that I'm in my own world and says nothing, only gives me a supporting look and puts her hand on my leg.

◆ ◆ ◆

When people think of war, they instantly imagine how combat soldiers look the enemy in the eye a second before firing, or the sight of the wounded covered in blood. Even I went to that place initially, which greatly simplifies what happened.

There must be an incident, a cause for my post-traumatic stress, and I must find it. "Have you been shot at?" they asked the first day I turned for help. But it's not the sights that caused my PTSD. It wasn't the soldier who screamed in pain when his entire body was crushed after the company's tank ran him over. It's probably not the hole in Stern's face either, and not even the bodies we carried.

When I searched for the most impactful experiences of the war, I didn't even consider that moment I took my helmet off and felt a million eyes staring at me. The incident wasn't something that happened in reality, my mind created it. How could something that didn't even happen shock my entire system like this?

◆ ◆ ◆

After an hour and a half of driving, Noya stops the truck at a gas station on the Arava Road. She brings us coffee and I give Shushu water. We get back into the truck and this time I drive.

It's noon and Tel Aviv is busy. We pass by a coffee shop on the boulevard and everyone turns their heads at my travel truck painted dust-blue, straight from the desert. Returning to the city moves me, and I choke on my tears. I manage to stop them for a moment, but then I decide to let it go.

Thoughts about everything I've been through this past month fill the truck. Noya sees the tears coming down from behind my blue sunglasses and runs her hand over my face to wipe them off. Shushu doesn't understand what's going on, but continues to look on with her typical curiosity and her bulging eyes.

Noya puts her hand on my leg, and I put my hand on her, and on Shushu. God, what a journey I've made and how happy I am to finish it. We roll through the city and I recall coping with the first nights, the amazing mornings up north, and the special people who came as if by invitation to meet me, and made me think. Something in me feels much more whole.

We approach my apartment and from a distance I can see that my favorite parking spot, right under the building, is vacant. After all I've been through this month, it's not at all surprising. Someone, or something, prepared this journey in advance. All the experiences sat there waiting for me to come pick them up.

We get out of the truck and stretch after a long time seated. Noya comes over to my side and hugs me tightly, tears in her eyes. Shushu moves from the passenger seat to the driver's seat and joins us through the open window. I look at the packed truck, at Noya who's emotional, and at Shushu who wags her tail with joy. It's time for me to move on.

♦ ♦ ♦

Over the years I realized that no matter where I go, "he" will also come and wait until it turns dark. This book was written to shed light and direct it back at him, with the hope of being less afraid.

Thank you so much for reading my story and being part of my journey.

To get an updated epilogue with everything that has happened since the book was published and hear about my next project send an email to:
out.there.update@gmail.com

or scan the QR code

I would love to hear about your reading experience.
Feel free to contact me directly:
www.omrigi.com
Instagram: **@omri.gin**

Made in the USA
Monee, IL
03 October 2023

43917093R00249